Nurturing Young Black Males

RONALD B. MINCY, EDITOR

Nurturing Young Black Males

Challenges to Agencies, Programs, and Social Policy

THE URBAN INSTITUTE PRESS
Washington, D.C.

Library of Congress Cataloging in Publication Data

Nurturing Young Black Males:
Challenges to Agencies, Programs, and Social Policy/[Ronald B. Mincy, editor].

1. Afro-American teenage boys—Services for. 2. Afro-American men—Services for. 3. Juvenile delinquents—Services for—Unites States. I. Mincy, Ronald B.

HV3181.N88   1994   93-32879
362,7'9796073--dc20   CIP

ISBN 0-87766-598-2 (alk. paper; casebound)

Urban Institute books are printed on acid-free paper whenever possible.
Printed in the United States of America.

HV
3181
.N88
1994

Distributed by National Book Network
4720 Boston Way   3 Henrietta Street
Lanham, MD 20706   London WC2E 8LU ENGLAND

THE URBAN INSTITUTE is a nonprofit policy research and educational organization established in Washington, D.C., in 1968. Its staff investigates the social and economic problems confronting the nation and public and private means to alleviate them. The Institute disseminates significant findings of its research through the publications program of its Press. The goals of the Institute are to sharpen thinking about societal problems and efforts to solve them, improve government decisions and performance, and increase citizen awareness of important policy choices.

Through work that ranges from broad conceptual studies to administrative and technical assistance, Institute researchers contribute to the stock of knowledge available to guide decision making in the public interest.

Conclusions or opinions expressed in Institute publications are those of the authors and do not necessarily reflect the views of staff members, officers or trustees of the Institute, advisory groups, or any organizations that provide financial support to the Institute.

ACKNOWLEDGMENTS

This book could not have been completed without the encouragement, support, dedication, and collaboration of many people. I wish to thank Isabel Sawhill—my mentor, friend, and critic—for encouraging me to be bold in my thinking about policy remedies. She opened many professional doors and modeled the work effort I needed to walk through them. Next, I would like to thank my colleague Susan Wiener, who shared in the original conception of this project, and saw it through to its completion.

I would like to thank the members of the advisory board, who reviewed first drafts of the chapters and lent their perspectives as practitioners, program officers, policymakers, and researchers. Special thanks are due to Kalman Hettleman, Elaine Blechman, Andre Watson, Willis Bright, Demetra Nightingale, Mary Phillips, Gloria Primm-Brown, Usini Perkins, Jewelle Taylor-Gibbs, John Wilson, Michael Andrews, Darryl Kennon, Margaret Beale-Spencer, Richard Majors, Sherman Bonds, and Roderick Watts.

Several Urban Institute colleagues deserve special thanks. Bill Gorham, president of the Urban Institute, lent his support and encouragement throughout the project. Felicity Skidmore, director of the Urban Institute Press, provided strategic advice at critical points, and Kyna Rubin provided excellent editorial assistance. Mitch Tobin provided superb research assistance. Mary Coombs organized the conferences, handled a variety of administrative tasks associated with the project, and generally kept communications between myself and the authors going smoothly.

Support from the Rockefeller Foundation is gratefully acknowledged. Specifically, I would like to thank James Gibson, former director of the Foundation's Equal Opportunity Division, and my program officers Erol Ricketts and Aida Rodriguez. They saw the value of the questions raised in this book before many others, and maintained support for the project throughout.

Finally, I would like to thank my family for their constant support. My wife, Flona, made many personal and professional sacrifices while I worked on this project. My sons Daru and Ronald Jr. modeled many of the competencies and challenges that are the subject of this book. Because of them, I understand these issues better. They also showed me that, though parents and other well-meaning adults can try to ease the process, maturity requires adolescents to make choices. After watching Daru and Ron Jr., I have both a profound respect for the independence that adolescents seek and great pride in the choices my sons have made.

CONTENTS

Appendices

Tables

Figures

The established link between single-parenthood and a multitude of social problems has concerned the research and policy community for more than two decades. And an important body of research, program evaluations, and policy proposals has resulted, to which the Urban Institute has made many contributions. These include *Time of Transition* (1975), by Isabel Sawhill and Heather Ross, which provided early documentation of the rising trend in single-parenthood, and *Single Mothers and their Children* (1986), by Irwin Garfinkel and Sara McLanahan, which was the first comprehensive review of the evidence documenting increased developmental hazards for the children in mother-only families.

But research and policy have generally focused on the females involved, to the relative neglect of the males. The nurturing supports so important to healthy human development are often missing from the homes of young black males in high-risk environments, the community institutions that used to fill the gap have disappeared in many areas, and, tragically, the public schools often hurt rather than help these students. The major public policy response to the needs of these young people has been to wait until they run afoul of the law and then spend billions of dollars annually on putting them through the criminal justice system. But these are the fathers of the next high-risk generation. Our inadequate public policies are not only wasting the potential of the current generation, they are also increasing the likelihood that these men will father sons who will suffer the same fate.

Mincy and colleagues document the scars left by lack of male nurturing at young ages, and the neglect of early adolescence as an intervention point for black male children. But this is fundamentally an encouraging book. It describes programs that offer young black males from high-risk environments the same nurturing opportunities other youth have to develop the competencies needed for adult-hood—*programs that work.*

But most of these programs are small and private. Mincy and his contributors recommend using this program experience as the corner-stone for a national youth development policy, and review existing, pending, and proposed legislation as a framework for developing such a policy.

Most people who witness the troubled outcomes of young black males in high-risk environments are inclined simply to wring their hands in despair. I hope, with Mincy, that this book will convince concerned observers to put those hands to work.

William Gorham
President

WHY THIS BOOK?

You are about to read a series of excellent papers about a critical though neglected area of social policy: the need to reform our public and private interventions that affect young black males in America. Despite the caliber of the papers and the deep commitment that each contributor brings to the subject, this scholarly material will at some point become dry for some readers. Some may not complete the book; others may leave it without being motivated to take any action on the contributors' recommendations. This would be tragic, in my view. Therefore, I would like to take the unusual step of sharing with readers aspects of my personal and professional background that explain why I have organized and persevered through this effort and why I believe it is so vital. I hope this candor will encourage you to persevere, and above all, to critically assess the analysis in the volume and to become involved in efforts to bring about reforms.

It is hard to say when the idea for this volume began. About three weeks before I graduated from high school, I was with a group of my black male peers dreaming about the future. Most of us had spent the first 18 years of our lives in a public housing project called Patterson in the South Bronx, just over the bridge from Harlem. Marvin, one of the members of my peer group, was scheduled to enroll in the John Jay College of Criminal Justice in the fall in order to become a detective and get a safe desk job. As a detective he would still carry a gun, which would impress the young women. He was always looking for ways to attract them. A week later, Marvin got into a fight over one of his girlfriends. His rival stuck a knife under Marvin's arm pit. The knife entered his heart and killed him instantly.

I had seen the chalk marks framing the body of a victim a few times before, usually after the police bands were down and the red blood stains had begun to turn yellow. But for the first time they outlined someone close to me. And the first time I wore the dark suit my mother bought for my graduation was to Marvin's funeral.

Our ability to attract young women, with sex as the goal, was fundamental to our concept of manhood. Sexual conquest was the grand game and our ability to score was an important determinant of our standing within the peer group. This puzzled me, because most of the children I knew were from mother-only families. Why did we fail to see that the result was to reproduce another generation of mother-only families, because young men had experienced the privilege of sexual intercourse before being prepared for the responsibility?

The Patterson Projects provided many opportunities for us to make other choices that would ruin our long-term prospects. Cocaine trafficking was rising and many of our friends were committing petty crimes. Violence was already increasing in our neighborhoods. Yet we looked up to the drug dealers and hustlers in our neighborhood, imitating their dress, speech, and deportment. Those of us with older brothers who were drug dealers or hustlers had a special status in the peer group. Stably employed adult black males with positive relationships with partners and children were rare.

Many of the single mothers in the projects worked full-time and full-year, as did my mother. For nearly 20 years she commuted two hours each way to her job as a nurse's aide in a hospital on Long Island. My brothers and I were left to supervise one another, with only the force of my mother's character to hold us in check. Nevertheless, delinquency was rare in my family, as with many families in the neighborhood, but there were also many whose boys were frequently in trouble.

My mother forbade us to "hang out" at night. On warm nights I would see a group of boys or young men hanging out under my window, laughing, smoking, drinking, and gambling. My brothers and I wanted to join them, but if we were not in the house before dark the punishment was swift, sure, and humiliating.

These unsupervised young male peer groups later took a turn for the worse. Plans for selling drugs or committing petty crimes were hatched during their night sessions, and there was almost always a dispute, settled by fighting—first with hands, then with knives, and sometimes with guns. My brothers and I would hear the full details of these events on the following day, including reports of group members who were seriously injured, killed, or arrested during the night. We were glad that our mother provided an excuse for us to exempt ourselves from these activities. Today, most of the young men who regularly hung out below my window are dead, physically debilitated, or incarcerated. My brothers and I were spared this fate by my mother's conviction, courage, and wisdom.

Thus, my family usually managed well. But there were certain days when we needed the input of another adult, especially a man. There are issues that boys will not share with their mothers, no matter how caring and supportive their mothers are.

For example, I recall hearing a man boast in the barbershop one day, "Every time I pass by the school yard, I reach in my pocket, take out a few pennies, and throw them over the fence. Who knows? Some of those children could be mine!" I wondered if my father, whom I knew little about, felt that way about me. I wondered if all black men, indeed all men, were this callous about their responsibilities toward their children and partners. I desperately wanted to ask someone, especially an older man, to clarify or refute this view. But who could I ask?

In 1970, when I left the Patterson Projects to enroll at Harvard, I chose to study economics because I wanted to know why people were poor. I also wanted to know why so many black men had deserted their families, leaving them to fend for themselves in awful places like the Patterson. How could anyone expect children like Marvin, my brothers, and me to survive in that environment, and to become productive contributors to our society?

Four years later, while doing graduate work in economics at M.I.T., my wife and I became involved in a prison ministry. Once a week we visited men in Massachusetts state prisons to conduct bible studies. I remember the sound of the gate clanging behind us as we went from the outer yard into the prison area, and the heavy smell of urine that seemed to permeate everything.

On our last visit to the prison we attended an inmate talent show. This was our first glimpse of the poets, singers, dancers, and comedians who made up the general prison population. I was shocked to see hundreds of young black men, my age, locked up. Everything about them was familiar. Their dress, walk, and speech were like the young men who used to hang out below my window in the Patterson. It occured to me, "There but for the grace of God, go I." It was sickening. Hundreds of my brothers. I could not go back.

Shortly after completing my Ph.D. at M.I.T, I went to work for the Urban Institute, a public policy think tank in Washington. My task was to continue the pioneering work of Isabel Sawhill and Erol Ricketts, who estimated the size, composition, and growth of the underclass based on nonincome dimensions. I was convinced that the dimensions of social distress that Sawhill and Ricketts had identified were critical determinants of youth outcomes. I knew from firsthand experience that many young people failed to build upon their parents' efforts toward upward social mobility because of the non-income dimensions of neighborhood ecology.

When we turned to policy remedies, our discussions often centered on welfare reform. I found this preoccupation with welfare reform and its exclusive focus on young women and teenage pregnancy prevention extemely irritating. There appeared to be no discussion of risks facing young men. I decided that this gender bias in the policy community was wrong and began to ask questions. What interventions could help young men in neighborhoods like the Patterson Projects avoid self-destructive choices? This volume begins to answer that question.

Many changes have occurred since I began graduate training. First, the spread of AIDS, the crack epidemic of the mid-1980s, and the escalation of semi-automatic weapons have increased the risks facing young black males in the Patterson Projects and in other high-risk neighborhoods. To survive today, these young males must have far more effective street skills than my brothers and I ever had. Moreover, there are many more of them without fathers, because the black men of my generation who grew up in these neighborhoods were sexually active early, and many who survived heroin addiction and alcoholism throughout the 1970s succumbed to AIDS, crack, and the gun-related violence in the 1980s. Second, while the policy and human services community has virtually ignored young males in high-risk environments, the criminal justice community has not. Today, prison ministries see tens of thousands of men from my generation, but hundreds of thousands of black males from my sons' generation.

Finally, I changed. I stopped relying on the income policy and human services community to learn what I needed to know about the structure of interventions for young black males. I learned that there are policymakers, researchers, social service practitioners, and program officers in community and human development who are vitally interested in what is happening to young black males in high-risk environments. In this volume I have asked members of this community to think collaboratively with me, to try to incorporate our collective knowledge about the human development needs and services relating to young black males into an income policy and human services framework.

Even if trends in mother-only families among low- and moderate-income blacks are irreversible, we cannot and should not expect black women (and taxpayers) to bear the responsibility of child-rearing alone. Even the heroes among them, like my mother, need support to meet the full range of their sons' needs.

But what are these needs? What is the best point in the life cycle to try to meet them? How do we begin to structure supports for meeting these needs? And what institutions should we try to enlist in the effort? Most of my colleagues put these questions on the back burner because budgets are limited and important questions about welfare reform and teenage pregnancy prevention still remain unanswered. This is impossible for me. And I hope that reading this book will make it increasingly difficult for you.

Ronald B. Mincy

Chapter One

INTRODUCTION

Ronald B. Mincy

Recently, I sat in an audience with other black men,
wondering whether to accept or reject the speaker's analogy
between us and cockroaches. "Despite being generally
despised and struggling for survival, with many advances and
setbacks," the speaker asserted, "black men, like cockroaches,
seem to be indestructible." Were the speaker not himself a
black man, I would have been insulted. Though the mental
picture of a cockroach was repulsive, I, and perhaps others in
the audience, could not easily dismiss this bittersweet
analogy. For a moment, I allowed myself to feel the attack,
from all sides, under which black men in America often labor.
I also felt the sense of loss, which I imagined a cockroach
must feel from repeatedly seeing members of his own kind—
especially the young ones—crushed in one way or another.
Finally, I was attracted by the cockroach's penchant for
survival, for, like the cockroach, I fully intend to keep coming
back. But what about the others, especially the young ones?
That thought snapped me out of it. I laughed nervously, with
others in the audience, then gave my attention to the rest of
the speaker's comments.

Advocates, researchers, policymakers, and journalists—hoping to
stimulate public and private action—are producing reams of reports
on the many signs of distress among black males. Most writing focuses
on young black males from poor, high-risk families and communities.
This documentation is needed, and the conclusion drawn by some—
that black males are becoming an endangered species—has some
merit (Gibbs 1988; Staples 1991). However, observers tend to ignore
evidence of progress to date and the potential for even greater progress
in the future. Rather than stimulating action to help young black
males from high-risk backgrounds, research and advocacy that focus
on the negative may encourage public and private apathy or, worse,

increase the pressure for criminal justice solutions to the public safety concerns created by black males.

To decrease the substantial developmental risks many young black men face due to high rates of poverty, nonmarriage, and dysfunction among their parents and neighbors, these risk markers must be eliminated or substantially reduced. A decline in the demand for low-skilled workers and housing segregation are at the root of much of the family and neighborhood dysfunction. We could wait and do nothing about the crisis indicators among black males until we resolved these stubborn and complex problems. But we have not chosen to wait. Instead, in the name of public safety our society has chosen to spend billions annually to incarcerate young black males who succumb to the risk markers. Even though this is a policy by default, it is suspect unless we balance our concern for public safety with a concern for the developmental needs of young black males. To do this we must provide services to help parents, especially single mothers, nurture their boys into manhood in high-risk neighborhoods, and offer services for boys who have to make it on their own because parents cannot or will not help them. But what kinds of services do black males 10 to 15 years old need? What kinds of agencies (public or private) now deliver or could deliver these services? What are or could be the sources of funding for these services? If there are gaps in the quantity or quality of services, how could those gaps be filled? This volume is organized around these questions.

WHY FOCUS ON YOUNG BLACK MALES?

Although some issues and programs discussed in this book apply to at-risk youth more generally, the contributors make every effort to focus on young black males. We do this to offer alternatives to the punitive public policies that disproportionately affect young black (and Latino) men.

The public response to suicides, pregnancies, prostitution, and drug and alcohol abuse among troubled youth (regardless of race) ranges from indifference to empathy. In extreme cases, we handle self-destructive youth problems privately, by placing youths in private juvenile facilities. But among some black male youths, behavior goes beyond the self-destructive to the victimization of other people through theft, violent crime, and drug trafficking. The public's response to this sort of behavior, which statistically occurs more among young black men than young white men, is more punitive than its response to at-risk youth generally. Custody rates in the last decade rose by 31 percent in public juvenile facilities (which, unlike private facilities, house persons convicted of crimes), where the typical inmate was a black or Latino male from a poor family (U.S. Department of Justice 1992).

These and other data suggest that there are systemic problems in the development of young black males. We can respond to these problems through several policy strategies. One method, used during most of the 1980s, is to ignore the crisis data while treating individual black males in fragmented social service systems, depending on the part of the bureaucracy corresponding to their main problem (e.g., mental health, general assistance, criminal justice, and so on). The high incarceration rates of black males are a result of this kind of default strategy. Another strategy is to target young black males for prevention, treatment, or remediation services to help them avoid or recover from particular problems. Federal agencies such as the Substance Abuse and Mental Health Services Administration and the Office of Juvenile Justice Delinquency Programs are currently pursuing this strategy. A third strategy, offered by the contributors to this book, is to develop strategies that nurture high-risk adolescent black males so that they develop the competencies needed for adulthood.

Without more information about the developmental needs of black males and the available structures to meet these needs, our society will continue to ignore the systemic problems and choose the first strategy above. This book provides a base of knowledge on which policymakers, practitioners, and policy analysts might begin to build public and private strategies that ultimately will be more humane and more effective.

To formulate strategies to help black males between 10 and 15 years old make successful transitions to adulthood, we need a sober assessment of the status of young adolescent black males. Below I attempt to identify the segment of the young black male population that one can reasonably argue is in crisis. These are the youth most in need of the services offered by the programs discussed in this volume. I do this by briefly describing what these programs are up against, i.e., the educational, labor market, criminal justice, and health dimensions of the crisis. I then draw on recent research to speculate on the causes of the crisis, concluding that program effectiveness depends critically on improvements in underlying family, economic, social, and neighborhood conditions. Despite the book's

Table 1.1 EDUCATIONAL ATTAINMENT BY PERCENTAGE, 1989

Age/Race	4 Years High School or Less	High School Graduate	High School Grad. or More	Some College	College Grad. or Higher
White Males					
18–24	24	42	76	28	7
25–34	14	40	86	20	26
Black Males					
18–24	32	45	68	20	3
25–34	20	46	80	22	12

Source: Author's calculations based on U.S. Bureau of the Census (1991), table 6.

focus on black males between 10 and 15 years old, I also look at older teenagers and young adults. These older cohorts are important because they are the fathers of these younger adolescents, and parental socioeconomic status is an important determinant of the schooling, employment, and delinquency outcomes of youth. My purpose here is not to contribute to the litany of negative statistics on young black males, but to provide a context for youth development programs serving young black males. Finally, I provide a "road map" to the remainder of the volume.

Which Black Males are in Crisis?

Given what we know about the determinants of education and its effects on employment status, earnings, and delinquency, young black men do reasonably well. In 1989, 80 percent of black men between 25 and 34 years old had completed four years of high school or more (table 1.1). Hauser (1992) estimated that about 43 percent of black males who had just completed high school enrolled in college the following semester. Throughout the 1970s and most of the 1980s, fewer white men would have graduated from high school and enrolled in college if they had had the same socioeconomic characteristics as black men (Hauser 1992; Clark 1992).

Gaps in academic attainment account for much of the gap between the employment and earnings of black and white men. In 1989, 76 percent of black men between 25 and 34 years old were employed, compared with 90 percent of white men (table 1.2). Black men earned 73 percent as much as white men in this age group (table 1.3). However, employment and earnings gaps generally decreased with the educational attainment of blacks. Thus, the employment rate of black

Table 1.2 EMPLOYMENT/POPULATION RATIO, 1989

Age/Race	Total	4 Years High School or Less	High School Graduate	Some College	College Grad. or Higher
White Males					
18–24	0.73	0.67	0.79	0.68	0.81
25–34	0.90	0.80	0.90	0.92	0.93
Black Males					
18–24	0.56	0.32	0.67	0.62	0.94
25–34	0.76	0.56	0.75	0.88	0.90

Source: U.S. Bureau of the Census (1991), table 6.

Table 1.3 BLACK/WHITE MEAN EARNINGS RATIO, 1989

Age/Employment Status	Total	4 Years High School or Less	High School Graduate	Some College	College Grad. or Higher
18–24 Year Olds					
All Earners	0.79	0.64	0.79	0.84	N/A
Full-Time/ Full-Year	0.87	N/A	0.96	0.76	N/A
25–34 Year Olds					
All Earners	0.73	0.68	0.77	0.85	0.79
Full-Time/ Full-Year	0.80	0.86	0.81	0.95	0.80

Source: Author's calculations based on U.S. Bureau of the Census (1991), table 6.

male college graduates between 25 and 34 years old was 90 percent, compared with 93 percent among whites in the same age group (table 1.2). Of those black male college graduates who had earnings, 77 percent worked full-time and full-year (table 1.4) and earned 80 percent of the amount that their white male counterparts earned (table 1.3). Black–white employment and earnings gaps are higher for males who never went to college. Nonetheless, 75 percent of black men between the ages of 25 and 34 who completed high school worked in 1989 (table 1.2), and those who worked full-time and full-year (68 percent of those with earnings—see table 1.4) earned 81 percent as much as their white counterparts (table 1.3).

These basic employment and earnings data suggest that no crisis exists for the vast majority of young black men. However, current trends and future prospects do not recommend complacency. Although the rate of high school completion among blacks was within a few percentage points of the corresponding figure for whites, the college entry rates of black males have fallen compared with whites

Table 1.4 PERCENTAGE OF EARNERS WORKING FULL-TIME, FULL-YEAR, 1989

Age/Race	Total	4 Years High School or Less	High School Graduate	Some College	College Grad. or Higher
White Males					
18–24	39	33	48	29	43
25–34	76	65	75	77	83
Black Males					
18–24	36	26	40	36	45
25–34	64	50	68	61	77

Source: U.S. Bureau of the Census (1991), table 9.

since the late 1970s. During the 1980s, college enrollment rates among black men (and women) declined, while enrollment rates of white men (and women) rose (Hauser 1992). By 1988, the college enrollment rates of black males were about 20 percentage points lower than those of white males. Unfortunately, college enrollment rates of black males were declining while employers were offering higher wage premiums to (black and white) workers with some college training. Finally, employment and earnings of black high school graduates also declined in the 1980s.

These trends suggest growing racial gaps in employment and earnings. They also suggest that growing numbers of black high school graduates could become stuck in low-wage jobs. Some might supplement their earnings with income through drug sales and, therefore, expose themselves to the violence and incarceration associated with drug selling (Fagan 1992; Reuter, MacCoun, and Murphy 1990). Therefore, some of the black males between 10 and 15 years old who are likely to graduate from high school in the next three to eight years could be counted among the population in crisis.

For young black men who have not completed high school, the picture is much more bleak. Only 56 percent of black male high school dropouts between 25 and 34 years old worked in 1989, and less than a third of those who were between 18 and 24 years old worked (table 1.2). Black men between 25 and 34 years old who worked full-time and full-year earned 86 percent of their white counterparts. However, only about half of the older cohort and just over a quarter of the younger cohort worked full-time and full-year.[1]

This evidence gives us a more conservative estimate of the size of the population "in crisis," and tells us what we would like future cohorts to avoid. Clearly, young black males who are at risk of becoming high school dropouts should be the major focus of crisis interven-

Figure 1.1 RATIO OF BLACK TO WHITE READING PROFICIENCY SCORES

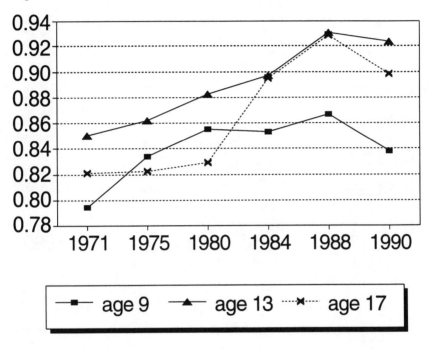

Source: U.S. Department of Education (1992).

tion. Unfortunately, this at-risk population is large. In 1986, 57 percent of blacks between 10 and 15 years old were two or more years behind their grade level. Though grade retention data are not available by race and sex, rates of grade retention for all races are generally higher for boys than girls (Resnick et al. 1992). Such grade retention often precedes dropping out, which is highly correlated with the employment and earnings difficulties just reviewed and with other social problems.

Even among young blacks who remain in school, improvements in basic skills are weakening. For example, figure 1.1 shows that after rising consistently since the early 1970s, the ratio of black to white reading proficiency scores has declined in recent years. Figures 1.2 and 1.3 show that the same is true of basic math and writing proficiency scores, except for the math proficiency scores of 17-year-old students and the writing proficiency scores of fouth graders. These recent declines in achievement are worrisome because of the increas-

Figure 1.2 RATIO OF BLACK TO WHITE MATH PROFICIENCY SCORES

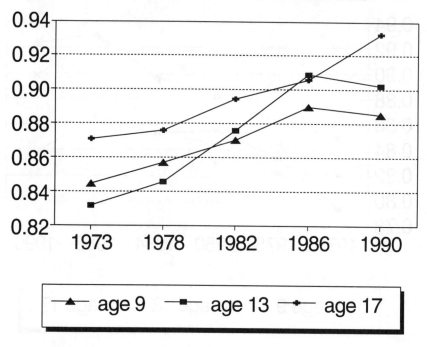

Source: U.S. Department of Education (1992).

ing relationship between academic achievement and earnings. Recent increases in the black–white earnings gap may have occurred because the black–white achievement gap was not closing fast enough to overcome increases in skill-based wage premiums (Bound and Freeman 1990; Ferguson 1992).

Now as in the past, poor labor market prospects for less skilled workers are correlated with increases in criminal activity. Hagedorn (1988) points out that the Great Depression prolonged delinquent behavior and gang membership, and increased criminal involvement among white immigrant youth and young adults in the 1930s. In a similar way, declines in the demand for low-skilled workers also prolonged participation in these activities among white, black, Chicano, and Puerto Rican teenage and young adult males in the 1980s (Williams and Kornblum 1985; Anderson 1991; Bourgois 1991; Hagedorn 1988; Jarret 1990; Taylor 1990; Fagan 1992).

However, changes in drug use patterns and criminal justice policies

Figure 1.3 RATIO OF BLACK TO WHITE WRITING PROFICIENCY SCORES

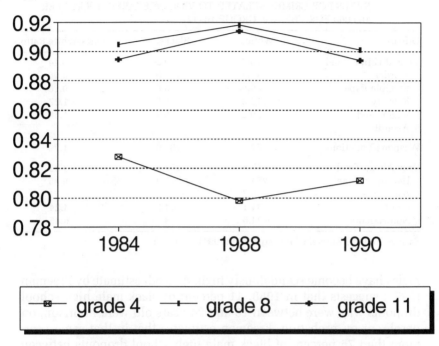

Source: U.S. Department of Education (1992).

have exacerbated the effects of poor job prospects on young black males. The introduction into the mid-1980s' urban drug markets of crack cocaine—an inexpensive and highly addictive drug—could have caused an increase in crime among jobless or low-earning men. On the other hand, drug use and crime might be joint activities that merely fill a void in the lives of young men idled by the dearth of high paying employment (McFate 1989). Whatever the reason for the increase in crime, changes in criminal justice policies have had an independent effect on incarceration rates. Despite fluctuating crime rates since the 1970s, incarceration rates have risen steadily. And criminologists expect that if new guidelines associated with Bush's War on Drugs are implemented, they will result in a 119 percent increase in the prison population between 1987 and 1997. The typical prisoner drawn into the system through these policies is a young, poorly educated, minority male (Mauer 1991).

Because of these trends, incarceration rates among young black

Table 1.5 PERCENT CHANGE BETWEEN 1980 AND 1990 IN JUVENILE ARREST
RATES FOR CRIMES RELATED TO VIOLENCE (ARREST RATE PER
100,000 FOR THE AGE GROUP 10–17)

Offense	Whites	Blacks	Black/White Ratio
Violent Crime Total	43.8	19.2	0.44
Murder	47.4	145.0	3.06
Forcible Rape	85.9	8.5	0.10
Robbery	12.3	− 15.6	− 1.27
Aggravated Assault	59.2	88.9	1.50
Weapons Violations	57.6	102.9	1.79
Drug Abuse Total	− 47.6	158.6	− 3.33
Heroin/Cocaine	251.1	2,372.9	9.45
Marijuana	− 66.7	− 47.5	0.71
Synthetic	− 34.1	144.7	− 4.24
Non-Narcotic	− 34.6	223.3	− 6.45

Source: Federal Bureau of Investigation (1991), table 5.1.

males have become scandalously high. A rough estimate by Freeman
(1992) suggests that in 1988, 41 percent of black male high school
dropouts who were between 18 and 24 years old were in prison, on
parole, or on probation. Freeman estimates that in that same year,
more than 75 percent of black male high school dropouts between
25 and 34 years old were in prison, on parole, or on probation.
Studies focusing on major metropolitan areas such as Baltimore,
Washington, D.C., and San Francisco also show that 30 to 60 percent
of young adult black males are involved in the criminal justice system
(Fry and Schiraldi 1992; Miller 1992a and 1992b; Reuter, MacCoun
and Murphy 1990). Thus, in 1988 nearly half a million black men
were in America's prisons and jails at a cost of almost $7 billion
(roughly $14,000 per man) per year (Edna McConnell Clark Founda-
tion 1992).

Drug abuse and drug-related crimes are also taking their toll on
younger black males. Between 1980 and 1990, black juvenile arrest
rates for drug abuse rose by 158.6 percent (table 1.5). The fact that
arrests of black juveniles for heroin or cocaine abuse grew by 2,373
percent shows the importance of crack cocaine in the recent upsurge
of juvenile arrests for drug-related offenses. While arrests of black
juveniles for heroin and cocaine grew ten times as fast as arrests of
white juveniles for abuse of these drugs between 1980 and 1990,
arrests of whites juveniles for abuse of all other drugs were falling.

Besides arrests for drug abuse, arrests of black juveniles for crimes

Figure 1.4 DEATH RATES FOR BLACK MALES BY HOMICIDE AND LEGAL
            INTERVENTION[a]

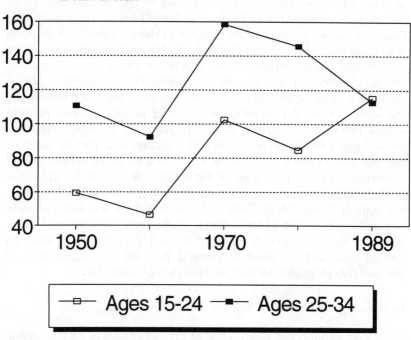

a. Number of deaths per 100,000 resident population.
Source: National Center for Health Statistics (1992).

associated with drug selling also have grown rapidly. Thus, between
1980 and 1990, arrest rates of black juveniles charged with weapons
violations grew by 102 percent. Arrest rates for murder and aggra-
vated assault grew by 145 and 89 percent, respectively.

Young black males are also the most common victims of drug-
related violence. Between 1950 and 1980, death rates due to homicide
and legal intervention (death at the hands of law enforcement officials) for black males between 15 and 24 years old were at least 50
percent lower than corresponding rates for black males between 25
and 34 years old (figure 1.4). This gap closed in the last decade
because the rate for the younger cohort grew by 27 percent, while
the rate for the older cohort fell by 29 percent. At the end of the
decade, death rates due to homicide or legal intervention for black
males were eight to nine times the corresponding rates for white
males in the same age groups.

Finally, prostitution and increases in the human sex drive associated with the sale and abuse of crack cocaine may be responsible for reversing favorable trends in the incidence of sexually transmitted diseases (STDs) among blacks. Growth in the prevalence of syphilis is a prime example. The incidence of syphilis declined sharply among whites and blacks between 1981 and 1985. Because of changes in sexual practices of white male homosexuals and bisexuals, these declines continued among whites between 1985 and 1989. But during the same period, the incidence of syphilis rose by over 40 percent among black males between 15 and 19 years old, by over 80 percent among black males between 20 and 24 years old, and by over 50 percent among black males between 25 and 29 years old (Rolfs and Nakashima 1990).[2] Increases in the incidence of syphilis and other STDs foreshadow high rates of mortality as today's black male teenagers mature (Cates 1991). Deaths due to HIV infection have already begun to rise among older cohorts. Thus, between 1987 and 1989, mortality rates due to HIV infection among black males between 25 and 34 years old increased 46 percent, from 52 per 100,000 to 75.9 per 100,000 (National Center for Health Statistics 1992).

Explaining the Crisis Indicators

What can explain the confluence of crisis indicators among young black males? Most black male adolescents who grow up in inner cities complete high school and avoid crime, substance abuse, and other problems. Individual personality traits help to explain why some young black males make harmful choices. However, there is a growing consensus that there are common antecedents to youth problem behavior and outcomes (regardless of race) such as delinquency, school failure, substance abuse, and early sexual activity. The most important antecedents are poverty, family dysfunction, and residence in a neighborhood with concentrations of families also experiencing poverty, family dysfunction, and other social problems (Bronfenbrenner 1979; Resnick et al. 1992).

Black children are more likely to be raised in poor, single parent households than children of other race and ethnic groups (Johnson et al. 1991). In 1991, 45.9 percent of black children were poor compared with 16.1 percent of white children and 39.8 percent of Hispanic children (U.S. Bureau of the Census 1992b). In the same year, 54 percent of black children were in mother-only households, compared with 16.5 percent of white children and 26.6 percent of Hispanic children (U.S. Bureau of the Census 1992a).

Poverty and family structure pose challenges to the development of black children, especially males. Parents of poor children are more likely to experience stressful events (such as illness, housing problems, and the death of friends or family members), and poverty diminishes their ability to respond positively.[3] Maternal depression and mental illness are more likely to occur among poor mothers, and poor maternal mental health status contributes to a higher incidence of infants with low birth weights (Parker, Greer, and Zuckerman 1988; McLoyd 1989). In turn, children with low birthweights are at greater risk for death in infancy, neurodevelopmental disabilities (such as cerebral palsy and seizure disorders), and other developmental problems that predict school failure (Institute of Medicine 1985). Poor children are also more likely to experience physical and emotional problems, and in adolescence are more likely to exhibit behavior problems (Dryfoos 1990).

Family members can inhibit the healthy development of youth because of what they do or fail to do. Families that engage in domestic violence, substance abuse, and child abuse and neglect create harmful environments for youth development (Resnick et al. 1992). These signs of dysfunction are high among black families in poverty (Ards 1989). Even without these signs of family dysfunction, parents who fail to support their children or who are uninvolved in their children's lives also inhibit youth development.

Children from single-parent households are more likely than other children to experience behavior problems and to drop out of high school. They are less likely than other children to enroll in or graduate from college. Recent studies show that boys are at greater risk when they are raised in single-parent households (Dryfoos 1990; McLanahan and Sandefur, forthcoming). In particular, verbal and physical abuse of toddlers by inner-city teenage mothers and liberal parental supervision of boys in female-headed families may predispose young black males to violent behavior, association with negative street peer groups, and disciplinary problems in school (Sampson 1987; Anderson 1993).

While several factors have adversely affected black family income, structure, and functioning, declines in the demand for low-skilled workers and persistent housing segregation surely play dominant roles. Since the mid-1970s, declines in the demand for low-skilled labor have undermined the economic status of black fathers and mothers who lack college training. The major factors responsible for this decline in demand are shifts in the industrial composition of U. S. output, increasing international trade, a decline in the minimum wage, and a decline in union representation and power in wage negotiations. Besides contributing to the decline in black family incomes, these economic changes have undermined the position of working-class males in black communities, individuals who once served as important socializing agents, especially for boys and young men (Anderson 1990). In some low-income black communities, drug gangs and street hustlers have now become the role models that children emulate (Taylor 1990).

Although economic changes have increased poverty among black adults, housing segregation concentrates this poverty, together with its related social problems, in black neighborhoods (Massey 1990). Blacks concentrate in large metropolitan areas, and low-income blacks concentrate in the poorest and most socially distressed neighborhoods in these areas. For reasons that are not clear, low-income whites tend to avoid these areas (Mincy, forthcoming, a). This compounds the adverse effects of low family income on black children with the adverse effects of neighborhood poverty and distress. About 6 percent of all black males between 5 and 14 years old live in under class neighborhoods and 18 percent live in extreme poverty neighborhoods. These data provide other measures of the size of the "in crisis" population. An extreme poverty area is a census tract in which 40 percent or more of the population is poor. An under class area is a census tract in which the fraction of adults detached from the labor force (or with barriers to labor force attachment) exceeds the national average. Significant barriers include being a high school dropout, a household head receiving public assistance, or a female head of household with children (see Mincy and Wiener, forthcoming). Thus, members of the "under class" are identified by types of behavior, not only extreme poverty. I use two words rather than the more typical "underclass" (one word) usage to emphasize the behavioral aspect, just as "middle class" and "lower class" conjure up types of labor force activity, not just income.

Concentrations of poor and nonworking people create additional ecological challenges to the development of black children. For example, under class areas are responsible for a disproportionate share of all foster care placements in Manhattan (Ards and Mincy 1991). Similarly, under class areas had the highest incidence of child mortality and morbidity due to AIDS (Mincy and Hendrickson 1988). In 1980, under class and extreme poverty neighborhoods in Cleveland and Washington, D.C., had higher rates of drug arrests and violent crimes than other neighborhoods in those cities. Between 1980 and

1988, these rates grew most rapidly in extreme poverty neighbor-hoods in these metropolitan areas (Wiener and Mincy 1991).

Though the quantitative evidence is mixed, qualitative evidence suggests that youths in neighborhoods with high rates of social prob-lems are likely to imitate negative role models or associate with peers involved in delinquency, sexual activity, and substance abuse (Hagedorn 1988; Anderson 1989, 1990; Jarret 1990; Taylor 1990).[4] Peers, family members, gang members, and neighborhood residents involved in drug selling are often the most important role models and caregivers for black boys in extreme poverty and under class neighborhoods. These role models and caregivers sometimes encour-age black boys to join them in their drug-selling activities as look-outs or carriers (Bing 1991).

The street culture that develops among black males in racially and economically segregated neighborhoods can also have adverse long-term consequences. Through this culture, black boys learn habits of dress, language, demeanor, and interpersonal skills that run counter to the expectations of teachers, school administrators, and employers (Majors and Billson 1992; Anderson 1990). In school these habits contribute to lack of engagement, poor grades, grade retention, drop-ping out, and disciplinary problems (Fordham and Ogbu 1986). In the labor market, these habits—compounded by poor math, reading, and writing skills—contribute to joblessness and low wages (Kirsch-enman and Neckerman 1991; Kirschenman 1991).

Some studies also point to the fear felt by black youth and parents living in neighborhoods where crime and violence are pervasive (Case and Katz 1990; Freeman 1992; Joint Center for Political and Economic Studies 1992). Boys who witness acts of violence or have a friend or relative who falls victim to violence are likely to experience trauma by such experiences. As a result, they anticipate a short life, which makes long-term investment in school, job skills, or health promotion seem trivial. They may become desensitized to violence or be motivated to arm themselves for protection (Brownstein et al. 1990). Both responses increase the number of young black men in crisis.

The Book

This volume provides an overview of youth development programs that help families nurture young black males from high-risk environments. Contributors come from diverse academic and professional backgrounds including economics, youth policy analysis, adolescent development, public welfare administration, and practice in the voluntary youth-service sector. The authors here focus on boys between 10 and 15 years old, because prevention is a cost-effective way to secure healthy development for all children and early adolescence is a neglected intervention point, especially for black males. For brevity, we call the programs under discussion YDBM programs, standing for Youth Development Programs Serving Young Black Males. Beyond the programs themselves, we focus on the boys and on the private financing arrangements and public youth policies that support the programs.

First, Courtland Lee discusses the goals of adolescent development generally, and the peculiar challenges that face young black males in the development process. He also examines the implications of these issues for social policy and program development. Next, Karen Pittman and Shepherd Zeldin call for a shift in thinking away from problem reduction toward youth development. They define youth development, review the supports needed to promote it, and emphasize the role of community-based organizations in providing these supports.

Following these two chapters on the services needed by black males between 10 and 15 years old, three contributors assess publicly and privately funded responses to these services needs. Ronald Ferguson provides an overview of programs that serve young black males. Agencies in the black community sponsor most of the programs in Ferguson's sample, and an Afrocentric world view is at the core of a subset of these programs. Morris Jeff then explains the basic principles underlying the Afrocentric world view and the reasons why some members of the black and white communities have been reluctant to accept this view. He illustrates how this world view is applied to youth development programming by drawing on his own personal experience with the Louis Armstrong Manhood Development Program in New Orleans. A large and well-developed youth service sector in this country possesses resources and experience that dwarf what is available in the black community. Black community efforts to help their own youth are a recent phenomenon whose effectiveness is constrained by the limited resources of these communities. Jane Quinn explains the history and structure of the youth service sector and the extent to which this sector is reaching young black males. While it is difficult to determine how many young black men are served, Quinn concludes that the number could be larger.

She urges the mainline youth-serving organizations to expand their YDBM programs, and she identifies several obstacles to such expansion.

These discussions of programmatic responses focus on programs and sponsoring agencies, with two notable omissions: black churches and public schools. The black church is among the most stable institutions in the black community, so it is natural to assume that it is a major sponsor of YDBM programs. Several of the programs in Ferguson's sample used the facilities of black churches. However, we cannot be sure if these programs were operated or supported by the church in any other way, and to date, no overview of black church-based YDBM programs has been conducted. We also know that a recent study found that only a quarter of black churches surveyed in the Northeast and North Central regions of the country offered youth programs of any kind (Rubin, Billingsley, and Caldwell, forthcoming). Therefore, it is unlikely that our omission of programs sponsored by black churches results in a serious gap in either the quantitative or qualitative assessment of available YDBM programs.

The exclusion of public schools was more deliberate. Most black males between the ages of 10 and 15 spend a significant portion of each weekday in the public schools. Public schools not only provide an opportunity for young black males to get basic skills, but also provide a rare opportunity for those who live in high-risk neighborhoods to interact with persons of different races and socioeconomic backgrounds. Thus, public schools have enormous potential to promote the development of young black males.

Unfortunately, complaints about the adverse effects of public schools on black children, especially males, are many. A recent survey by Kozol (1991) details the deplorable conditions of the segregated public schools many black children attend in urban areas. There are also complaints about particular public school policies that adversely affect low-income, minority children. For example, homogenous ability-tracking segregates students by race and class in integrated schools and adversely affects students' "academic achievement, extracurricular participation, self concept, peer relationships, career aspirations, and motivation" (Irvine 1991, p. 4). Arbitrary disciplinary practices discriminate against black students, especially males, resulting in suspensions and expulsions that remove and alienate them from the classroom. These and other failings of public schools with respect to poor and minority children are the subjects of legislative and programmatic reforms, which are beyond the scope of this book.[5]

Together, the programs reviewed by Ferguson, Jeff, and Quinn suggest a variety of nonpunitive ways to compensate for the ecological barriers to healthy development faced by many young black males. While there is no magic bullet, these programs provide a structure that policymakers, youth development practitioners, and private and corporate philanthropies can test, revise, and gradually improve. Though some of the keys to successful strategies are clear, significant challenges to progress remain.

In the final part of this volume, contributors assess the most important challenges affecting youth—social policy and funding. Andrew Hahn discusses how policy changes needed to increase public support of programs for young adolescents, including young black males, might occur. Hahn's view of social policy affecting young black males is pragmatic, covering several instruments available to policymakers to effect change. While he recommends that the United States develop a deliberate policy to help young adolescents make successful transitions to adulthood, how that policy should be targeted, the kinds of services it should support, and the methods for evaluating the effectiveness of those services are open questions. Susan Wiener (see Appendix A) shows how little funding is available for YDBM and other youth programs and discusses dramatic disparities among youth-serving agencies in access to existing funding sources. The agencies most likely to serve youth in high-risk environments rely primarily on meager public funding. This reliance limits the quantity and quality of youth services available to young black males. She makes several recommendations for changing the way youth-serving agencies seek private funding and the ways private sources provide such funding, and suggests that policy changes will be needed to increase public funding for young black youths.

In the concluding chapter, I draw on the work of the contributors to make recommendations to public and private agencies at national and local levels that wish to expand YDBM programs. This discussion is based on the original research of Richard Majors of the University of Wisconsin at Eau Claire, who has followed the evolution of national minority research and advocacy groups addressing the needs of black males in America. I end with a review of existing, pending, and proposed legislation that provides a framework for the national youth development policy recommended by several of the authors here.

Given the crisis indicators for young black males who have been the main focus of research to date, we can understand the hand-wringing response of most people who witness the troubled outcomes of young black males in high-risk environments. It is hoped that this book will inform and inspire concerned observers, so that they may put their wringing hands to work.

Notes

1. Employment among white high school dropouts was not much higher. Only 65 percent of white high school dropouts between 25 and 34 years old worked full-time and full-year. About a third of white male high school dropouts between 18 and 24 years old worked full-time and full-year.

2. The growth in the incidence of syphilis was even higher among black women between 1985 and 1989.

3. The unemployment and poverty experienced by black men may also contribute to their low marriage rates or their inability and unwillingness to play more active and supportive parenting roles. Unfortunately, studies attempting to relate unemployment and poverty to the mental health, marital status, and parenting skills of black fathers are yet to be conducted.

4. See Mayer and Jencks (1989) and Mincy (forthcoming, b) for recent reviews of the literature on neighborhood effects.

5. See Comer (1992) and the Commission on Chapter 1 (1992) for discussions of needed reforms.

References

Anderson, Elijah. 1993. "Drugs and the Inner-City Family." Research Paper. The Urban Institute, Washington, D.C., May.

_____. 1991. "Neighborhood Effects on Teenage Pregnancy." In *The Urban Underclass*, eds. Christopher Jencks and Paul E. Peterson. Washington, D.C.: The Brookings Institution.

_____. 1990. *Streetwise: Race, Class and Change in an Urban Community.* Chicago: University of Chicago Press.

_____. 1989. "Sex Codes and Family Life Among Poor Inner-city Youths." *The Annals of the American Academy of Political and Social Science* 501 (January): 59–78.

Ards, Sheila. 1989. "Estimating Local Child Abuse." *Evaluation Review* 13, 5: 45–49.

Ards, Sheila, and Ronald B. Mincy. 1991. "Foster Care and Underclass Areas." Research Paper. The Urban Institute, Washington, D.C., July.

Bing, Leon. 1991. *Do or Die.* New York: Harper Collins Publishers.

Bound, John, and Richard B. Freeman. "What Went Wrong? The Erosion of the Relative Earnings and Employment of Young Black Men in the 1980s." *Quarterly Journal of Economics* 107, 1(February): 201–32.

Bourgois, Phillippe. 1991. "In Search of Respect: The New Service Economy and the Crack Alternative in Spanish Harlem." Mimeo. Russell Sage Foundation, New York, May.

Bronfenbrenner, U. 1979. *The Ecology of Human Development: Experiments by Nature and Design.* Cambridge, Mass.: Harvard University Press.

Brounstein, Paul J., Harry P. Hatry, David M. Altschuler, and Louis H. Blair. 1990. *Substance Abuse and Delinquency Among Inner City Adolescent Males.* UI Report 90-3. Washington D.C.: Urban Institute Press.

Case, Anne C., and Lawrence F. Katz. 1990. "The Company You Keep: The Effects of Family and Neighborhood on Disadvantaged Youths." Mimeo. Harvard University, Cambridge, Mass., July.

Cates, Willard, Jr. 1991. "Teenagers and Sexual Risk-Taking: The Best of Times and the Worst of Times." *Journal of Adolescent Health* 12: 84–94.

Clark, Rebecca L. 1992. "Neighborhood Effects on Dropping Out of School Among Teenage Boys." Discussion Paper Series, Population Studies Center, the Urban Institute, Washington, D.C., December.

Comer, James. 1992. "Organize Schools Around Child Development." *Social Policy* 22 (Winter): 28–30.

Commission on Chapter 1. 1992. *Making Schools Work for Children in Poverty.* Washington, D.C.: The Commission on Chapter 1, December.

Dryfoos, Joy. 1990. *Adolescents at Risk: Prevalence and Prevention.* New York: Oxford University Press.

Edna McConnell Clark Foundation. 1992. *Americans Behind Bars.* New York: The Edna McConnell Clark Foundation.

Fagan, Jeffery. 1992. "Drug Selling and Licit Income in Distressed Neighborhoods: The Economic Lives of Street-Level Drug Users and Sellers." In *Drugs, Crime, and Social Isolation: Barriers to Urban Opportunity,* eds. Adele V. Harrell and George F. Peterson. Washington, D.C.: Urban Institute Press.

Federal Bureau of Investigation. 1991. *Uniform Crime Reports for the United States, 1991.* Washington, D.C.: U.S. Government Printing Office.

Ferguson, Ronald F. 1992. "Social and Economic Prospects of African–American Males: Why Reading, Math, and Social Development Should Be Leadership Priorities." In *What a Piece of Work Is Man!* ed. Bobby W. Austin. Kalamazoo, Mich.: W. K. Kellog Foundation.

Fordham, Signithia, and John U. Ogbu. 1986. "Black Students' School Success: Coping with the 'Burden of Acting White.' " *The Urban Review* 18, 3: 176–206.

Freeman, Richard B. 1992. "Crime and the Employment of Disadvantaged Youths." In *Urban Labor Markets and Job Opportunity,* eds. George E. Peterson and Wayne Vroman. Washington, D.C.: Urban Institute Press.

Fry, Susan, and Vincent Schiraldi. 1992. *Young African American Men and the Criminal Justice System in California.* San Francisco, National Center on Institutions and Alternatives.

Gibbs, Jewelle Taylor. 1988. "Young Black Males in America: Endangered, Embittered, Embattled." In *Young, Black, and Male in America: An Endangered Species,* ed. Jewelle T. Gibbs. Dover, Mass.: Auburn House.

Hagedorn, John M. 1988. *People and Folks: Gangs, Crime and the Underclass in a Rustbelt City.* Chicago: Lake View Press.

Hauser, Robert M. 1992. "Trends in College Entry Among Whites, Blacks, and Hispanics, 1972–1988" Mimeo. Institute for Research on Poverty, no. 958-91, Madison, Wisc., March.

Institute of Medicine, Committee to Study the Prevention of Low Birthweight. 1985. *Preventing Low Birthweight*. Washington, D.C.: National Academy Press.

Irvine, Jacqueline Jordan. 1991. *Black Students and School Failure: Policies, Practice, and Prescriptions*. New York: Greenwood Press.

Jarret, Robin L. 1990. "A Comparative Examination of Socialization Patterns Among Low-Income African Americans, Chicanos, Puerto Ricans, and Whites: A Review of the Ethnographic Literature." Mimeo. Social Science Research Council, New York, May.

Johnson, Clifford M., Leticia Miranda, Arloc Sherman, and James D. Weil. 1991. *Child Poverty in America*. Washington D.C.: Children's Defense Fund.

Joint Center for Political and Economic Studies. 1992. *Joint Center/HBO Survey*. Washington, D.C., Summer.

Kirschenman, Joleen. 1991. "Gender Within Race in the Labor Market." Presented to "The Urban Poverty and Family Life Conference," University of Chicago, Chicago, Ill., October.

Kirschenman, Joleen, and Kathryn M. Neckerman. 1991. " 'We'd Love to Hire Them, But...': The Meaning of Race for Employers." In *The Urban Underclass*, eds. Christopher Jencks and Paul E. Peterson. Washington D.C.: The Brookings Institution.

Kozol, Jonathan. 1991. *Savage Inequalities: Children in America's Schools*. New York: Crown Publishers, Inc.

Majors, Richard, and Janet Mancini Billson. 1992. *Cool Pose: The Dilemmas of Black Manhood in America*. New York: Lexington Books.

Massey, D. 1990. "American Apartheid: Segregation and the Making of the Underclass." *American Journal of Sociology* 96, 2: 329–57.

Mauer, Marc. 1991. *Americans Behind Bars: A Comparison of International Rates of Incarceration*. Washington, D.C.: The Sentencing Project, January.

Mayer, Susan, and Christopher Jencks. 1989. "Growing Up in Poor Neighborhoods: How Much Does It Matter?" *Science* 243: 1,441–45.

McFate, Katherine. 1989. "Crime, Drugs and the Urban Poor." Joint Center for Political and Economic Studies, Urban Poverty Roundtable No. 5, November.

McLanahan, S., and G. Sandefur. Forthcoming. *Uncertain Childhood, Uncertain Future*. Cambridge, Mass.: Harvard University Press.

McLoyd, V. 1989. "The Impact of Economic Hardship on Black Families and Children: Psychological Distress, Parenting and Socioemotional Development." Mimeo. University of Michigan, Ann Arbor.

Miller, Jerome G. 1992a. *Hobbling a Generation: Young African American Men in the Criminal Justice System in American Cities: Baltimore, Maryland*. Alexandria, Va.: National Center on Institutions and Alternatives.

_____. 1992b. *Hobbling a Generation: Young African American Men in DC's Criminal Justice System*. Alexandria, Va.: National Center on Institutions and Alternatives.

Mincy, Ronald B. Forthcoming, a. "Ghetto Poverty: Black Problem or Harbinger of Things to Come?" In *African American Economic Thought: Vol. Two, Methodology and Policy*, ed. Thomas D. Boston. New York: Routledge.

————. Forthcoming, b. "The Under class: Concept, Controversy, and Evidence." In *Poverty and Public Policy: What Do We Know, What Can We Do?* eds. S. Danzinger, D. Weinburg, and S. Sandefur. Cambridge, Mass.: Harvard University Press.

Mincy, Ronald B., and Susan E. Hendrickson. 1988 "AIDS and the Underclass." Statement before the Presidential Commission on the Human Immunodeficiency Virus Epidemic, April.

Mincy, Ronald B., and Susan Wiener. Forthcoming. "Underclass Growth During the 1980s: Changing Concept, Constant Reality." Mimeo. The Urban Institute, Washington, D.C.

National Center for Health Statistics. 1992. *Health United States 1991*. Public Health Service DHHS Pub No. (PHS) 92-1232. Washington, D.C.: U.S. Government Printing Office, May.

Parker, S., S. Greer, and B. Zuckerman. 1988. "Double Jeopardy: The Impact of Poverty on Early Child Development." *Pediatric Clinics of North America* 35, 6: 1–14.

Resnick, Gary, Martha R. Burt, Lisa Newmark, and Lorraine Reilly. 1992. "Youth At Risk: Definitions, Prevalence, and Approaches to Service Delivery." Mimeo. The Urban Institute, Washington, D.C., July.

Reuter, Peter, Robert MacCoun, and Patrick Murphy. 1990. *Money From Crime: A Study of the Economics of Drug Dealing in Washington, D.C.* Washington, D.C.: RAND Corporation.

Rolfs, Robert T., and Allyn K. Nakashima. 1990. "Epidemiology of Primary and Secondary Syphilis in the United States, 1981 through 1989." *Journal of the American Medical Association* 264, 11(September): 1,432–37.

Rubin, Roger H., Andrew Billingsley, and Cleopatra H. Caldwell. Forthcoming. "The Role of the Black Church in Working with Black Adolescents." *Adolescence*.

Sampson, Robert. 1987. "Urban Black Violence: The Effect of Male Joblessness and Family Disruption." *American Journal of Sociology* 93: 348–82.

Staples, Robert. 1991. "Black Male Genocide: A Final Solution to the Race Problem in America." In *Black Adolescents: Parenting and Education in the Community Context*, ed. Benjamin P. Bowser. Lanham, Md.: University Press of America.

Taylor, Carl S. 1990. *Dangerous Society*. East Lansing, Mich.: Michigan State University Press.

U.S. Bureau of the Census. 1992a. *Current Population Reports, Marital Status and Living Arrangements: March 1991*. Series P-20, No. 461. Washington, D.C.: U.S. Government Printing Office.

_____. 1992b. *Poverty in the United States, 1991.* Current Population Reports, Series P-60, No. 181. Washington, D.C.: U.S. Government Printing Office.

_____. 1991. Current Population Reports, Series P-20, No. 451. *Educational Attainment in the United States: March 1989 and 1988.* Washington, D.C.: U.S. Goverment Printing Office.

U.S. Department of Education, National Center for Education Statistics. 1992. *The Condition of Education, 1992.* Washington, D.C.

U.S. Department of Justice, Office of Juvenile Justice and Delinquency Prevention. 1992. *National Juvenile Custody Trends 1978–1987.* Washington, D.C.

Wiener, Susan J., and Ronald B. Mincy. 1991. "Social Distress in Urban Areas: Variations in Crime, Drugs, and Teen Births During the 1980s." Mimeo. The Urban Institute, Washington, D.C., April.

Williams, Terry M., and William Kornblum. 1985. *Growing up Poor,* Lexington, Mass.: Lexington Books.

Part One

ASSESSING NEEDS

Chapter Two

ADOLESCENT DEVELOPMENT

Courtland C. Lee

Social and economic indicators for black male youth in America today provide a profile of a group whose quality of life is in serious jeopardy (Gibbs 1988). It has become increasingly apparent that adolescent black males are confronted with a series of obstacles in their attempts to attain academic, professional, and personal success.

Because achieving manhood has historically been a complex task for black males in this country, black manhood must be carefully nurtured by major socializing agents and institutions (Lee 1992). The challenge is to develop, implement, and evaluate initiatives that foster the social and economic empowerment of adolescent black males. But policy formulation and program implementation must be based on an understanding of the dynamics associated with adolescent psychosocial development from a black perspective. In this chapter, I examine adolescent development generally, adolescent male development in an African/African-American cultural context, and the social policy and program implications associated with the developmental issues especially relevant to black male adolescents.

ADOLESCENCE AS A LIFE STAGE

Theorists and researchers have suggested that major aspects of human development unfold in a series of life stages and are influenced by both heredity and environment (Erikson 1950; Havighurst 1972; Kohlberg 1966; Piaget 1970). As individuals progress through various life stages they must master a series of developmental tasks. Mastery of tasks at one stage influences success with mastery of tasks in subsequent stages. Conversely, failure to master developmental tasks at one stage can negatively influence success in later stages.

Adolescence is the developmental transition between childhood and adulthood, and is characterized by significant physical and psychological changes. This period marks a sudden increase in body size and strength as well as a change in many physiological functions, including reproductive capacities. It also marks major personality changes designed to attain self-esteem and independence. According to Havighurst (1972), there are eight significant developmental tasks that must be accomplished during adolescence: 1) accepting one's physique and using the body effectively; 2) achieving emotional independence from parents and other adults; 3) achieving a masculine or feminine social role; 4) achieving new and more mature relations with peers of both sexes; 5) desiring and achieving socially responsible behavior; 6) acquiring a set of values and an ethical system as a guide to behavior; 7) preparing for an economic career; and 8) preparing for marriage and family life.

More than 40 years ago, Erikson (1950) linked adolescence with the development of a sense of personal identity, which involves discovering "who I am" and increasing understanding of one's existence. An adolescent's failure or frustration in developing a personal identity will result in self-doubt and role confusion. During the transitional years of adolescence, the development of a personal identity is greatly influenced by three important socializing institutions: the family, the secondary school, and the peer group. These three institutions contribute significantly to the mastery of adolescent developmental skills.

The family is the chief socializing influence on adolescents. Home atmosphere, parental involvement, and family relationships shape adolescent personality and instill modes of thought and behavior important for impending adult life. Important role modeling from parents and other family members can promote socially responsible behavior and contribute to the acquisition of values and ethics. Such role modeling can also help prepare adolescents for eventual marriage and family life.

With the achievement of virtually universal secondary education in the United States, high school is the central organizing experience in the lives of most adolescents. Secondary school, through both academic and social activities, offers adolescents the opportunity to learn information and master skills important for later life. Junior and senior high school also provide the opportunity to preview career choices in preparation for choosing a profession.

The influence of peers is also a major factor in the adolescent socialization process. The concept of peer group refers specifically to a cluster of associates who know one another and serve as one another's source of reference or comparison. In adolescence, the significant peer group consists of age-mates in the neighborhood or school who have a direct and dominant effect on the adolescent's daily life (Newman 1982). Within a peer group, adolescents can test their developing identities, evolving independence, and emerging behaviors.

In order for young people to successfully master the developmental tasks of adolescence, a commitment must be made to their education, personal growth, and career preparation. Social policy aimed at promoting adolescent development should focus on empowering healthy and capable young people with critical thinking skills, a sense of purpose, economic opportunities, high expectations, and significant social support. Such a policy should emphasize cooperation among home, school, and community. Strong families, good schools, and responsive communities form the basis of support that young people need to master adolescent developmental tasks and realize their full potential.

IMPEDIMENTS TO THE DEVELOPMENT OF BLACK MALE ADOLESCENTS

For black males, successfully completing the tasks associated with adolescent development has often been problematic due to a complex set of interacting historical and social factors that often inhibit success. This significant lack of mastery negatively influences black adolescents' academic, professional, and social success in later life.

Historically, manhood has not been a birthright for black males, who have not generally been granted traditional masculine privilege or power in the United States (Hernton 1965; Lee 1992; Staples 1978). Social, cultural, and economic forces manifested in racism and oppression throughout American history have combined to keep black males from assuming traditionally accepted masculine roles (Staples 1983; Wilkinson and Taylor 1977). The persistence of such barriers to the achievement and expression of manhood has contributed to black males' failure, in many instances, to master crucial adolescent developmental tasks.

Racism and socioeconomic disadvantage often converge to impact negatively on the adolescent development of black males, who are often confronted with extreme environmental stress during the crucial early years of life (Hilliard 1985; Myers and King 1980). For example, a significant number of black males, particularly in urban areas, are born into home and community environments characterized by traditions of poverty, crime, unemployment, inequitable educational opportunities, and a perceived sense of social and cultural alienation. Young males nurtured in such environments may experience difficulty in mastering the developmental tasks that characterize the childhood and adolescent years.

Successful completion of these developmental tasks can be further hampered by school experiences often distinguished by ineffective teaching strategies and educators' predetermined negative views of black males and their learning potential (Hale 1982; Patton 1981; Washington and Lee 1982). Rather than developing a sense of industry that comes with mastering reading, writing, and computing skills in elementary school, many young black male students experience frustration with the teaching–learning process, thus laying the groundwork for future academic and social failure.

It is not unusual, then, for black males to reach adolescence with a basic mistrust of their environment, doubts about their abilities, and confusion about their place in the world. This makes developing an identity during the adolescent years extremely problematic. Compounding this problem is the fact that many adolescent black males may have to engage in the process of identity formation with minimal or no positive adult male role modeling. The developmental passage to adulthood thus becomes a confusing experience for many black male youths because the evolution of gender-appropriate roles and behaviors for black men has often been stifled by historical and social powerlessness.

By the age of 18 or 19, the sum total of these impediments to adolescent development can often be seen in negative and self-destructive values, attitudes, and behaviors among young black males. These, in turn, have resulted in academic underachievement, unemployment, delinquency, substance abuse, homicide, and incarceration in disproportionate numbers for black male youth (Cordes 1985; Gibbs 1988).

Policy formulation and program implementation for nurturing black male youth must be based on an understanding of the complex dimensions associated with adolescent black male development. These dimensions are challenging in a society that has historically placed black men at social and economic risk.

AFRICAN/AFRICAN-AMERICAN CULTURE AND ADOLESCENT BLACK MALE DEVELOPMENT

Appreciating the development of adolescent black males requires an understanding of the cultural dynamics that can positively shape that development. Over the past several decades, black educators and psychologists have found aspects of the black cultural experience in America that have evolved out of African tradition and that have a significant effect on the psychological and social development of blacks in this country (Cross 1974; Harper 1973; Nobles 1980; Pasteur and Toldson 1982; White and Parham 1990). These findings have led to a framework for understanding African-American behavior and personality.

Black culture is comprised of the attitudes, behaviors, values, and lifestyles that have developed in relatively homogeneous black communities in which rudimentary Afrocentric ways of life have been largely preserved. Examining the core of this culture reveals that Americans of African descent have developed a world view that reflects the historical experience of black people in America and is based on African cultural and philosophical traditions. These traditions stress harmony among people and harmony between people and their external environment, and foster self and group development through behavioral expressiveness (Nobles 1980). From an early age, black male youth tend to be socialized into these traditions in the home and larger black community (Allen 1981; Staples 1983; Wilson 1987). These traditions form the basis of survival strategies, coping mechanisms, and forms of resistance to the racial and gender bias that has confronted black males in American society.

A synthesis of these cultural traditions is readily apparent in the personality dynamics of black male youth, and can be considered the basis of a distinct black male culture (Hale 1982; Kunjufu 1986; Lee 1992). Majors (1986) refers to these personality dynamics as "cool pose" and considers them to be the cornerstone of urban black male identity. These dynamics are manifested in the following ways:

Social behavior. There is a unique dynamism associated with the social behavior of urban adolescent black males. For instance, their peer group interactions are often characterized by high levels of energy that tend to be very physical and demonstrative.

Authenticity. Adolescent black males have a propensity to exhibit real, honest, and authentic behavior in all interactions—that is, for "being for real" or "telling it like it is." They tend not to stifle their true thoughts, feelings, or behaviors in most social situations. While such authenticity may not always be appreciated or understood by others, black male youths tend to cut to the heart of a matter with their genuineness.

Language and Speech. The language and speech of urban adolescent black males are highly expressive and exhibit considerable creativity. Colorful slang expressions, "woofing" (making verbal threats not backed up by actions), "playing the dozens" (trading verbal insults), and the popular "rap" vernacular are innovative ways to communicate both the trivial and the profound. Often these expressive linguistic traditions are used in order to diffuse tension between young males that could lead to physical aggression. For example, the often harsh verbal volleying that accompanies "woofing" can prevent two young black males from coming to physical blows.

Style. Adolescent black males in urban areas find creative ways to put their personalities on display. One has only to examine the style and flair exhibited in the play of black males on a basketball court, the swagger associated with walking, hats worn at a jaunty angle, distinctive handshakes, fancy sneakers, or flashy articles of clothing to appreciate this expressiveness. For young black males, these displays of style are attempts to make a proud statement about themselves.

Successful mastery of the developmental tasks of adolescence is facilitated by the healthy expression of the above dynamics on the part of black male youth. As Majors (1986) suggests, these personality dynamics have also been an important coping mechanism. Rather than use anger and frustration to confront the racism and oppression that characterize the black experience in America, black males have channeled their energies into the development of expressive personality dynamics. Such dynamics significantly contribute to black male survival.

POLICY AND PROGRAM IMPLICATIONS

The negative effects of poverty, alienation, and racism have taken their toll on the development of many adolescent black males in contemporary American society. The future status of black men in America depends, in large measure, on the ability of agencies, programs, and social policy to nurture the development of black male youth. Helping to empower adolescent black males so they can live productive adult lives will require a comprehensive and systematic approach.

Below is a synthesis of policy strategies and options for nurturing the development of adolescent black males. This synthesis represents recent social policy ideas concerning adolescent development from a variety of sources (American Association of School Administrators 1990; Children's Defense Fund 1990; Congressional Task Force on the Future of African Americans 1989; Maryland State Department of Education 1989; Mosqueda and Palaich 1990; National Black Child Development Institute 1990; Office of Educational Research and Improvement 1991; Scales 1990; House of Representatives 1989; Solomon 1988; Spencer, Swanson, and Cunningham 1991; Strickland and Cooper 1987; Taylor 1987; William T. Grant Foundation 1988). These policy recommendations call for aggressive private and public sector support of efforts by families, schools, and communities to facilitate the mastery of adolescent developmental tasks by black male youth.

Educational Empowerment

Education is power. Black people have always placed a great value on education. Indeed, the social and economic progress that blacks have made in this country has been in direct proportion to the educational opportunities available to them.

Adolescent black males face formidable challenges to their educational development. The achievement, aspiration, and pride of many black males in school systems throughout the country are seriously stifled. Frustration, underachievement, and ultimate failure comprise the educational reality for scores of black male youths. Indeed, data on the educational development of adolescent black males from a variety of sources (House of Representatives 1990; Jones 1986; Congress of the United States 1991; National Black Child Development Institute 1990; Reed 1988; House of Representatives 1989) reveal a troubled profile. Policy recommendations to address the challenge of educational development for adolescent black males include the following:

☐ Introduce a flexible secondary school curriculum for black males that is based on the acceptance and application of African and African-American cultural traditions in the teaching–learning process;
☐ Increase the number of black male educators at the secondary level who can serve as significant role models, adequately assess the

developmental and learning needs of black male youth, and link youth with needed services, opportunities, and/or programs. This will involve attracting and facilitating increased enrollment of black men in education degree programs at universities;

□ Enhance parent involvement through school efforts to help parents and educational professionals understand their mutual responsibilities in the educational development of black male adolescents;

□ Make non-academic educational pursuits available through churches and other centers of community activity, including physical education, recreation, exposure to the arts, social skills development, and cultural education.

Career Preparation

Preparing for an economic career is a major developmental task of adolescence. However, for many adolescent black males the world of work is landscaped with unfulfilled dreams, wasted potential, and economic struggle. Policy initiatives must take into consideration the social pressures on black male career development, and restructure traditional adolescent career guidance accordingly. Below are some of the main policy recommendations for preparing black male youth for the world of work:

□ Create relevant secondary school career education and counseling programs that focus on non-stereotyped jobs and careers for black males;

□ Focus public and private sector attention on workable approaches to easing the passage from school to work for black male adolescents including cooperative education, internships, apprenticeships, and other forms of experiences in the work world, wheneverˌpossible with black businesses and/or black male professionals;

□ Encourage efforts by parents, teachers, and employers to help black male youth plan reasonable part-time work schedules.

Personal Social Growth

Developing a positive self-identity is the essence of successful mastery of the developmental tasks of adolescence. Racism and alienation have profoundly influenced black male well-being in America, often leaving young black males wondering who they are, where they belong, and where they are going. Policy recommendations to facilitate a positive transition from boyhood to manhood include the following:

☐ Promote initiatives to foster the integrity of black family life to insure the transmission of values, facilitate the achievement of emotional independence, and help adolescent males prepare for marriage and family life;
☐ Encourage cultural experiences that promote an understanding and appreciation of the black man in history and culture;
☐ Create mentoring programs in schools, churches, and community agencies that involve adolescent male youth in ongoing relationships with successful adult black males;
☐ Conduct "rites of passage" ceremonies in schools, churches, and community agencies to formally acknowledge the transition from boyhood to manhood among black male youths;
☐ Expand fatherhood programs that include parenting and family planning education;
☐ Create opportunities to achieve socially responsible behavior by promoting relationships and experiences that encourage a sense of community;
☐ Increase structured leisure activities in community social centers that provide opportunities for positive peer interactions after school, on weekends, and during the summer months;
☐ Offer comprehensive community health initiatives to assess and address health attitudes, behaviors, values, and needs to insure strong minds and healthy bodies;
☐ Increase emphasis on the development of spiritual values among adolescent black male youths.

CONCLUSION

The future status of black men in America depends, in large measure, on policy and program initiatives aimed at nurturing the development of adolescent black males. Empowering young black males will require a comprehensive and systematic approach. Black male adolescence needs to be understood in the context of African and African-American culture and norms. Facilitating healthy black male adolescent development cannot be done without support from home and family resources, leadership from educational institutions, and the careful tapping of the cultural strengths of black communities.

The challenge to agencies, programs, and social policies is to insure that black male youths master adolescent development tasks in a social and economic system that has historically been stacked against them.

References

Allen, W. R. 1981. "Moms, Dads, and Boys: Race and Sex Differences in the Socialization of Male Children." In *Black Men*, ed. L. E. Gary. Beverly Hills, Calif.: Sage Publications.

American Association of School Administrators. 1990. "Healthy Kids for the Year 2000: An Action Plan for Schools." Arlington, Va.: American Association of School Administrators.

Children's Defense Fund. 1990. "S.O.S. America! A Children's Defense Fund Budget." Washington, D.C.: Children's Defense Fund.

Congress of the United States. 1991. "The Economic Status of African Americans: Hearing Before the Subcommittee on Investment, Jobs, and Prices of the Joint Economic Committee." Washington, D.C.: U.S. Government Printing Office.

Congressional Task Force on the Future of African Americans. 1989. *The Future of African Americans to the Year 2000. Summary Report.* Washington, D.C.: U.S. Government Printing Office.

Cordes, C. 1985. "Black Males Face High Odds in a Hostile Society." *American Psychological Association Monitor* (January): 9–11, 27.

Cross, A. 1974. "The Black Experience: Its Importance in the Treatment of Black Clients." *Child Welfare* 52: 158–66.

Erikson, E. 1950. *Childhood and Society.* New York: Norton.

Gibbs, J. T. 1988. "Young Black Males in America: Endangered, Embittered, and Embattled." *Young, Black, and Male in America: An Endangered Species*, ed. J. T. Gibbs. Dover, Mass.: Auburn House.

Hale, J. E. 1982. *Black Children: Their Roots, Culture, and Learning Styles.* Provo, Utah: Brigham Young University Press.

Harper, F. 1973. "What Counselors Must Know About the Social Sciences of Black Americans." *Journal of Negro Education* 42: 109–16.

Havighurst, R. J. 1972. *Developmental Tasks and Education.* New York: McKay.

Hernton, C. 1965. *Sex and Racism in America.* New York: Grove.

Hilliard, A. G. 1985. "A Framework for Focused Counseling on the African American Man." *Journal of Non-White Concerns in Personnel and Guidance* 13: 72–78.

House of Representatives. 1990. "Hearing on the Office of Educational Research and Improvement. Hearing Before the Subcommittee on

Select Education of the Committee on Education and Labor." Washington, D.C.: U.S. Government Printing Office.

————. 1989. *Barriers and Opportunities for America's Young Black Men. Hearing Before the Select Committee on Children, Youth, and Families.* Washington, D.C.: U.S. Government Printing Office.

Jones, K. M. 1986. "Black Male in Jeopardy." *Crisis* 93: 16–21, 44–45.

Kohlberg, L. 1966. "Moral Education in the Schools: A Developmental View." *School Review* 74: 1–30.

Kunjufu, J. 1986. *Countering the Conspiracy to Destroy Black Boys.* Vol. II. Chicago: African American Images.

Lee, C. C. 1992. *Empowering Young Black Males.* Ann Arbor, Mich.: ERIC/CAPS.

Majors, R. 1986. "Cool Pose: The Proud Signature of Black Survival." *Changing Men: Issues in Gender, Sex, and Politics* 17: 5–6.

Maryland State Department of Education. 1989. *On the Brink: Students at Risk During Times of Transition: Technical Team Report.* Baltimore: Maryland State Department of Education.

Mosqueda, P. F., and R. Palaich. 1990. *Mentoring Young People Makes a Difference.* Denver: Education Commission of the States.

Myers, H. F., and L. M. King. 1980. "Youth of the Black Underclass: Urban Stress and Mental Health." *Fanon Center Journal* 1(January): 1–27.

National Black Child Development Institute. 1990. *The Status of African American Children: Twentieth Anniversary Report, 1970–1990.* Washington, D.C.: National Black Child Development Institute.

Newman, P. R. 1982. "The Peer Group." In *Handbook of Developmental Psychology,* ed. B. B. Wolman. Englewood Cliffs, N.J.: Prentice Hall.

Nobles, W. 1980. "African Philosophy: Foundations for a Black Psychology." In *Black Psychology,* ed. R. L. Jones. New York: Harper & Row.

Office of Educational Research and Improvement. 1991. *Youth Indicators 1991: Trends in the Well-being of American Youth.* Washington, D.C.: U.S. Government Printing Office.

Pasteur, A. B., and I. L. Toldson. 1982. *Roots of Soul: The Psychology of Black Expressiveness.* Garden City, N.Y.: Anchor Press/Doubleday.

Patton, J. M. 1981. "The Black Male's Struggle for an Education." In *Black Men,* ed. L. E. Gary. Beverly Hills, Calif.: Sage Publications.

Piaget, J. 1970. *Science of Education and the Psychology of the Child.* New York: Onion Press.

Reed, R. J. 1988. "Education and Achievement of Young Black Males." In *Young, Black, and Male in America: An Endangered Species,* ed. J. T. Gibbs. Dover, Mass.: Auburn House.

Scales, P. 1990. "Developing Capable Young People: An Alternative Strategy for Prevention Programs." *Journal of Early Adolescence* 10, 4(November): 420–38.

Solomon, B. 1988. "The Impact of Public Policy on the Status of Young Black Males." In *Young, Black, and Male in America: An Endangered Species,* ed. J. T. Gibbs. Dover, Mass.: Auburn House.

Spencer, M. B., D. P. Swanson, and M. Cunningham. 1991. "Ethnicity, Ethnic Identity, and Competence Formation: Adolescent Transition and Cultural Transformation." *Journal of Negro Education* 60, 3(Summer): 366–87.

Staples, R. 1983. *Black Masculinity: The Black Male's Role in American Society*. San Francisco: Black Scholar Press.

————. 1978. "Masculinity and Race: The Dual Dilemma of Black Men." *Journal of Social Issues* 34: 169–83.

Strickland, D. S., and E. J. Cooper. 1987. *Educating Black Children: America's Challenge*. Washington, D.C.: Howard University Bureau of Educational Research.

Taylor, R. L. 1987. "Black Youth in Crisis." *Humboldt Journal of Social Relations* 14: 106–33.

Washington, V., and C. C. Lee. 1982. "Teaching and Counseling Black Males in Grades K to 8." *Journal of the National Association of Black Social Workers* 13, 1(Spring): 25–29.

White, J. L., and T. A. Parham. 1990. *The Psychology of Blacks: An African-American Perspective*. Englewood Cliffs, N.J.: Prentice Hall.

William T. Grant Foundation Commission on Work, Family and Citizenship. 1988. *The Forgotten Half: Pathways to Success for America's Youth and Young Families*. Washington, D.C.: W. T. Grant Foundation.

Wilkinson, D. Y., and R. L. Taylor. 1977. *The Black Male in America: Perspectives on His Status in Contemporary Society*. Chicago: Nelson-Hall.

Chapter Three

FROM DETERRENCE TO DEVELOPMENT: SHIFTING THE FOCUS OF YOUTH PROGRAMS FOR AFRICAN-AMERICAN MALES

Karen Johnson Pittman and Shepherd Zeldin

"Adults tend to think of kids they just as you know . . . they're troublemakers . . . put 'em somewhere, let 'em do something, it's like, it's like putting your, like, when you get a three-year-old, if they're messing with something, you're gonna throw 'em in a room just to play with a toy or something, just to get them out of the way."

—Youth speaking on pending cuts in the Washington, D.C., Summer Youth Jobs Program, WAMU-FM, July 31, 1992

There is a sharp tension in this country between what society wants from young African-American males—fewer crimes, fewer unclaimed children, fewer unemployment claims—and what these youths need from society—more respect, responsibility, participation, opportunities, and rewards. This kind of tension affects all youth, but is greater and historically more deeply rooted in reference to young African-American males (see chapter 2).

Most institutionalized youth programs focus on "fixing" youth problems by deterring negative outcomes and correcting deficits. The assumptions underlying this approach are that adolescents have little to offer society, and that because they have marginal attachments to mainstream social values, they cannot be trusted with significant responsibilities. These assumptions have distorted the shape of youth policy and youth services in this country.

In this chapter we argue that prevalent assumptions about adolescents, and about adolescent black males in particular, are barriers to creating and supporting services that effectively meet their needs. The programmatic emphasis on deterring problems distorts the primary goal of promoting positive youth development. To assume that youth have little to contribute to society is to fail to provide them opportunities to participate. To believe that youth do not care about community is to fail to *empower* them to make full use of their skills.

These assumptions foster an attitude that considers at-risk youths "lost causes" unworthy of investment.

Society magnifies these assumptions all the more when considering black male (and other minority) youths. Much of adult society views young black men as "less than" their peers, and hence less deserving of society's resources (Smith 1990; Batts 1988). Inequalities are magnified for black male youths because they receive even fewer developmental opportunities than other youths (National Research Council 1993). As long as existing youth programs overlook the developmental needs of young black men, this group will continue to be placed at increasing risk of failure.

NEGATIVE ASSUMPTIONS ABOUT YOUTH

Young black males need what every parent strives to offer his or her child—caring, continuity, connections, challenges, and community. These forms of nurturing help young people acquire the skills necessary for emotional health and achievement—commitment, compassion, conviction, and competence. But most youth programs today are not designed to provide this nurturing because of society's negative assumptions about adolescents.

Assumption One: The Goal of Policy is to Deter and Correct Deficits Among Young People

Adherence to the goal of deterring youth's deficits leads to the belief that, with the exception of education, services for at-risk youth should exist in response to youth problems. The assumption of "fixing" is clearly reflected in the services offered to at-risk youth. When a young person starts to show anger or hopelessness, for example, or begins to perform poorly in school or experiment with drugs, the first recourse is often to place the adolescent in a counseling, tutoring, or "remedial" program. Consequently, there is a strong assumption that the best way to deal with the "problem" of black males—the demographic group often deemed at greatest risk—is through highly structured programs that carefully target deficits or deter serious behaviors. Dropout recovery, second chance training, substance abuse prevention, pregnancy prevention, and diversion programs are all examples of this approach.

But "problem free" does not mean "fully prepared." Preventing high-risk behaviors, even if achieved, is not the same as helping young people prepare for their future. Preparation requires an equal commitment to helping youths understand life's challenges and responsibilities and teaching them the necessary skills for success as adults. It demands a response that includes not simply problem prevention, but also opportunities that require the young person to take responsibility for self, engage in collaborative action with peers and adults, and participate in activities that require the acquisition and use of basic academic, social, and vocational competencies.

Assumption Two: Youths Are Poor Investments Because They Have Little To Offer Society

This second assumption reflects the deep ambivalence toward youth in the United States. In response to this ambivalence, advocates for youth programs have adopted an "investment" strategy, arguing that investing in youth will increase productivity and decrease anti-social behaviors, and in the long term, public dependency. There are two problems with this line of thinking. First, investing in problem pre-vention is a low-yield approach, whether the focus is on preventing academic failure, alcohol use, or early sexual behavior (Office of Technology Assessment 1991). Second, investment implies that there can be good and bad investments. Unfortunately, adolescents labeled "at-risk," especially black males, are not viewed as lucrative invest-ments in 1993. Consequently, disproportionately high investments are made in those youth who are likely to be strong adult contributors anyway (William T. Grant Commission on Work, Family and Citizen-ship 1988).

Assumption Three: Youths Do Not Desire to Become Contributing Members of Society

This third assumption suggests that, for some reason, young people are different from everybody else. Certainly, many young people appear not to share societal values, but this is not surprising given current conditions and limited opportunities that exist for many of them. Being reared in a deteriorating neighborhood or being viewed as a "problem" is not likely to foster the attachments that society and adolescents desire. Attachments, like all aspects of youth devel-opment, need to be nurtured. Absent this support, young people will meet their needs for connection by attaching themselves to destructive entities such as gangs.

A MORE POSITIVE APPROACH TO YOUTH DEVELOPMENT

How does a youth become not merely "problem free" but also confident and competent? A more promising approach than the current one is to look at youths as resources rather than as problems, and to provide them with opportunities and reasons to build attachments to positive social institutions.

In the words of two Washington, D.C., poor, black, "at-risk" youths speaking about pending cuts to a summer youth jobs program:

> There's a lot of buildings right here that's empty, you know, they have . . . boards up and stuff. You could get a group of teenagers to go there, fix it up, and I'm sure they'll love what they see when it was all finished.
>
> I live in Northeast. If you wanted me to fix a house in Northwest, you have to pay me. But if you want me to fix a house on the other end of my block, I would be glad to help.
>
> —WAMU-FM, July 31, 1992

It is well documented that at-risk adolescents can make substantial contributions to their communities in ways that at the same time promote youth development (Hedin and Conrad 1982; Hamilton 1990; Pittman and Cahill 1992). Providing youth with opportunities to contribute to the community and with choices of how to do so strengthens their social, academic, and vocational competencies. In the same vein, cooperative learning—whereby peers help peers to learn academic subjects, enhance decision-making skills, or reduce anger or violence—has been shown to have similar benefits for young people (Hedin and Conrad 1982; Slavin 1991; Hamilton 1980; Weissberg, Caplan, and Bennetto 1988).

Getting youths to build attachments to social institutions or to the values that underlie them will not automatically follow as the result of building adolescent competencies. As documented frequently, for example, schools may have programs that, on the face, should impart academic knowledge. But because young people are not always given the opportunity to feel ownership over their work, learning and attachment to school do not always occur. Attachments are emotional as much as competency-based. Youth will respond when given participatory roles, when trusted, and when they perceive they are valued members of schools and communities. Without such empowerment, there is little chance that young people will form attachments to institutions.

At-risk youths such as those quoted above are black, male, poor, and live in the inner-city. They do not view themselves in need of "fixing" or "repair." What they do talk about is the desire for nurturing, respect, and opportunities to develop skills and responsibility. Their statements confirm the need for a shift in the way we perceive our youth and the programs that serve them. We need to move our program focus away from intervention to interaction, away from programs to people, and away from content to context. This new vision of services for youth is based on the following assertions.

Assertion One. Youth development is an ongoing process throughout which young people seek ways to meet their basic physical and social needs and to build the competencies and connections they perceive as necessary for survival and success. All youth are engaged in the process of development (see table 3.1).

Youth development occurs in the context of people, places, and institutions that form the ecological environment in which young people mature. It is not the domain of families or any single set of organizations or actors. To the contrary, all institutions and individuals that touch youths' lives can have an impact on their development. Whether and how young people acquire the maturity, confidence, and skills critical to full societal participation depends on the quality and constancy of the influences in their lives.

Assertion Two. Youth development is marked by the acquisition of a broad range of competencies and the demonstration of a full complement of connections to self, others, and the larger community. Confidence, compassion, commitment, and character are terms commonly used to express the attitudes and behaviors that determine if and how learned competencies will be used.

Promoting youth development requires attention not only to the content of what is taught or shared, but to the contexts in which learning and social interactions take place, and how these interactions are experienced by adolescents. Engagement—the active connection of youth to self, peers, adults, group, and community as both recipient and giver—is a prerequisite of competency development. Skill building is best achieved when young people are confident of their abilities, contacts, and resources. This means that youth need

Table 3.1 CRITICAL COMPONENTS OF YOUTH DEVELOPMENT

Meeting Needs	Plus	Building Competencies
Young People have basic needs critical to survival and healthy development. These include a sense of:		*To succeed as adults, youth must acquire adequate attitudes, behaviors, and skills in five areas:*

Young People have basic needs critical to survival and healthy development. These include a sense of:

Safety and structure;

Belonging and membership;

Self-worth and an ability to contribute;

Independence and control over one's life;

Closeness and several good relationships;

Competence and mastery;

Self-awareness/Spirituality.

To succeed as adults, youth must acquire adequate attitudes, behaviors, and skills in five areas:

Health:
Good current health status and evidence of knowledge, attitudes, and behaviors that will assure future well-being; for example, exercise, good nutrition, and effective contraceptive practices.

Personal/Social Skills:
An ability to understand emotions and practice self-discipline, and interpersonal skills such as working with others, developing and sustaining friendships through cooperation, empathy, negotiation, and developing judgment skills and a coping system.

Knowledge, Reasoning, and Creativity:
A broad base of knowledge and an ability to appreciate and demonstrate creative expression; good oral, writing, and problem-solving skills, and an ability to learn; interest in life-long learning and achieving.

Vocation:
A broad understanding and awareness of life options and the steps to take in making choices; adequate preparation for work and family life, and an understanding of the value and purpose of family work, and leisure.

Citizenship:
Understanding of their nation's, community's and racial/ethnic/cultural group's history and values; desire to be ethical and to be involved in efforts that contribute to the broader good.

to be nurtured, guided, empowered, and challenged by important work that they perceive as relevant. It means that they have to be engaged in constructive relationships with peers and adults.

These assertions suggest needed changes in the way services and supports for youth are planned, structured, delivered, and assessed. They call for an examination of the fact that a disproportionate share of policy attention and funding is focused on the narrow goals of academic training and vocational placement, without understanding the importance of developing "non-credentialed" competencies such as personal and social skills, health, and citizenship. Finally, these assertions demand that priority attention be given to the basic human needs of young people—confidence, emotional well-being, structure, healthy relationships, membership, and participation. In brief, policymakers need to nurture all of youth development, not just part of it.

COMMUNITY-BASED YOUTH ORGANIZATIONS AND YOUTH DEVELOPMENT

As currently structured, community-based youth organizations (and the programs they sponsor) are better equipped to promote youth development than institutional services such as schools, the justice system, and the health care and social service systems (Pittman 1991). This fact, documented in this volume, is increasingly acknowledged by policymakers and researchers (Carnegie Council on Adolescent Development 1993).

There is no way to concisely summarize the vast array of services that community organizations offer to young people. Their fundamental link is that they seek to empower young people. In almost every effective program, for example, adolescents are given choices and expected to take responsibility for themselves and the well-being of the program. Typically, young people are given opportunities to develop functional competencies through service to peers, neighborhood residents, or the community in general.

But it is not the activities that capture the essence of successful youth programs as much as it is the environment offered. Translated into another setting and structure, in fact, the same activities may become burdensome or even intimidating to many youth. I have argued that the necessary component to effective youth programs is caring (Pittman and Cahill 1992). Caring is what differentiates such programs from institutions such as schools and employment programs.

In the research literature, caring is a "protective factor" separate and distinct from high expectations and opportunities for participation. It is the essential quality that underlies the development of social competence, problem-solving skills, autonomy, and a sense of purpose and future (Bronfenbrenner 1979; Ianni 1989; Bernard 1991). Yet, as the term "caring" makes its way from research into policy and practice (Pittman and Cahill 1992), it can be usefully broken down into four components:

☐ *Caring As Nurturing:* Consistent support, comfort, and attention to basic needs;

☐ *Caring As Healing and Treatment:* Adequate identification and treatment of problems, and amelioration of unhealthy circumstances;

☐ *Caring As Empowerment:* Development of young people's sense of independence, control, and mastery; assistance in understanding, analyzing, and engaging in the immediate and larger environments in which they live;

☐ *Caring As Development:* Clear expectations and resources to help young people develop competencies in academic, vocational, social, civic, and health areas.

The strength of the most exemplary community youth programs is that they offer services that address all four aspects of caring. It is far too simplistic to determine that a young person living in a distressed neighborhood or attending a dysfunctional school needs only to be nurtured and healed. All young people need all four components. Through observations of youth programs, interviews with program staff and young people, and literature reviews, we have come to believe that caring is established by:

☐ Creating environments in which young people feel welcome, respected, and comfortable, and where they are offered legitimate choices for participation;

☐ Structuring opportunities for the development of sustained, personal, and collaborative relationships with adults and peers;

☐ Providing information, counseling, and expectations that enable young people to define what it means to care for themselves (by focusing on health issues, risk avoidance, coping skills, assertiveness skills, life planning) and to care for a definable group (by focusing on respect for others, conflict resolution, teamwork, leadership skills); and

☐ Providing opportunities, training, and expectations that encourage young people to contribute to the greater good through service, advocacy, philanthropy, and active problem-solving on important issues.

Genuine affection cannot be manufactured, but caring relationships and environments can be reliably crafted if caring is recognized as an important ingredient of youth development. And while caring environments are more easily created in community youth programs, caring must, and can be, incorporated into schools and other institutions. To do so, such efforts must be an explicit goal, not a "tangential benefit" to a given initiative (Sizer 1992; Comer 1987).

CONCLUSIONS AND POLICY RECOMMENDATIONS

The reduction of problem behaviors among young people is a necessary policy goal. But it is not enough. We must be equally committed to articulating and nurturing those attributes that we wish adolescents to develop and demonstrate. This goal should not be limited to a subset of the adolescent population that does not generally include young black males. Rather, we should intensify our efforts to reach these goals for African-American males, a population greatly in need of the attention typically offered to more socially and economically advantaged populations.

There is an unprecedented opportunity to move a national youth agenda in this country, and to create an institutional and community-based infrastructure that nurtures development for young black men. The tasks are clear. First and foremost, *policy must adopt youth development, rather than deterrence, as its base.* This will require a shift away from problem prevention, to a belief that adolescents have, or can develop, the competencies to contribute to society, and that they can and wish to develop attachments to communities and institutions. Once this framework is accepted and moved into the public domain, it will become possible to more adequately answer the question, "What is it that young blacks (or Latinos, Asians, or Native Americans) need that is different from the core set of socialization inputs and opportunities required for positive youth development?"

Adopting positive youth development as a policy goal will also require *full-scale acceptance and support for community-based youth organizations* and the socialization and development services they provide. This acceptance will require a major expansion of the types of organizations and institutions involved in offering socialization and development programs. To implement a strategy of youth development beyond community-based organizations, sustained efforts will be necessary to encourage the national youth-serving organizations to expand service delivery to a broader array of youth populations. Lessons learned from community-based programs need to be explicitly incorporated into existing sports, parks, religious, and recreational programs, both public and private.

Investing in community-based, voluntary youth programs, however, is only part of the solution. The policy goal of *facilitating youth development must be translated and incorporated into the public institutions* of education, employment and training, juvenile justice, and health services. Until these institutions demonstrate caring, which they currently fail to do for many young people (National

Research Council 1993), the potential effectiveness of community-based programs will be severely diminished.

Youth development is not the sole responsibility of any specific organization. Effective policy, therefore, will *move from building strong programs to also building strong communities.* Since all youth-serving organizations contribute to youth development, the goal is for communities to provide the essential inputs necessary for positive youth development, a goal independent of the specific settings or programs where this occurs. The task becomes one of assessing and mobilizing communities based on their collective ability to promote youth development. Are there places where all adolescents, including African-American males, have a legitimate opportunity to develop a sense of belonging, a feeling of safety, and a positive self-image? Are there places where all adolescents, including African-American males, have opportunities to develop the interpersonal, problem-solving, and citizenship skills and attitudes necessary to move successfully into adult roles? When policymakers can answer these questions affirmatively, and act to institutionalize a full array of community supports, progress toward facilitating positive youth development will be achieved.

Finally, full-scale success of a youth development strategy will require *sustained attention to poverty and racism,* the two factors that necessitate the creation of focused programs for minority youth. Community-based youth programs are well-suited to assist young blacks in crossing these barriers. There is an emerging research base suggesting that through open discussion, through opportunities to learn about different cultural backgrounds, and through experiential problem-solving activities, these programs can successfully promote youth development among groups with a long history of oppression (Camino 1992). However, even the best youth programs cannot over-come the formidable obstacles of poverty and racism without compa-rable attention from all social institutions.

References

Batts, V. 1988. *Modern Racism: New Melodies for the Same Old Tunes.* Cambridge, Mass.: Visions, Inc.

Bernard, B. 1991. *Fostering Resiliency in Kids: Protective Factors in the Family, School, and Community.* Portland, Ore.: Northwest Regional Educational Laboratory.

Bronfenbrenner, U. 1979. *The Ecology of Human Development: Experiments by Nature and Design*. Cambridge, Mass.: Harvard University Press.

Camino, L. 1992. *Racial, Ethnic, and Cultural Differences in Youth Development Programs*. Paper prepared for Carnegie Council on Adolescent Development, New York.

Carnegie Council on Adolescent Development. 1993. *A Matter of Time: Adolescents in the Non-School Hours*. New York: Carnegie Council on Adolescent Development.

Comer, J. 1980. *School Power*. New York: Free Press.

Hamilton, S. 1990. *Apprenticeship For Adulthood*. New York: Free Press.

————. 1980. "Experiential Learning Programs for Youth." *American Journal of Education* 88: 179–215.

Hedin, D., and D. Conrad. 1982. "The Impact of Experiential Education on Adolescent Development." In *Youth Participation and Experiential Education*, eds. D. Hedin and D. Conrad. New York: Haworth Press.

Ianni, F. 1989. *The Search for Structure: A Report on American Youth Today*. New York: Free Press.

National Research Council. 1993. *Losing Generations: Adolescents in High-Risk Settings*. Washington, D.C.: National Academy Press.

Office of Technology Assessment, U.S. Congress. 1991. *Adolescent Health—Volume II: Background and the Effectiveness of Selected Prevention and Treatment Services*. Washington, D.C.: U.S. Government Printing Office.

Pittman, K. 1991. "A Rationale for Enhancing the Role of the Non-School Voluntary Sector for Youth Development." Paper prepared for Carnegie Council on Adolescent Development, New York.

Pittman, K., and M. Cahill. 1992. "Youth and Caring: The Role of Youth Programs in the Development of Caring." Paper prepared for the Lilly Endowment, Indianapolis, Ind.

Sizer, T. 1992. *Horace's School*. New York: Houghton Mifflin.

Slavin, R. 1991. "Synthesis of Research on Cooperative Learning." *Educational Leadership* 48, 5: 71–82.

Smith, T. 1990. *Ethnic Images*. GSS Topical Report no. 19. Chicago: University of Chicago, National Opinion Research Center.

Weissberg, R., M. Caplan, and L. Bennetto. 1988. *The Yale-New Haven Social Problem-solving Program for Young Adolescents*. New Haven, Conn.: Yale University Press.

William T. Grant Commission on Work, Family and Citizenship. 1988. *The Forgotten Half: Pathways to Success for America's Youth and Young Families*. New York: William T. Grant Foundation.

Wynn, J., et al. 1987. "Communities and Adolescents: An Exploration of Reciprocal Supports." Chapin Hall Center for Children, University of Chicago.

Part Two

ASSESSING RESPONSES

HOW PROFESSIONALS IN COMMUNITY-BASED PROGRAMS PERCEIVE AND RESPOND TO THE NEEDS OF BLACK MALE YOUTH

Ronald F. Ferguson

INTRODUCTION

African-American males, particularly those from low-income female-headed households, are vastly over represented among the under-educated, the jobless, and the jailed. Reversing this waste of human potential is among the most important challenges facing the nation. This paper offers a framework and some illustrative examples from the field for understanding the potential role of community-based education and socialization programs in responding to this challenge. We pay particular attention to boys age 10 through 15. The passage from childhood to adolescence occurs during these years and brings dramatic changes in physical, cognitive, and social development. (Hamburg 1990; Task Force for Education of Young Adolescents 1989) As they experiment with new identities and life styles, boys choose teen peer associates and make important decisions about the types of men they aim to become. These decisions are too often misinformed and doomed to produce trouble for themselves, their families, and society at large.

Based on visits to programs in six cities, we argue here that timely and well-managed interventions targeted at high-risk youth and armed with well-packaged information and social support, can make the difference between wasted and productive lives. We describe what such interventions do and, in appendix 4.C, summarize what the request for proposals for an ideal program might look like. The life skills and strategies that programs address stretch beyond standard categories to include, for example, ways of managing the anger and emotional pain that are often by-products of social and economic disadvantage. We use quotations liberally in order to capture personalities and nuances of expression that convey important sentiments. While the examples and the concerns that motivate the research center on black males, many of the issues and much of the basic framework apply to black girls and to other racial and ethnic groups as well.

Ideas from the social sciences provide additional conceptual structure. The notion of "engagement" is the most central. It helps bring together into one framework a progression of functions that good programs perform. These functions motivate and facilitate the involvement of youth in activities that improve the quality of their present lives, foster healthy human development, and protect them from the environmental risks associated with less wholesome preoccupations.

This paper aims to serve academics, practitioners, and policymakers. Our approach is purposefully eclectic. We rely on social science literature for bits of evidence and for elements of a conceptual framework, but we do not formulate nor test hypotheses directly. We use quantitative and qualitative data to illustrate ideas and practices but not to evaluate particular programs. Finally, while the paper is primarily about ideas and practices that seem to work, and while we advocate a programmatic vision, we also emphasize the need for formal evaluations that carefully measure program impacts.

THE PROGRAMS

This project relied on local informants to identify programs serving black male youth in Baltimore, Md.; Boston, Mass.; Cleveland, Ohio; Hartford, Conn.; Pittsburgh, Pa.; and Washington, D.C. The 23 programs visited range in focus from dropout, drug abuse, and teen pregnancy prevention, to general cultural enrichment. Even most of the specific-focus programs, however, provide more general forms of socialization and address a broad array of issues.

None of the programs is affiliated with a mainstream national youth-serving organization such as the YMCA, Boy's and Girl's Clubs, Boy Scouts, 4-H, or Big Brothers/Big Sisters, though a few have ties to the local Urban League. For reasons we did not investigate, local informants in the cities we visited did not direct us to such agencies. Instead, they led us to programs in public housing, churches, social service agencies, community recreation centers, reformatories, and universities. All of the programs were primarily the result of local initiatives by officials and agencies whose concerns and responsibilities included but were not limited to the well-being of youth.

Most of the visits took place in summer 1989. Most programs targeted youth from low-income single-parent households. Programs were small and highly varied in design. Most served fewer than 100 children per year. Funding came primarily from local foundations, corporate sponsors, and local government, with smaller amounts from private donations. Staff size ranged from one to about eight, rather evenly distributed through this range. Executive directors typically had master's degrees in fields related to youth. Despite the variation in program design, the ideal visions that executive directors expressed had much in common across cities and programs. This paper reports the common core of their shared vision and offers some fragmentary evidence of its practicality. (See appendix 4.A for a brief discussion of methodology, and appendix 4.B for a list of programs visited and the ages they serve.)

CONCEPTUAL FRAMEWORK AND TERMINOLOGY

Literature on resilience in childhood and adolescence suggests that the net effect of environmental forces on developmental outcomes for youth depends on the relative balance in the environment of "risk factors" versus "resistance resources" or "protective factors" (Jessor 1991; Rolf et al. 1990; Rutter 1987; Werner and Smith 1982, 1991). In various ways, all of the programs cited in this report aim to shift the balance—to overcome risk by fostering resistance and providing protection.

A common mission statement of these programs might be, "To promote and facilitate the engagement of African-American male children in endeavors that enhance personal development and thereby enable social and economic mobility." Accordingly, "engagement" in activities that foster healthy adolescent development is a key concept in this paper. In other contexts, say marriage, for instance, engagement connotes the selection of someone or something upon which to concentrate effort and attention. Similarly, engagement here is the concentration of effort and attention on particular activities and associated goals.

Skinner, Wellborn, and Connell (1990) have done important research on children's engagement in school. They emphasize the importance of strategy beliefs in addition to skills (i.e., capacities or competencies). They write:

(a) *Strategy beliefs* are expectations about "what it takes for me to do well in school [or in other roles]" (such as effort, ability, powerful others, luck, and unknown factors); (b) *capacity beliefs* are expectations about whether "I have what it takes" (i.e., Can I exert effort? Am I smart? Liked by powerful others? Lucky?); (c) *control beliefs* are expectations about "whether or not I can do well in school" without reference to specific means (pp. 23–24).

The idea is that when a child knows a strategy that, if implemented competently, will produce a desired outcome, and perceives that he has the capacity to implement it, he is more likely to perceive that he has *control* over the relevant outcome and to *engage* in an attempt to implement that strategy.

Inducing adolescents to engage in healthy activities thus requires programmatic attention to opportunities, strategies, skills, rewards, and goals. More specifically, the best programs do most of the following: 1) create new *opportunities* for youth while also deepening their knowledge of options that already exist; 2) teach *strategies* (i.e., recipes for exploiting particular varieties of opportunity); 3) help youth in acquiring and practicing the *skills* and confidence necessary for implementing particular strategies; and 4) provide *rewards* (incentives) aimed at inducing young people to invest in learning the strategies and skills necessary for achieving the *goals* that they select from an expanded menu of available opportunities.

Various other ideas from the social sciences help to complete the paper's framework. First, all humans share basic motives (or drives or needs) that are the fundamental aims of human behavior (McClelland 1987). Psychologists do not agree on one precise list, but few would dispute that achievement, affiliation, influence, security, avoidance of discomfort, and freedom from hunger are primary. Self-esteem is also a basic motive, closely related to achievement and affiliation (Maslow 1970). However, due to several forms of ambiguity in measuring and interpreting self-esteem as a concept, especially between lay people and psychologists, this paper avoids that term by using other terminology (see Ferguson 1990, pp. 3–5, for further discussion).

Conceptually, one can imagine decomposing preferences for particular objects or activities into component desires for the good feelings associated with achievement, affiliation, influence, security, freedom from hunger, and so on. Consider some simple examples. A good student may like school because it permits him to experience achievement and to have influence with peers and teachers. A poor student may be ambivalent: repeatedly failing exams is uncomfortable but is partially compensated by the affiliative payoffs of being with friends during the school day. Hence, in trying to understand why a young black male (or anyone else) seems more attracted to one activity than to another, it is often useful to ask what payoffs the two activities provide in terms of affiliation, achievement, influence, and so on.

Other useful ideas concern roles. People find affiliation, achievement, and influence through performing standard and not so standard roles in their families and communities. Roles are fundamentally social. They constitute patterns of interaction through typically well-defined relationships, in which actors engage in "exchanges" of goods, services, and sentiments that affect satisfaction on both sides of the transaction. We play several roles simultaneously (leader, follower, helper, student, employee, father, bully) and may move through many roles in a given day. When a person has difficulty succeeding in a given role, psychologists predict that the person will experience "role strain" and may adapt or mal-adapt by shifting to other more manageable roles (Bowman 1989). Preparing people to assume socially useful and personally satisfying roles in families and communities is the essence of a healthy nurturing process and the central purpose of the programs discussed here.

Children may perceive that satisfaction is more readily available through playing some roles (such as bully, class clown, casual student) than through others (such as teacher's helper, serious student). The roles that children choose are those that they expect may yield the greatest satisfaction and for which they feel most competent and worthy. The sources of satisfaction that we emphasize in this paper are achievement, affiliation, influence, and security. Programs can offer opportunities to experience these satisfactions in the present, while simultaneously broadening the range of potentially satisfying roles that participants feel qualified to pursue for the future. Programs achieve these outcomes through a combination of teaching, caring, providing, and manipulating the youth's environment so that it nurtures him more positively. In these ways, programs expand opportunities, teach strategies, nurture skills, offer rewards, and facilitate the pursuit by youth of goals associated with healthy human development. (For a similar perspective, also based on examining programs that serve youth, see Brice-Heath and McLaughlin 1991.)

Below we discuss in specific terms how the programs visited succeed in providing affiliation and security; teaching about strategies; teaching skills, confidence, and feelings of worthiness; and teaching about reward structures and values. These sections are followed by a discussion of goal setting by youth, of disagreements among program approaches, and of some practical recommendations for policymakers and funders.

Providing Affiliation and Security

Every child needs at least one adult who cares about him and who is an effective confidant, guide, broker, advocate and, at times, disciplinarian in helping to manage his development. Many parents provide only the caring, and many social service professionals may provide the rest, but every child needs at least one adult who combines both. In other words, children need adults who "care and deliver." In the words of Shawn Satterfield, age 17, of Project Roadmap, Baltimore:

> [Other programs for high school dropouts] didn't work. That's why I'm here now. This program has been the best so far. People ask me what's so special about this program. It's the people. They care and they deliver. Whereas, the other programs they never put their personal feelings in it; it was just like a nine to five type thing. Here, it's the counselors, the mentors, everybody involved in the program . . . they want to help you . . . it's real. It's nothing false about it. You just get a feel for what's real and what's not real—these people are in it with their heart.

Without the affiliation and security of caring relationships, youth often hesitate to incur the costs or take the risks that conventional success may require. Adults asking children to pursue life options that seem unattainable (e.g., graduate from high school) or to practice behaviors of which peers disapprove (e.g., abstain from sex or avoid drugs) are asking them to forego popular pleasures and to risk failure and social ostracism. Caring relationships are critical in programs because friendships between program-related youth and adults can compensate to some degree for lost affiliation and influence with the old peer group. Further, before "stepping onto thin ice," a youth needs the security of *trusting* that the advisor has good intentions, can deliver required assistance, and knows the youth well enough to have made an accurate assessment that he has (or can acquire) the skill to succeed. Finally, expecting that the adult cares enough to share in celebrating his potential success constitutes an additional incentive.

Program operators say that how deeply an adult should become involved in a child's life depends on how much of a commitment he or she is willing to make to the child, how much support the child wants, and how the child's parents respond. An ever-present danger for the child is that an adult will once again make a commitment and not keep it. Children understand that program staff have families and other responsibilities that limit the frequency and intensity of contact. What they desire from adults is clarity, consistency, and clear evidence of concern. Adults who are clear about their commitments, consistent in living up to those commitments, and show unmistakable evidence of concern have the most success in working with children over extended periods. Examples below help illustrate this point.

Even though a child may settle for what he can get, a minimum of one interaction per week of at least a few hours in duration seems to be the standard for programs where adults play major supplemental parenting roles. Program professionals testified that the greatest need of the children who *most* need neighborhood-based programs is for love, attention, and brokering from a strong responsible adult who can see them regularly.

This level of involvement can initially threaten parents. However, most become supportive as they learn to trust that the program is operating in the child's best interest and is not demeaning the parent. Home visits and communication that keep parents informed about program activities facilitate this adjustment. Invitations to attend special events help to get some parents involved but, for various reasons, failure to respond to such invitations is common even when parents strongly encourage their children to participate. Encouragement to children to participate can be particularly strong from single-parent mothers who themselves are reluctant to come out but who recognize their children's needs for such programs.

A LOVING, MALE ROLE MODEL

Among the most recurrent themes in interviews was the special need that children from black female-headed households have for a relationship with a responsible black adult male. Even mothers for whom parent and provider roles are otherwise quite manageable recognize that their sons (and daughters) sometimes need a man's guidance and affection. Some mothers rely on male friends and relatives, while others actively search for programs. Black adult males were present in all the programs we visited.

Hartford's (Conn.) "Always on Saturdays" is a good example of a small program with a low budget that seems to make an important difference for youth. Always on Saturdays, a teen pregnancy prevention effort that teaches life skills, began around 1985 as part of the Hartford Action Plan on Infant Health. It focused initially on African-American males age 9 through 13 from low-income single-parent families. The age range is wider now because some boys need their relationship with staffer Amos Smith and have continued over several years, despite the fact that it is supposed to be a 12-week program. Amos Smith is a 40-year-old black male who holds a master's degree in social work and receives a part-time salary for his work in the program.

Each Saturday, Smith meets with participants for a few hours in the early afternoon to hold life skills training and discussion sessions. Since time is short and he wants to keep the sessions serious, he explicitly rules out sports as an activity. About 25 to 30 boys participate over the course of a year; some come year-round. Smith has become a father figure for about 10 long-term participants. He knows their mothers well, helps with school and occasional court visits, and occasionally with discipline during the week. When we visited, he had just returned from taking participants to New York City. His exuberance overflowed: "It was like seeing your kid walk for the first time. The feeling! And their expressions—the joy that I experienced looking at those kids marvel about being in a hotel in New York!"

The following are excerpts from our interview with Smith that show the central role of love and feelings in the program.

> What we wanted to do was try to give kids a fresh start—that is, to grow up learning about themselves, their bodies, how they grow, how they mature, what makes sense in developing and negotiating friendships. . . . At first, the program was generally focused around the issues embodied in most traditional prevention programs. There were four concepts, but we have added a fifth. We call the first four concepts keys: decision-making, problem solving, planning, and goal setting. In the process of talking with the kids and finding out a lot about what they felt regarding growing up in the environment that they're in, we added another key: feelings. We call it the "master key."

What we realized is [that we needed to] teach them how to deal with feelings regarding being in a household where there was no man, being in a neighborhood where there was no positive model of a man with whom they could identify or talk on an ongoing basis. In fact, many of the kids were unable to identify any single man with whom they could identify or talk. Their models, their leaders, the people whom they respect, were primarily all women, starting with their mothers. . . . The other thing that kids tell me is that they come because I'm the only man in their lives that takes some time with them.

I've worked with kids and adults. If you prove to kids that you are going to be consistent in being there for them, they will walk through walls for you if you ask them to. I have tried to be consistent.

Over five years, Smith has missed one Saturday—the morning that his wife was killed in an auto accident.

Similar testaments of love and involvement in children's lives came up again and again in our interviews.

When the staff of various programs responded to questions concerning their techniques for building successful relationships with children, they gave a variety of answers. Some answers (such as mirroring youth body language) seemed to come from formal training. But most answers came from more personal experience in relationships. The most common answer was that they get personally involved in the lives of children when necessary, with few firmly preconceived limits to that involvement. They are good listeners. They treat both children and their parents with respect but also with a gentle firmness that refuses to condone breaches of reasonable and clearly defined norms. They are dependable and "they practice what they preach." This was how people described Amos Smith and men who work in other programs.

Several programs also work on "building community." A school teacher in Pittsburgh who works with youth in several settings contrasted churches with schools as sites for life skills programs, arguing that:

[T]he sense of family, community, belonging, and connectedness happens differently in the church than it happens in most schools. . . . The church is a real fitting place for life-skills programs because you have access to the whole family unit. And even if it isn't the whole family, you have surrogate families and extended families in the context of the church. Any individual automatically has a family once they come to the church. It's a context—a whole context—where a person can be holistically nurtured.

Staffers at the Friendly Inn Settlement House in Cleveland made similar statements about extended family relationships in the public housing development that they serve: "We use the extended family norm. We try to find the 'together' adults who are actually or potentially helping to raise Johnny (e.g., if his parents need help) and work with them to help Johnny. This community is like a tribe. The challenge for the program is to get into it and become part of the tribe."

The most emphatic point that community-based professionals make is that addressing feelings and building one-on-one relationships are absolutely necessary to effectively serve disadvantaged children. Without these, little else works because little else gains children's trust.

VOLUNTEER MENTORS

Given the importance of caring adult-youth relationships and the difficulty of achieving very low staff-youth ratios, most programs try to use volunteer mentors to supplement the love and attention that their paid staff provides to children. But programs that have tried have experienced only limited success at finding mentors and keeping them active. Staff have discovered that fulfilling mentors' needs is as important to sustaining their involvement as meeting youths' needs is to sustaining youths' participation.

Few programs have the resources to serve the needs of both mentors and youths. However, the few programs that have had some success in this regard have techniques that are worth reviewing. One program in Columbus, Ohio, is an Afrocentric rites-of-passage program. Such programs provide opportunities for African-American youth to master a series of lessons and skills that qualify them to pass symbolically into black manhood (or womanhood) in a rites of passage ceremony at the end of the program. The concept is similar in its purpose to the Boy Scouts and Girl Scouts, but its teachings come from adaptations of traditional African beliefs, and place great emphasis on African and African-American identity, culture, history, and spirituality (see chapter 5 of this volume). Many such programs have developed rather independently, but members of a young Afrocentric program network are currently in the process of working toward more standardization of these kinds of programs. Programs for boys and girls are part of the same network, but programs work with boys and girls separately; men work with boys and women with girls. The Rites of

Passage Network held its third annual national conference in July 1990 in Detroit, Michigan. It was at the group's second national conference in July 1989 that we met Byron Cunningham, the young African American who runs the Columbus program.

Cunningham's program is sponsored by the county government, which refers participants from social service agencies. The county runs a personal background check on each mentor. All the mentors and boys in the program are black males.

Each child in Cunningham's program has a personal one-on-one mentor. Children and mentors meet separately in adult-only and child-only activities, as well as in activities in which both youth and mentors participate. Mentors and youth also meet one-on-one away from the group at least once a week. Among representatives from some ten rites of passage programs participating in a conference session for experienced program operators, Cunningham was by far the most satisfied with his success at finding and retaining volunteer mentors. Most other program operators at the session were from programs run by small cores of committed volunteers which, because of the difficulty of retaining other mentors, typically ended up with ratios of about ten boys to one mentor. This is an especially heavy burden for an unpaid volunteer with another full-time job, but those who are most committed are willing to pay the price. Cunningham, on the other hand, manages his program full-time, serving (at that time) about 70 mentor-child pairs.

Our notes from the discussion recall the following techniques for managing and sustaining mentorship. Much of the list reflects Cunningham's practices, but some of the ideas are from other programs as well (see Walsh 1989 for similar insights).

1. Use existing mentors to recruit new mentors. This serves as quality control, and also takes advantage of bonds between existing mentors and those whom they recruit to keep *both* active in the program.
2. Define the initial commitment to be for a limited time, such as six months. This makes potential mentors more inclined to give it a try. The experience of Byron Cunningham's program is that almost all mentors develop a strong enough relationship with the youths that they remain in the program when the first six months have ended. Asking for only six months is "bait."
3. Make frequent telephone calls (biweekly) to each mentor to remind him of his commitment and to keep his attention on the program. It is especially important to call a mentor after he fails to attend a group activity.

4. Include activities that are fun for mentors as well as for youths. It is important to try to understand the needs that the mentors are trying to fulfill through their involvement and, where not inconsistent with program goals and procedures, to try to serve these needs. For example, give recognition and praise to mentors who are doing a good job. Offering athletic activities for men within the mentoring program may help to keep the men's interest. Of course, this could attract men with the wrong motives, but appropriate oversight and initial screening should minimize this problem.

5. Structure the program so that volunteers who want different levels of involvement can all find ways to contribute. Think hard about the appropriate balance between program flexibility and structure, and try hard to keep a balance that serves your program's multiple purposes.

6. Screen as carefully as possible. Where possible, letters of recommendation from associates and background checks for criminal records are advisable.

7. Design well-organized and thorough orientation sessions where mentors learn what is expected of them and what they can expect from the program.

All of the programs that use one-on-one mentoring stress the importance of flexibility in making matches. Most describe an informal process whereby the boys and men become acquainted over a period of a few weeks through joint participation in recreational activities, and then express their tentative preferences to someone whose job it is to make the matches. Sometimes first matches are not comfortable and partners change. The length of time that it takes for relationships to jell varies, but Cunningham's experience (contingent, of course, on his management techniques and resources) is that close to 100 percent of mentors stay after the first six months.

Another program that makes one-on-one matches is Project Roadmap, where the mentors are black male employees of an IBM service center in Baltimore. Dave Johnson, head of the IBM service center, directs the mentoring arm of Project Roadmap. The mentoring operates in partnership with an academic skills and counseling component managed by the Baltimore Urban League. LaFon Porter, a mentor in Project Roadmap, describes the bonding process as follows:

> It's had its ups and downs. Getting a relationship started, it takes a lot of time and at first—with any type of relationship—it may not go as smooth as you would like. You may not be able to get the trust. I can imagine that if I were a client coming into a situation like this—seeing

a whole lot of professional young blacks in white shirts—it could be intimidating. We had avenues to break that down. For instance, on the weekend, we would play basketball—the IBM mentors against the clients.

It was a lot of just one-on-one personal type things that took place. . . . I let him meet some of my friends. Actually, we played racquetball once with some of my friends. A lot of interpersonal things took place to try to gain that relationship that I think was needed.

When this particular mentoring relationship began, the interactions were about once a week. At the time of our interview, about eight months into the mentorship, he reported that he talked with his assigned youth "every day or every other day." Porter Dave Johnson says that in his own case, "We talk to each other every day, maybe twice a day. We usually see each other every week or during the weekend; and they [the youth] come down to visit the office. It's almost like family."

Group mentoring in which a group of children relates to a group of adults seems to be the most common model in programs with paid staff. Programs that use paid staff find that each staff member develops special relationships with several children, and any given child may have special bonds to several staff members. As suggested above, many programs resemble extended families.

Though several people had strong opinions about the need for matching children and mentors by sex and race, we saw evidence of strong across-sex and across-race child-adult bonding. However, it was impossible to tell from our brief visits whether some *potential* participants are turned off by the unavailability of staffers and mentors with whom they might more closely identify and to whom they might more easily relate. We suspect, for example, that at one site where the majority of the staffers are white and some are female, some of the more street-wise youths in the neighborhood may not identify with the program as much as they might if more of the staffers were "cool" black males.

Peer-to-peer and child-to-adult bonding grow over time as participants interact in activities that staff members oversee. Most people endorse the importance of both types of bonding and claim that their programs accomplish both. As bonding and trust grow, so also does the degree to which programs can both formally and informally address children's more personal concerns. Similarly, children's certainty that behaving and performing well will draw praise and other reinforcing feedback grows and provides strong motivation.

It is difficult to find useful and accurate statements about how much time is needed for adults to establish enough rapport to be able to influence a child. Obviously, every relationship has its own timeframe. However, children say that some effects, such as the incentive of knowing that program staffers are going to look at school report cards, can have immediate influence. Also, an adult's encouragement and attention regarding school performance are among the signals that a youth may use early in a relationship to gauge how much the adult cares.

Teaching About Strategies

Let us begin with an extreme example. The young man is a black 17-year-old honor student with a 3.8 grade point average at a prestigious Catholic high school. His mother is a single, unemployed alcoholic. We learned about him because he approached a counselor seeking help for his mother. The boy told the counselor that he was selling drugs to save money for college because he expected that his mother could not afford to send him. Selling drugs was his strategy for funding his education. He was uninformed about financial aid. He did not know that the most expensive private universities in the nation offer comprehensive financial aid packages to African-American males with his profile, and he had never spoken to a guidance counselor about college. Nor had he encountered a program such as those described here that, even by age 15, might have introduced him to less risky and more socially acceptable ways to finance his education. This illustrates that even children with skills and laudable purposes may choose tragically uninformed and misdirected strategies in the absence of appropriate adult guidance.

Boys 10 to 15 years old need a great deal of information. They are at a pivotal stage in their lives, making fundamental choices about what roles they want for themselves now, later as older teens, and eventually as adults, and what strategies they will use to pursue those roles. Our interviews found widespread agreement that, though older teens are more impressionable than we often assume, pre-teenage and early teenage boys are clearly the most eager to accept help in understanding life. Through their everyday interaction with others, they study the roles that people play and see a roster of potential options.

Which roles a child chooses from the roster depends on: a) what options he is aware of (e.g., does he know about careers in investigative reporting?); b) for which of these he knows the strategies (does he know the steps to becoming an investigative reporter?); c) which strategies he thinks he has the ability to implement (does he think he has the resources and smarts to do what it takes?); and d) which roles he expects will bring the greatest satisfaction—the good feelings associated with influence/power, achievement, affiliation, and security.

Judging from what we learned in our visits, boys age 10 to 15 are eager to learn strategies for living healthy and productive lives. In addition to long-range strategies, they want ideas that they can apply in commonplace everyday situations. For example, according to Lonnie Hudspeth, leader of a group of three African-American men (from the Pittsburgh chapter of One Hundred Concerned Black Men) who volunteer weekly with a group of about 15 black male adolescents:

> What they wanted from us was help with intellectual and emotional development. They wanted to deal with issues of manhood—what being a man is all about, with issues like sexuality and drugs. They wanted to deal with violence in the schools and protecting themselves. These are experiences that they encounter and they wanted to know how to handle them. They wanted to demonstrate their creativity—to produce a play that would portray their ideas about things. They wanted to go on trips and to see different things and have different experiences.

> A number of them had a desire to learn how to control their emotions, for example, when they don't agree with a teacher or don't appreciate the way a teacher or an authority figure 'comes off' to them: belittling them or making them feel like they're stupid. They wanted to know how to react to that. Typically, if it's a teacher, their usual reaction was to get smart, get into an argument, and to get kicked out of class. If it's a fellow student who they have a problem with, they get into an argument and it breaks out into a fight. In other words, in reaction to feeling put down they would lose control of their emotions and get into trouble. One of the things that we observed was that the young men had a difficult time respecting one another. On the one hand they wanted to receive respect, but on the other hand they didn't have the proper training to respect one another. We had to work on this with them.

The men in Pittsburgh had structured the program around the interests of the children, augmented by advice from child development experts like the well-known black educator Barbara Sizemore at the University of Pittsburgh. Their intent, according to Hudspeth, was "to address physical, intellectual, spiritual, emotional, and social development." However, when asked, most of the interests that the boys expressed were in intellectual, social, and emotional development. To the adults' surprise, the boys did not ask for sports or physical development.

The programs we visited teach a broad range of strategies relating to an equally wide range of roles and issues. None of the programs claims to cover more, or in a more culturally cognizant way, than the Black Male Youth Health Enhancement Project of the Shiloh Baptist Church Family Life Center in Washington, D.C. This program uses an Afrocentric rites-of-passage format, augmented by peer counseling, after-school study halls, recreational skills development, a yearly conference on issues facing black males, and other activities. The curriculum occupies weekly classes that covered the following topics during the 1988–1989 year:

> September—AIDS education
> October—Self-esteem
> November—Sexuality/teen pregnancy
> December—The human body
> January—Drug abuse education
> February—Cultural awareness
> March—Nutrition
> April—Physical fitness/exercise
> May—Communication skills
> June—Employment readiness skills
> July—Coping with anger and anxiety
> August—The human body

In addition to topical issues, programs try to frame lessons with general principles and techniques that apply broadly. For example, Amos Smith's Always on Saturday program incorporates general decision-making, problem solving, planning, and goal-setting techniques into its curriculum. Though Smith says that these are the same principles taught in most "prevention" programs, he teaches them using real life examples that both he and the youths provide.

Programs rely on combinations of commercially available and home-grown instructional materials, though the staff of several programs express the desire for a greater variety of culturally tailored curricular options. The strategies that programs convey to youth are easy to understand and essentially the same as those that parents and teachers would ideally teach in other settings. For example, the basic strategies to avoid making a baby are abstaining or using birth control. Programs teach about alternative kinds of birth control, and address techniques for avoiding sex in the face of social pressure.

Other strategies are similarly straightforward: Lessons in study skills provide strategies for improving academic performance; discussion of spirituality and God provide strategies for making ethical choices and for finding inner peace; employability training teaches interviewing techniques, résumé writing, proper dress, budgeting, and other strategies for finding and keeping jobs; health, nutrition, and exercise lessons provide strategies for staying healthy; violence prevention lessons teach strategies for avoiding or defusing conflict; and cultural awareness lessons give youth reasons for feeling more positive and confident about their race and culture.

Programs apply combinations of standard techniques to teach strategies. They use both formal instruction and informal conversations to describe strategies; they demonstrate strategies and show students role models who are applying the strategies; they provide relevant reading materials; they facilitate discussions in which the youths figure out strategies for themselves; and they help youths to practice strategies and then to review the results, focusing on the causal connection between the outcome and what the youth did to cause it. Some programs use quizzes to review strategies and test comprehension.

In addition to strategies for roles that youngsters already recognize, programs provide exposure to roles and associated strategies that participants never knew existed or never thought were realistic possibilities. In some cases, the new roles would actually not be open if programs did not procure resources from schools, businesses, and other institutions to make them feasible.

Not surprisingly, the most popular techniques for providing exposure are field trips and guest visits from role models. A more unusual approach (for youths under 16) is to place youngsters at non-traditional job sites, as is done in the Cambridge (Mass.) Public Housing Authority's Work Force Unemployment Prevention Program. This program teaches standard employability skills to youth beginning at age 13. It then places those 14 to 16 years of age in try-out jobs at sites such as law firms, health spas, and universities; participants can rotate to different job cites in 12-week cycles. They learn new skills, new strategies, and new options from people with whom they would not likely come into contact if not for the program. While employed, youths in this program spend one two-hour session each week in discussion sessions with peers and program staffers during which they continue to learn life skills. Staffers also oversee youths' academic progress, act as advocates between schools and families, and generally provide supplemental parenting.

Teaching Skills, Confidence, and Feelings of Worthiness

Familiarizing a child with a role and giving him strategies for attaining and performing that role are necessary but not sufficient for motivating engagement. The child must also expect that he is skilled enough, that external conditions are amenable, and that he is deserving.

Most programs teach strategies and skills and simultaneously create opportunities. A list of the skills that programs teach would basically duplicate the strategies discussed above. Therefore, for example, when adults tell a child that working hard on homework is a strategy that will improve his grades in school, these same adults will often arrange for that child to receive the tutoring and social support that he needs for acquiring requisite skills and for developing confidence. After-school study halls and tutoring, for example, are among the methods programs use to reinforce the strategy for academic success. Even for recreational activities, programs emphasize the importance of skill and help youth to acquire it by encouraging them to practice and by providing instruction and necessary equipment.

Teaching skills to youth is complicated by the fact that children vary in their talents and learning styles. Readings that program managers found useful on this topic were Howard Gardner's (1983) *Frames of Mind: The Theory of Multiple Intelligences* and Janice Hale-Benson's (1982) *Black Children: Their Roots, Culture, and Learning Styles*. A number of people also cited other popular books, especially Jawanza Kunjufu's (1983) *Countering the Conspiracy to Destroy Black Boys*. Program professionals clearly believe that work in this vein is important. However, none of the staff we interviewed seems to have a set of materials and easily transferable instructional techniques for identifying and responding to distinguishable learning styles among children in neighborhood-based programs. This is an area ripe for development.

Another way that programs assist children in developing skills and confidence is by helping them to understand their successes and failures. For example, Jeffrey Howard, executive director of the nonprofit Efficacy Institute in Lexington, Massachusetts, helps program staff at Freedom House in Boston (as well as other institutions across a number of cities) to understand the psychology of "efficacy" and to incorporate it into their interactions with children. Ideally, the adult builds the child's confidence relative to a particular goal by emphasizing to him that he knows (or can learn) the strategy *and* that he has (or can develop) the skill to implement it.

Theoretical and empirical studies in psychology find that attributing success to effort and ability helps people to justify further engagement in similar efforts (Garber and Seligman 1980; Marsh et al. 1984). Attributing failure to *lack* of ability or to stable, uncontrollable external influences is among the surest ways to discourage further effort. For example, incorrectly attributing failure to lack of ability sets up an expectation that can be self-fulfilling because it reduces the child's belief in the efficacy of effort. The child will under-invest in his own skills and over time will accumulate fewer skills than if he had more accurately estimated his own ability, and better understood the cause-and-effect relationship between effort and outcomes.

Insights such as these infuse the work of people like Bob Harrison, who runs Pittsburgh's Second Step Program and works with youngsters in the public schools using a framework that he calls "success modeling." The idea that we want to emphasize here is the role of self-esteem. For Harrison, the self-esteem issue concerns whether a person feels that he deserves to attain what he envisions. Most people feel uncomfortable receiving or pursuing what they feel they do not deserve. Hence, a child may not wholeheartedly engage in building skills if he feels that someone like him does not deserve the rewards for which those skills would otherwise qualify him.

The feelings of unworthiness that youth need to overcome may be as vague as a general uneasiness at the thought of being in a particular situation. Theories of cognitive dissonance and other ideas associated with psychological needs for cognitive and moral consistency help to explain such feelings and their effects on motivation. For our purposes, the lesson is that children need help in making judgments about what they deserve, and that without such help feelings of unworthiness may hold them back. Adults need to be aware that such feelings may be lurking and must consciously deliver off-setting messages.

Feeling disliked and unworthy is said by program professionals to be a common problem for children with disciplinary problems. Such feelings may be the consequence of self-fulfilling prophesies that operate through cycles that caring adult interventions may be able to break. Caring adults affiliated with programs (or not) can mediate with others who "don't like" the child and can help the child in other ways. For example, Earnest "Lucky" Dotson of the Boston Youth Collaborative, which provides case management and program services for middle-school children with disciplinary problems, applies a simple technique. He has the child list one or two adults whom he thinks *do* like him. Then he sends the child to get a list from these adults of what it is about him that they like. The children usually come back with long lists and with statements like "I guess I'm better than I thought I was." No doubt they also feel more worthy.

When youth feel confident and worthy, they are more inclined to invest time in developing skills for achieving conventional (instead of unconventional) goals.

Teaching About Reward Structures and Values

Different people perceive different rewards for similar behaviors and face different options for finding given types of satisfaction. One should expect that behaviors will reflect expectations about how to achieve satisfaction. Even so, casual observers often conclude that "values" differ, when what actually differs are real or perceived opportunities. Here, the most relevant opportunities are those that satisfy basic human drives for such things as friendship, achievement, influence, security, and freedom from hunger. The prospect of achieving satisfaction along one or more of these dimensions is a powerful incentive for undertaking particular activities.

Much of the activity that claims to be teaching values to children is actually teaching them about reward (and penalty) structures. Most of socialization is the process that teaches people the specific ways in which their culture rewards and punishes various behaviors. Note that even religion does not simply teach values: it promises affiliation with God, emotional security, and other satisfactions that can be regarded as incentives, in return for faith and observance of religious practices. Thus, even moral values have some basis in reward structures.

Hence, molding healthy and socially constructive values among youth requires providing constructive reward (and penalty) structures and making sure that youth understand them. Programs we visited do this in a variety of ways.

Most programs recognize the importance of celebration. The good feelings associated with celebration become incentives to value and to excel in the celebrated activities in anticipation of future celebrations. Several programs that monitor report cards and academic performance take pains to provide ongoing attention and celebration as rewards both for academic improvement and for steady high-level performance. Only one program (Work Force Unemployment Prevention in Cambridge, Mass.) provided a small financial incentive for performance in school, but participants said that the attention and excitement motivated them more than the money. A group of about 20 participants in the program voted unanimously that they work harder in school because they know that program staff are watching, and because they look forward to rewards and celebration.

Celebration is especially important for children from households that neglect it. We came to appreciate the subtle distinction between how much parents care about academic performance and how actively they celebrate and promote it. Several youths in the Cambridge program said that their parents do not pay much attention to their performance on report cards and almost never communicate with school teachers. These same parents nevertheless express a strong preference for their children to continue participating in the Work Force Unemployment Prevention Program, and gratitude to the staffers for the roles they are playing in the children's lives. Staff argue that these parents care as much as any other parents, but that the infrequency and ambiguity in the feedback they give to their children reflect their own feelings of insecurity and uncertainty about how to provide the right level and mix of support.

Another values modification strategy that programs use is to foster discussion that helps young people to empathize with the people whom their own behaviors affect. The feelings that boys have toward mothers and younger siblings, for example, are a lever for encouraging good behavior. Youths want mothers and siblings to be happy, and they feel satisfaction when they think they are adding to rather than detracting from the household's happiness. Satisfaction may come in the form of warm affiliative feelings or from feelings of power and importance that come from being protective. Conversely, hurting mothers (by disappointing them) or younger siblings (by setting a bad example) causes feelings of guilt and also may cause social ostracism. For example, during a focus group discussion in a Cleveland reformatory, an incarcerated teenager admitted to having stolen from his mother in order to buy drugs. The group immediately expressed its disapproval, with one young man saying, "To steal from your mother is the worst crime in the world—I don't steal from my mother! That's cold!" (Jackson 1988, p. 76)

However, the most poignant example of empathetic consciousness-raising is the method used by Amos Smith from Always on Saturdays in Hartford, Conn., to develop in his boys a distaste for teenage fathering. His technique is simply to engage youth in discussions about their own fathers. Almost all the boys live in single-parent households with their mothers and siblings. Discussions about fathers awaken deep-seated and intense feelings. These are by far the strongest peer bonding experiences in the program. Recall that this is the program that dubbed "feelings" to be the fifth and "master key." Smith says that he moves the boys:

> . . . to think about the fathering process and what it involves by asking them to think about their own fathers if they are familiar with them; if they are not familiar with them, getting them to think about what they would like it to be like if they did have a father. There is a traditional question that I ask: "How old should you be before you become a father?" The answer to that question [that the boys discover for themselves during the discussion] is generally that there is no age requirement—there is a maturity requirement and a level of economic responsibility and emotional commitment that are the requirements.

> Most bonding occurred around discussions about their fathers—about either not having a father present or about having a father come around and knowing that he's not going to stay.

In Always on Saturdays, these discussions produce a shared resolve among participants not to put their own children through the pains that they themselves have experienced.

The other strategy that Smith and most other program staff employ is to heighten youths' appreciation of what economists call "opportunity costs." The aim is not that youths should "value" any given activity more or less in absolute terms. Instead, the point is that they should think more clearly and more often about trade-offs—what they have to give up in exchange for a given choice. Again, we quote Smith in relationship to fathering:

> Part of my concern was that we were asking kids to delay a decision that was a popular part of behavior in that neighborhood, i.e., sexual expression is a very popular part of one's identity in that neighborhood. You have to give kids some reason to believe that waiting is worthwhile. We had to begin to show them that there was life outside of the neighborhood, and that life outside of that neighborhood wasn't much different from life within the neighborhood, but only that people were exposed to much broader options and opportunities. So, if they waited, and didn't get bogged down or tied down with the issues and anguish of fathering a child early, then they would be exposed to or have the advantages and opportunities that life had to offer.

> So field trips became a very important part of the program, getting out and gaining exposure, being around people that they would not

ordinarily be around, having contact with people whom they would not ordinarily meet. So, in a sense, being a "speakers bureau" where kids are able to talk with people and ask questions is a very important part of the program.

Evidence from other programs, however, suggests that some youngsters may not buy the idea that having a baby causes anguish. Providing alternative sources of fulfillment and emphasizing opportunity costs are particularly important for dealing with boys who *want* to have children as teenagers because it will give them "a reason to live." As one teenage father in Cleveland's Teen Father program says about parenthood, "It makes you feel like living! Because that's your flesh. You see yourself in that child. Not only yourself, but you see your maker in that one person!"

Obviously, childless teenagers who anticipate the feelings articulated by this speaker should *not* be told to value children less. Instead, we need to persuade them to empathize with the unborn child, and to recognize that both they and their children will be happier in the long run (if not in the short run) if they wait. While they wait, programs like those we visited can help to quench some of the hunger for affiliation, achievement, influence, and other satisfactions that boys might otherwise seek through fatherhood.

GOALS: PERFORMANCE VERSUS GROWTH AND LEARNING

Throughout this paper we have been talking indirectly about helping youth to set and reach "goals"—the last item in our earlier list of what programs do to promote positive and healthy engagement. By shaping knowledge of opportunities, strategies, skills, and rewards, programs guide youth toward selecting more wholesome and life-enhancing goals. How and why youth set particular types of goals is an especially important issue for programs aiming to influence youth goals.

Experimental psychologist Carol Dweck and various coauthors have conducted a series of studies in which a clear relationship has emerged between the types of goals that children choose and their beliefs about whether ability is a basically fixed entity or, alternatively, a malleable quality (see, for instance, Dweck and Leggett 1988; Dweck 1991). She finds that children who believe intellectual capacity is a fixed entity are much more likely to choose what she calls "performance goals." This holds true regardless of whether the child believes that the level of his or her ability is high or low. Performance goals aim to demonstrate or document high ability and avoid demonstrating low ability.

Conversely, children who believe that intelligence can be changed, even if they believe that their ability is presently low, are more likely to choose learning or mastery goals. They appear to understand that effort mobilizes, rather than substitutes for, ability. They anticipate the pleasure that comes from accepting challenges and mastering them, instead of being preoccupied with the pride or embarrassment associated with successful or unsuccessful performance. Failure for such youths often has a different meaning. For them it is an opportunity to learn how to devise and implement a new problem-solving strategy.

Dweck's characterization of children who believe that ability and other traits are fixed, and who therefore choose performance over mastery goals, is very relevant to African-American youth culture. The "oppositional culture" among African-American youth that Ogbu (1978), Fordham and Ogbu (1986), Fordham (1988), Solomon (1992), and others study, and the "cool pose" about which Richard Majors (1986) writes, both emphasize performance over mastery goals. Moreover, both "oppositional culture" and "cool pose" appear to embrace the idea that working hard is a negative behavior, except perhaps in athletics. For youths adhering to these attitudes, working hard is a sign of low ability or of cultural betrayal ("acting white").

Dweck's work is not explicitly prescriptive. She has not tested whether a larger percentage of black than white youth believe that ability is a fixed entity. Nor has she tested for racial differences in performance versus mastery goal setting. Nevertheless, her work has powerful implications for youth programs serving black males if, as this author suspects, black youth tend to believe that ability is fixed and tend to choose performance over mastery goals.

While more research needs to be done to help us better understand how beliefs about ability and other traits are formed, one suspects that race plays a central role for black youth. Perhaps the most dominant message of racism against blacks in the United States is that mental aptitude is relatively fixed and, for blacks, is low. As most blacks know from personal experience, this is a powerful message to overcome. One implication of Dweck's work is that what African-American children need to internalize is not necessarily that their current ability is high (though it often is), but that their potential ability is much higher than they will ever know if they fail to make the effort to activate it. Children need to believe that ability can be ever expanding. As young black males come to believe this, they will aim more often to learn instead of simply to perform. Through all that they do, community-based programs can cultivate and reward this reorientation of beliefs and goals.

DISAGREEMENTS AND UNKNOWNS

Above we have synthesized the insights and experiences of many youngsters and adults who participate and work in programs serving African-American male children. We do not evaluate their programs. Instead, we present what we think is a common vision that program staff share of what an ideal program for this target group should resemble.

Substantive disagreements, which we have not emphasized, are few. One, however, concerns the primacy of filling significant adult roles with African-American males. Some of the people whom we interviewed argued that having black males in these roles is absolutely critical. Others argued that all else equal, black males are preferable, but that all else is not always equal. When necessary, they maintained, women and non-black men can work with black male youths quite effectively. One related difference in perspective concerns the salience of an Afrocentric philosophy and focus. Some respondents strongly supported a heavily Afrocentric orientation, while others questioned its relative importance vis-à-vis the many needs that remain unmet for African-American youngsters. In the end, these differences paled relative to the range of agreement.

No one dissented from the view that it is very important for African-American children to learn more about their culture and history, and that neighborhood-based programs have a role to play in teaching it to them. Nevertheless, a source of confusion is the lack of a clear, common interpretation of what "Afrocentric" means. Some program staff are not sure what to think of programs that claim to be Afrocentric, nor are they sure whether to apply the label to their own programs. Also, the deficiencies in adults' own cultural training is often an impediment to more effective cultural training for youth.

Many unknowns remain. The most obvious one concerns the effectiveness of the programs. Most appear to be effective but, as far as we know, none has undergone a complete and careful evaluation. Since next to none of them keep careful records on participants who have graduated, dropped out, or aged out of their programs, a careful evaluation of long-term results is close to impossible. This is not a criticism. It is a statement of fact. All of these programs operate on tight budgets. Their priority is serving children, not collecting ex-post data for researchers and evaluators.

However, if persuaded that formal evaluations might be a bridge to more resources for the children they serve, many programs directors would surely welcome the intrusion. For example, several programs claim to raise children's grades in school. Simple studies comparing grades before the program with grades during and after the program would not be difficult to carry out if school administrators, parents, and program operators were willing to cooperate.

RECOMMENDATIONS

Small-scale neighborhood-based programs provide relationships and information that can profoundly influence young people's goals and life chances. Effective programs alert youth to positive options, and teach them strategies for pursuing those options and the skills for implementing them. Programs can alert youth to the efficacy of effort in realms such as academic ability, where black male youth are often prone to giving up. Celebration and other activities that affect reward structures provide important incentives for "doing the right thing." These are common elements of programs we visited for this project.

Despite these commonalities, however, every program has unique capacities and idiosyncratic preferences among its leaders and staff for achieving particular ends. Therefore, policymakers and private sector funders aiming to utilize the insights that this paper offers should not respond with narrowly conceived ideal prototypes. Instead, within clearly but loosely defined parameters, they should invite potential grantees to offer their own ideas for how they would provide the caring and services that our research suggests are the most important. This would provide both the flexibility necessary for creativity and the structure to ensure that programs are well-conceived. A funder issuing a request for proposals could provide supportive materials to give applicants ideas for how to structure their responses (including, for instance, chapters of this book; Mincy and Wiener 1990; Walsh 1989) or could leave them to their own devices to test their knowledge and resourcefulness. Below, in appendix 4.C, I have outlined the essential features of such a request for proposals, including attention to accountability and evaluation mechanisms. If administered by local review boards, the process of judging and selecting among respondents might be quite manageable, even for a nationally funded program.

Scaling up the number and coverage of programs discussed here may appear to be so large and expensive a venture that it is not worth considering. However, the need is easy to overestimate. The most intensive versions of these programs are not necessary for every child in every low-income neighborhood. Planned variation in the intensity of interaction with children (and their families) can occur even within single programs. The key to efficient management of time and resources is targeting. School teachers, program managers, and law enforcement officials are well positioned to select children who appear to need supplemental nurturing. Children most in need are often easy to identify.

Both new and existing programs will benefit from assistance with staff training and curriculum development. Few programs have the resources to search extensively for curricula materials, to review the materials that they find, and to make judgments about relative strengths and weaknesses. Therefore, funders could provide a very useful service by sponsoring and widely disseminating annotated bibliographies of published curricula, especially materials that incorporate racial and ethnic themes. Sponsoring production of additional curricula materials is also warranted. In addition, conferences where people trade ideas informally and where workshops provide staff training received strong endorsements from the people whom we interviewed. Funders might consider supporting more such networking opportunities for community-based youth program staff.

The time has come for society to take a closer look at the potential of neighborhood-based programs. Careful evaluations are likely to show that the benefit-to-cost ratio can be substantial for programs that are carefully targeted, well conceived, and well managed.

Note

Many of the interviews on which this paper is based were conducted by Margo Saddler, a Ph.D. student at the Heller School for Social Welfare Policy at Brandeis University. Sincere thanks go to her and to the many people who gave their time and wisdom in interviews. The paper does not discuss by name all of the programs and people whom we visited, but the choice of whom to mention was in the end rather arbitrary, since so many programs could be used as illustrations for any given point. Appendix 4.B lists the programs visited. David Ellwood, Olivia Golden, Naomi Goldstein, Ronald Mincy, Kyna Rubin and two anonymous reviewers provided helpful comments on earlier drafts.

References

Bowman, Phillip J. 1989. "Research Perspectives on Black Men: Role Strain and Adaptation Across the Adult Life Cycle." In *Black Adult Development and Aging*, ed. R. L. Jones. Berkeley, Calif.: Cobbs & Henry.

Brice-Heath, S., and M. W. McLaughlin. 1991. "Community Organizations as Family: Endeavors that Engage and Support Adolescents." *Phi Delta Kappan* (April): 623–27.

Dweck, Carol. 1991. "Self-Theories and Goals: Their Role in Motivation, Personality and Development." In *Nebraska Symposium on Motivation, 1990*, ed. R. A. Dienstbier. Lincoln, Nebr.: Lincoln University Press.

Dweck, Carol, and Ellen L. Leggett. 1988. "A Social Cognitive Approach to Motivation and Personality." *Psychological Review* 95, 2: 256–73.

Ferguson, Ronald F. 1990. "The Case for Community-Based Programs that Inform and Motivate Black Male Youth." Research paper. The Urban Institute, Washington, D.C., November.

Fordham, Signithia. 1988. "Racelessness as a Factor in Black Students' School Success: Pragmatic Strategy or Pyrrhic Victory?" *Harvard Educational Review* 58, 1: 54–84.

Fordham, Signithia, and J. U. Ogbu. 1986. "Black Students' School Success: Coping with the Burden of 'Acting White.' " *The Urban Review* 18, 3: 176–206.

Garber, Judy, and Martin E. P. Seligman, eds. 1980. *Human Helplessness Theory and Applications*. New York: Academic Press, Inc.

Gardner, Howard. 1983. *Frames of Mind: The Theory of Multiple Intelligences*. New York: Basic Books, Inc.

Hale-Benson, Janice E. 1982. *Black Children: Their Roots, Culture, and Learning Styles*. Baltimore, Md.: The John Hopkins University Press.

Hamburg, Beatrix A. 1990. *Life Skills Training: Preventative Interventions for Young Adolescents*. Washington, D.C.: Carnegie Council of Adolescent Development.

Jackson, Mary Speed. 1988. "Drug Use and Delinquency in the Black Male Adolescent: A Descriptive Study." Case Western Reserve University School of Applied Social Sciences, unpublished dissertation.

Jessor, Richard. 1991. "Risk Behavior in Adolescence: A Psychosocial Framework for Understanding and Action." In *Adolescents at Risk: Medi-*

cal and Social Perspectives, Proceedings of the Seventh Conference on Health Policy, Cornell University Medical College.

Kunjufu, Jawanza. 1983. *Countering the Conspiracy to Destroy Black Boys.* Chicago: African American Images.

Majors, Richard. 1986. "Cool Pose: The Proud Signature of Black Survival." *Changing Men: Issues in Gender, Sex and Politics* 17: 83–87.

Marsh, Herbert W., Len Cairns, Joseph Relich, Jennifer Barnes, and Ray L. Debus. 1984. "The Relationship Between Dimensions of Self-Attribution and Dimensions of Self-Concept." *Journal of Educational Psychology* 76, 1: 3–32.

Maslow, A. H. 1970. *Motivation and Personality.* New York: Harper.

McClelland, David C. 1987. *Human Motivation.* New York: Macmillian.

Mincy, Ronald B., and Susan J. Wiener. 1990. "A Mentor, Peer Group, Incentive Model for Helping Underclass Youth." Research paper. The Urban Institute, Washington, D.C., September.

Ogbu, John U. 1978. *Minority Education and Caste: The American System in Cross-Cultural Perspective.* New York: Academic Press, Inc.

Rolf, J., and A. Masten, D. Cicchetti, K. Nuechterlein, and S. Weintraub, eds. 1990. *Risk and Protective Factors in the Development of Psychopathology.* New York: Cambridge University Press, Inc.

Rutter, M. 1987. "Psychosocial Resilience and Protective Mechanisms." *American Journal of Orthopsychiatry* 57 (July): 16–331.

Skinner, Ellen A., James G. Wellborn, and James P. Connell. 1990. "What It Takes to Do Well in School and Whether I've Got It: A Process Model of Perceived Control and Children's Engagement and Achievement in School." *Journal of Educational Psychology* 82, 1: 22–32.

Solomon, Patrick R. 1992. *Black Resistance in High School.* Albany, N.Y.: State University of New York Press.

Task Force for Education of Young Adolescents. 1989. *Turning Points Preparing American Youth for the 21st Century.* New York: Carnegie Council of Adolescent Development, Carnegie Corporation of New York.

Walsh, Joan. 1989. *Connections: Linking Youth with Caring Adults.* Oakland, Calif.: Urban Strategies Council.

Werner, Emmy E., and Ruth S. Smith. 1991. *Overcoming the Odds: High Risk Children from Birth to Adulthood.* Ithaca, N.Y.: Cornell University Press.

————. 1982. *Vulnerable But Invincible: A Longitudinal Study of Resilient Children and Youth.* New York: McGraw Hill.

METHODOLOGY

During the summer and fall of 1989, this project interviewed staff and participants of more than 20 neighborhood-based programs that address the developmental needs of African-American males age 5 through 25. The goals of the project were to understand: 1) what neighborhood programs were actually doing; 2) how program operators understood the nature of the challenge; and 3) what difference they thought their work was making. Most program participants were from low-income single-parent households in Baltimore, Boston, Cleveland, Hartford, Pittsburgh, and Washington, D.C. (see list in appendix 4.B).

Interviews were conducted on site with program directors and were often supplemented by follow-up telephone calls. Most interviews were tape-recorded. Written materials from programs supported the interviews. Other staff members joined in about half the meetings. Information that the project sought from each program included: history and context of the program; target population and salient characteristics of participants; race, sex, age, and professional backgrounds of staff; program design and underlying theory and philosophy; materials used, instructional styles, program duration, frequency of contact, family involvement, use of volunteers; forms, sources, and uses of financial and other resources and judgments about program effectiveness and associated measures. We interviewed program participants at about one-third of the sites and, in four cases, administered written questionnaires. Two of the four groups that completed questionnaires were youth in the 10-to-15 age range (see Ferguson 1990, for a brief summary of replies on the questionnaires).

Given the brevity of contact, it was not always possible to judge the difference between a program director's ideal vision of what the program could be, given adequate resources, versus what the program actually did in practice. However, in many cases we discussed programs with outside informants and found little discrepancy. In one case, outsiders suggested that a program director had exaggerated the scale of his program. In two other cases, outsiders reported that directors were overextended and that, despite good program models, they were failing to provide quality management.

PROGRAMS SERVING YOUNG BLACK MALES: SITES VISITED

(Specific information on the programs listed below, including contacts, addresses, and phone numbers, can be found in Ferguson (1990).)

Program	Target Group
Addison Terrace Learning Center Pittsburgh, Pa.	Young adult males, ages 18–25, out-of-school youth
African American Men's Leadership Council Males Rites of Passage Program Baltimore, Md.	Black male adolescents
Always On Saturday Hartford Action Plan Hartford, Conn.	Black males, ages 9–15, in-school youth
Black Male Youth Health Enhancement Project Shiloh Baptist Church Washington, D.C.	Black males, age 9–17, in-school youth
Boston Youth Development Project Roxbury Multi-Service Center Boston, Mass.	Middle school youth
Bringing Black Males to Manhood Family Enhancement Project Pittsburgh Urban League Pittsburgh, Pa.	Black males, age 13–17, in-school youth
Choice The University of Maryland Baltimore, Md.	Mostly black males, age 15–18, in-school youth

Program	Target Group

The D.C. Youth Initiative
National Center on Institutions and
  Alternative Sentencing
Alexandria, Va.
	Black males, age 15–17,
	  juvenile offenders, out-
	  of-school youth

The Friendly Inn Settlement House Cleveland, Ohio	Black males and females, age 6–18
I Have a Dream Program Cleveland State University Cleveland, Ohio	Black males and females, age 15–16
Invest Now University of Pittsburgh Pittsburgh New Futures Project Pittsburgh, Pa.	Black males, age 12–13, in-school youth
Mali Yetu (Wealth) Cleveland State University Cleveland, Ohio	Black males and females, age 6-14
One Hundred Black Men of Pittsburgh Pittsburgh, Pa.	Black males, age 14–17

Pittsburgh in Partnership with Parents
Young Fathers Program
Hill House Association
Pittsburgh, Pa.
	Black males, age 15–25,
	  youth fathers, out-of-
	  school youth

Positive Futures
Urban League of Eastern
  Massachusetts
Roxbury, Mass.
	Black males, age 6–12,
	  in-school youth

Project Roadmap IBM Baltimore, Md.	Black males, age 17–21, school dropouts

The Robert and Jane Meyerhoff
  Scholarship Program
University of Maryland
Baltimore, Md.
	Black males, age 17–18,
	  entering freshman,
	  Univ. of Maryland,
	  Baltimore County

Roxbury Youthworks, Inc. Clinical Services Unit Roxbury, Mass.	Black males, age 14–17

Program	Target Group
SIMBA East End Neighborhood House Cleveland, Ohio	Black males, age 9–17
Success Model The Second Step P.B.A. Inc. Pittsburgh, Pa.	Males and females, age 14–18, in-school youth
Teen Father Program The Hough Multi-Purpose Center Cleveland, Ohio	Black males, age 15–25, young fathers
Work Force Unemployment Prevention Program Cambridge Housing Authority Cambridge, Mass.	All races, age 13–18, in-school youth
Young Fathers Program Urban League of East Boston Roxbury, Mass.	Young fathers, age 15–21, in-school and out-of-school youth
Youth Leadership Council Mayor's Commission on Families, Health & Welfare Planning Pittsburgh, Pa.	Black males and females, age 14–18, in-school youth

A MODEL "REQUEST FOR PROPOSALS"

The framework in this paper emphasizes how neighborhood-based programs can encourage and facilitate youths' engagement in activities that are satisfying and that enhance their prospects for wholesome and productive lives. This appendix considers what needs to be in the request for proposals (RFP) if a funding agency wants to support a program with the characteristics that this research suggests are most desirable. (The RFP would specify the maximum length of the reply in each category in order to limit what could otherwise be quite lengthy responses.)

Identity and Qualifications of the Proposed Program Director

Most directors of programs visited had master's degrees in social work, education, or psychological counseling. It is difficult to know the degree to which the academic credential is merely a sorting device for identifying the people with the most commitment to children, versus a measure of a person's preparation to serve children effectively. The RFP should not have strict degree requirements, but should weigh degrees heavily in choosing among respondents. Of course, the ideal is the combination of an appropriate degree with several years of relevant experience in administering programs and working with children. This is especially the case where the applicant proposes to serve special needs populations such as delinquents, drug-involved children, abused children, or chronic truants.

However, even more important than an appropriate degree is evidence that the director genuinely cares for the welfare of disadvantaged children. Applicants should list personal references who will attest to their past successes in communicating with and caring for the target population. For example, the RFP might require the applicant to provide letters from or telephone numbers of two parents and two professional colleagues familiar with his or her work.

If the respondent proposes to employ other professionals, their identities (if known) and qualifications should be given. Any staff training that the director would provide should be described.

Identity of Target Population and Methods of Outreach

The RFP would specify only a few demographic characteristics of the target population: for example, males age 8 through 16 who, because of household structure, socio-economic status, neighborhood, or past behavior, appear to be at-risk for developmentally problematic choices and behaviors. Each program would be allowed to choose its own target neighborhood(s) and other characteristics of a target population that fit within the broad outlines of the eligible range. Once funded, programs would be expected to stay roughly with the populations described in their proposals, but the funding agency would allow flexibility at the margins.

The proposal should say where the program would find participants and how it would persuade them to participate in the program. If the applicant is proposing to attract a generally hard-to-reach population (e.g., truants, youths who have been selling drugs, or delinquents) the proposal should show some evidence that the applicant recognizes the difficulties of attracting and retaining such participants and has strategies in mind for meeting this challenge.

Substantive Program Content and Instructional Methods

Here, the RFP would ask applicants what they expect to teach participants and how. It might provide headings such as those that this paper employs. For example, the RFP might ask respondents to discuss what ideas, materials, activities, techniques, and philosophies they would consider most important for addressing each of the following:

1. *EXPOSURE TO OPTIONS:*
   a. Jobs/careers (present and future)
   b. Lifestyles (present and future)
   c. Other

2. *STRATEGIES and SKILLS:*
   a. For managing relationships (with parents, peers, teachers, . . .)
   b. For managing feelings (anger, sadness, . . .)
   c. For managing identity issues (race, class, . . .)
   d. For recreation (sports, games, trips, . . .)

    e. For employability (dress, interviewing, conduct, . . .)
    f. For academic success (studying, taking tests, . . .)
    g. Other
 3. *VALUES AND REWARD STRUCTURES:*
    a. Celebration (for academics, conduct, sports, . . .)
    b. Consciousness raising (regarding teen fatherhood, crime, . . .)
    c. Conduct and performance standards in the program
    d. Other

These categories roughly parallel the discussion of this paper, covering options/roles, strategies, skills, and reward structures. The RFP might ask applicants to select a primary outcome target (e.g., dropout prevention) for which they would agree to be most accountable, but to select a number of secondary emphases as well, taking into consideration the needs of the target population.

Ideally, the respondents would find it appropriate to weave together issues of race, class, culture, and identity through coverage of several categories on the list. Similarly, topics such as decision making, problem solving, planning, goal setting, and related principles might appear under several headings. Funders would not necessarily restrict programs to organize their formal curricula using the headings in the above list, but nevertheless would require some attention to each.

Staff-Participant Ratio and Frequency of Contact

The most important point that our interviews produced was that relationships between staff and participants, and among participants, are critical foundations for achieving other programmatic goals. In answering this item, respondents should specify staff-to-participant ratios and frequencies of contact to allow development of the necessary relationships. Also, the response should suggest specific methods for fostering personal interaction and communication.

Programs may specify a "core" and a "non-core" level of participation, where youngsters in the non-core may use program facilities but will not have as much personal support and attention as youngsters in the core program. Programs proposing this option should say how they would ration access to the core slots. If the applicant expects that staff will meet with core participants less than once per week or that the program will have a core participant-to-staff ratio of greater than about 12 to 1 (numbers that our interviews suggest are typical), they should explain what effect they expect this to have on forming and maintaining relationships. Volunteer mentors may supplement staff (see below).

Peer Bonding and Peer Support

Programs use a variety of mechanisms including peer tutoring, team sports, rap sessions, and other group activities to foster peer bonding and peer support. Experienced program operators will have plenty of ideas here. This section of the RFP should have applicants spell out the methods that they expect to use in the proposed program.

Methods and Mechanisms for Using Unpaid Assistance

It is worthwhile soliciting in some detail how applicants plan to use and manage volunteer resources. Common problems include: a) the inability to find and sustain participation by the number of volunteer mentors that programs expect; and b) the hassle of screening volunteers and directing their involvement. Respondents who expect to use volunteers should comment on their familiarity with the issues involved here and with their expectations regarding how they will address the associated problems.

Parental Involvement

Uniformly, people who work with children from disadvantaged families talk about the value of having access to the whole family in order to help resolve family problems and to secure more in-home support for the program participant. The RFP should ask respondents to anticipate problems involved in securing parental support for youths and to describe the techniques that they would expect to apply.

Interaction with Schools, Courts, and Other Service Agencies

Applicants should discuss how they would expect to interact with other institutions. Frequently, for example, parents of disadvantaged youths are intimidated by teachers and court personnel and invite program staffers to come along on visits. The respondent should say whether the program will be willing to interact with other agencies and how. Any existing relationships between the applicant and other agencies should be described here. The proposal should mention any special ideas for inter-organizational collaboration.

Record Keeping and Tracking of Progress

Funders might, for example, require records on program attendance, retention, participation in activities, important staff/participant contacts outside of regular activities, and staff ratings of participant performance and development. In addition, they might want records (where possible) on school attendance and school grades. In a demonstration project, the funders would have to carefully consider what they were trying to demonstrate and then fine tune data requirements with this in mind. Respondents to the RFP would address both their willingness to comply with data collection requirements and their planned mechanisms for doing so. An appropriately flexible RFP might ask respondents to suggest what *they* want to demonstrate, what performance measures they want to be judged on, and how they plan to organize and present their evidence. One can imagine a process in which the candidates selected to receive funding would participate as a group in setting the final parameters of the demonstration.

Additional Comments on Accountability

Here, respondents would supplement the discussion of performance measures under the preceding heading with a discussion of other accountability issues. For example, they might spell out what they perceive to be the already present accountability pressures in their own socio-political environments. They might also respond to the idea, for example, that they should be willing to tolerate some given number of visits (perhaps three per year) on short notice (e.g., three days notice) of agents from the funding agency.

A Short Profile of the Organization Sponsoring the Application

This section would be a fairly straightforward description of the sponsoring organization. It should include, for example, the organization's primary mission, organizational structure, board composition, experience with programs similar to the one it is proposing, and a statement of what resources it is willing to commit to the proposed program.

An Evolutionary Vision

Respondents would be invited to speculate how their programs might evolve over time under alternative assumptions about available funding. For example, some might suggest potential roles for program alumni (e.g., use them as mentors, tutors, etc.), or potential links with other organizations that may take time to develop. This section could be used to speculate about contingencies and to suggest how the program would be likely to adapt.

Chapter Five

AFROCENTRISM AND AFRICAN-AMERICAN MALE YOUTHS

Morris F.X. Jeff, Jr.

What can we do to make a positive difference in the lives of troubled young Black men in America's cities? How can we help to enhance their self-image and increase their capacity to survive and flourish in an often hostile world? Instilling Black youth with the cultural values of their ancestors is one promising way to make them strong again. In this paper I argue for the incorporation of Afrocentric models into social programs for African-American youths, briefly tracing the history behind these models and the basic theoretical tenets on which they are based. I also examine the reasons that segments of both the white and Black communities may resist Afrocentrism, and discuss in some detail how the Louis Armstrong Manhood Development program operated by the New Orleans City Welfare Department successfully uses an Afrocentric approach to better the life chances of young urban men.

THE LIMITATIONS OF PREVIOUS EFFORTS TO HELP BLACK YOUTHS

The United States has never had a comprehensive youth policy with clearly articulated strategies and goals. As a result, cities and localities have developed their own programs. Historically, initiatives targeted specifically at African-American urban youths have been few and short-lived. Harlem Youth Opportunities Unlimited (HARYOU) was created in the early 1960s to address the problems facing Black youths in Harlem, New York (Clark 1965). Its goal was to develop and deliver a set of strategies to promote positive youth development through community development. About the same time, the city of Chicago under Mayor Richard Daley initiated the Chicago Youth Commission, structured to address the issue of youth development and the elimination of street gangs. HARYOU never evolved beyond the planning stages, primarily due to funding problems. The Chicago effort was initially successful but it too encountered difficulties. The city of Philadelphia, once a pioneer in addressing the needs of urban youths, ran up against similar fiscal constraints, causing a demise in urban youth initiatives.

As discussed elsewhere in this volume, some urban strategies are in place to deal with America's urban social problems. But these programs are based on traditional models of yesteryear that do not necessarily meet the needs of today's youth, especially African-American youths. For example, the Boy Scouts, Boys' Clubs, settlement houses, community centers, the YMCAs, and the YWCAs might have worked 20 years ago, but all have failed to some degree in translating earlier successes with white urban youths into successes with Black urban youths. Most of these not-for-profit and public-funded agencies have undergone significant budget cutbacks as America's urban social ills have multiplied.

In the absence of a strong commitment to enfranchise urban youths, Black community leaders have turned away from traditional agencies for help in addressing today's problems. They have instead begun to initiate their own models that are culturally relevant to their communities.

THE HISTORY OF AFROCENTRISM IN THE UNITED STATES

The teaching of traditional African culture and social values is an effective way to respond to the needs of socially alienated African-American youths within the context of their own cultural heritage and history. Afrocentrism is not a new phenomenon in America.

Even before emancipation in 1863 and the addition of the 13th, 14th, and 15th amendments (granting African Americans freedom, citizenship, and civil rights) to the U.S. Constitution, Bishop Richard Allen (1760–1831) and other leaders fostered ties between Africans in America and their African homeland. With the intent of basing his church on African precepts, Allen named the place of worship he founded in Philadelphia the African Methodist Episcopal Church. After emancipation, efforts to link Blacks in America to African traditions continued. Henry McNeal Turner, a member of the U.S. Congress representing South Carolina during Reconstruction (Redkey 1969), was a Methodist Episcopal bishop who called for Black people to return to Africa, or, if they chose to remain in the United States, center their lives around African values. It was also after emancipation that the free Black Masons created their movement to adopt the world view of the traditional African culture of Kemet (Egypt).

During the era of legal separation and segregation of the races in the United States (1896–1954), leaders such as Booker T. Washington, Southern founder of the Tuskegee Institute, and his northern counterpart William E.B. DuBois, founder of the Pan-African movement,[1] based their freedom movements on the premise of maintaining links with Africa and the African world view. For example, Washington established trade relationships with Africa, an effort that was waylayed by the start of World War I (Harlan 1972).

Marcus Garvey, a native of Jamaica, was a great admirer of Booker T. Washington and took up the latter's efforts after his death in 1915. Garvey established the United Negro Improvement Association, a Pan-African movement based on the belief that the African world view lies at the heart of liberation for Africans worldwide. As he explains in 1921, ". . . why Africa? Because . . .[it] looms as the greatest commercial, industrial and political prize in the world" (Barbour 1968, p. 54).

Though Garvey was deported back to Jamaica because of U.S. government charges that he defrauded his constituents, he had helped plant the seeds of the Afrocentric movement in the minds of African Americans.

In the 1950s and 1960s the African nations of Egypt, Nigeria, Ghana, and Kenya won their independence from European colonial powers (Lewen 1990). In the late 1960s the government-appointed Kerner Commission, named after its chair, then Illinois governor Otto Kerner, acknowledged that America was "moving toward two societies, one Black, and one white, separate and unequal" (Kerner Commission 1968). African Americans' increasing perception of isolation from American mainstream society and their continuous quest for rootedness gave birth to the Black Power and Civil Rights movements.

The Civil Rights movement changed U.S. laws, granting equal rights to African Americans. The Black Power movement changed the self-perceptions of Black people, who discarded the term Negro for Black, which better conveyed a new consciousness and pride of color and culture. Black and African studies programs were created on college campuses. Cornell University still has a well-developed Black studies program that has existed for 25 years. Temple University is known for its B.A., M.A., and Ph.D. degrees in African studies. From the Black studies movement on American campuses grew the

National Association of Black Studies and a plethora of African studies organizations. Moreover, it was during this era that Black caucuses
in mixed race organizations "seceded," forming independent Black
organizations and associations (e.g., the National Association of Black
Social Workers and the National Association of Black Psychologists).

Afrocentrism is thus an outgrowth of the African Americans' search
for identity in the face of the social, political, and economic alienation
that they have experienced in the United States. Its growth has also
been influenced by the phenomenon of Africa and Africans being
denied center stage in world history. At the same time, Afrocentrism
is rooted in scholars' growing documented evidence of Africa's
importance in world civilization.

THE THEORY BEHIND AFROCENTRISM

All theory is the offspring of observation, experience, and reasoning.
Afrocentricism, as theory, is the residual of observations and experiences of African people. It emerges from the history of Africa, and
from the minimal portrayal of Africans in the records of documented
world history. Its assumptions are based upon Africa's unique role
in the origin of the human species. Thus, the African world view is
the foundation of the Afrocentric paradigm in juxtaposition to the
prevalent Eurocentric worldview.

> Afrocentricity is concerned with systematic reconstruction of the
> human record to accurately reflect the prodigious influence African
> people have had on world history . . . It represents the single most
> significant paradigmatic shift in intellectual thought in modern time.
> (Rowe 1991)

In African tradition the cosmos is viewed as a whole made up of
interconnected parts. African ideals, thoughts, and social conduct
are guided by the view that human beings are organic elements of a
divine totality, and that they must follow the divine law in their
social conduct. Like the components of the universe, they too are
interdependent and must cooperate with one another. Therefore, in
the African tradition there is an imperative for values and beliefs to
be made manifest through "right conduct. . . if a person's actions are
not good, the person is not good. Doing good is equivalent to being
beautiful" (Asante 1988, p. 12).

Afrocentrism is a confluence of African world view and African-

American need. It affirms the need to be both African and American without shame, doubt, or feelings of inferiority vis-à-vis other cultures in the United States. Afrocentrism is based on the belief that it is proper and good to reconnect with the best aspects of one's historical, cultural, and social identity. As applied to current social problems, Afrocentrism refers to internalizing structures, values, and practices that are African derived, and applying the best of them to present-day situations. In the words of Paul Hill, Jr. (1992):

> . . .this uniquely Africentric world view provides the key to identifying those elements in African-American life and culture which are distinctively African and using those differences to define principles for socializing African-American male children. Purposeful and constructive transformational strategies will then emanate from those principles. (p. 36)

Some argue that, in contrast, the Eurocentric world view maps the universe into separate objects functioning as independent units. As Nobles (1982) writes:

> . . .the Euro-American cultural orientation reflects an ethic order that principally suggests the importance of "separation" and "domination." The values coming out of this cultural tradition emphasize "competition," "individualism," "individual rights," "independence," and "difference." (p. 49)

The implication here is that Afrocentrism serves to bind African people together and reduces competitive conflict and tensions while building strong character and self-esteem.

African Family Values: The "Seven Rs"

Afrocentrism is based on African institutions, the most important of which is the family. There are certain ethical principles that guide the conduct of African family members. These are what I refer to as the "Seven Rs."

Anthropologist Niara Sudarkasa (1980) identifies four ethical principles on which the African family is based: respect, responsibility, reciprocity, and restraint. To these I have added three more: religion, rhythm, and redemption (Jeff 1988). These seven principles define the proper social conduct of Africans wherever they reside in the world.

Respect, according to Sudarkasa (1980), is the cardinal principle guiding behavior both within the family and within society at large.

It not only applies to the behavior of family members toward the household head, but also governs relations among siblings. Responsibility is the obligation to give of oneself to make family life harmonious and productive. The good deeds coming from responsible behavior are expected to be returned in kind by other family members. Thus reciprocity is a primary principle in the regeneration of the life process and is considered important to the continuation of good deeds. Restraint, in her view, means that the rights of any one individual must always be balanced against the needs of the group.

Religion in African societies is written not on paper but in people's hearts, minds, oral history, [and] ritual. . . Everybody is a religion carrier. . . belief and action in African traditional society cannot be separated: they belong to a single whole. (Mbiti 1969, p. 4)

Rhythm is another ethical premise for African people. As Pasteur and Toldson (1982) write, "[Rhythm] is paramount in the black man's self-image. . . [it] resounds in customs, work, play, war, sex, speech, worship, song, [and] dance. . ." (p. 71)

Finally, redemption underpins the African world view because of Africans' belief that life is cyclical and never dies. Thus, it offers people a chance to redeem past mistakes and move on to a better future. The Seven Rs have implications for social conduct and it is in this context that they are relevant to Afrocentric socialization.

RESISTANCE TO AFROCENTRISM

Afrocentrism is struggling as a relevant concept because its basic precepts call into question generally accepted theories about the origins of Western civilization. Proponents of Afrocentrism argue that Western civilization has its origins in Africa rather than Greece, and that the European view precludes acknowledging Africa as the source of Western thought and civilization. Because of its iconoclasm, Afrocentrism has not fully found its place in mainstream Western academic and social circles.

Many social agencies groping for ways to help young African-American males have avoided the Afrocentric approach for a variety of reasons. For some, it is new and untested. Others fear the reaction of funders who may think that African-centered programs are anti-white rather than pro-Black. Some shy away from this approach because of the absence of knowledgeable staff with experience in the application of Afrocentric concepts and constructs. Still others appreciate the impact such programming is having, but are waiting for wider community sanctions.

Hill (1992) identifies two reasons that the African-American community at large may resist Afrocentrism. First, "blacks who have been inconvenienced and/or denied opportunity for development are naturally afraid of anything that sounds like discrimination or resegregation" (pp. 68–69). Second, some "established institutions within the community such as churches and mosques have resisted the model because it is perceived as a competitor that is contrary to their belief system" (p. 105).

Despite these reservations, the Afrocentric model is growing in concept and practice, and is achieving positive results in its impact on African-American youths. Afrocentrism is proliferating in schools, religious institutions, and social programs.

APPLICATION: AFROCENTRISM'S RELEVANCE TO BLACK YOUTHS IN AMERICA

Afrocentrism offers African-American youths positive values such as incorporation and enfranchisement that can help reduce the distance between them and their social environment. It fosters knowledge and human development through critical thinking, diligent study, and analysis. Afrocentrism has the potential to empower those who study and incorporate it as a guide to social conduct, and to produce a new person who adheres to strong kinship and family bonds (Coppock 1990).

Afrocentrism ". . .seeks to include African American children in the mainstream of education by providing information regarding the positive influences that persons of African descent have had on world civilizations" (Rowe 1991).

Current Program Use of Afrocentric Models

There are numerous Afrocentric program models aimed at Black youths throughout this country. Most are volunteer efforts initiated by highly motivated adults who, out of frustration and compassion, have chosen to cast their lives with young African Americans. One example is the network of "Simba Wachanga"(Kiswahili for Young Lion) programs (Kunjufu 1991; Hill 1992, p.73) in which older men serve as mentors, leaders, and spiritual guides for African-American youths who might otherwise be educated only on the street (Perkins 1975). These programs operate without budgets and are terribly underfunded and understaffed.

Some social service agencies have initiated Afrocentric programs with grants secured from foundations and public sources. The East End Neighborhood House in Cleveland, Ohio, which began the Simba Wachanga program in 1984, is a classic example of this model now nurturing both male and female youths in African culture.

There are a number of private, independent Afrocentric schools that are unique in that they combine the educational and social services modules into a social praxis starting at the preschool level. The Institute of Positive Education in Chicago fits this model. It offers an all-day Afrocentric school, the New Concept of Positive Development, as well as Youths with a Future, a manhood development program for males age 16 to 29 that operates after school and on weekends. Below I describe the program for young urban males that for the past five years has operated under my direction in New Orleans, with some background on the social conditions of that city which fueled the need for such a program. The program is an example of how the Afrocentric approach can be used effectively to improve the life chances of urban youths.

The Creation of the Louis Armstrong Manhood Development Program

The Louis Armstrong Manhood Development Program grew out of a crisis of funding and survival faced by the Milne Boys Home in which it is housed. The Milne Boys Home was named after Alexander Milne, a wealthy slave owner who, before his death around 1833, willed funds for an orphanage exclusively devoted to male children. A century after his death, Milne Boys Home was established by the Milne Trust and later leased to the city of New Orleans to operate for 99 years at a rate of one dollar a year. From 1954 to 1987, the Home was operated by the New Orleans city government as a residential treatment program for males between the ages of 8 and 18 who were declared by law to be non-delinquent, dependent, or neglected. It cared for a maximum of 64 youths.

In 1987, the Milne Boys Home was caring for 15 boys at a cost of $450,000 a year ($30,000 per child). The city gave the New Orleans Welfare Department, which manages the Home, the choice of serving a larger constituency of boys, finding a more cost-effective way to achieve its goals, or closing down. The Welfare Department chose the first two options, creating the Louis Armstrong Manhood Development Program. The Home's program restructuring was designed to preserve male youths in their own homes while developing their survival skills and their ability to make positive contributions to society. Disgarding the residential component of Milne Boys Home enabled staff to expand its constituency to 200 male youths a year on the same $450,000 budget. The annual cost of $30,000 per child was thus reduced to $2,250.

The Louis Armstrong Manhood Development Program was designed to address the problems faced by male youths, particularly African Americans, in New Orleans. A few statistics illustrate these problems. In 1992, 88 percent of the 1,260 juveniles in detention in the city were African-American males (City Welfare Department 1987). In 1988, African-American children made up 85 percent of the city's public school population, but 94 percent of all children suspended. Sixty-five percent of all youths suspended from school in grades 1 to 12 were African-American males. Eighty-six percent of all school dropouts were African-American students (Orleans Parish School Board 1988).

Youths participating in the city's 1992 Save Our Youths Summit identified many of the major problems they face. Among them were school suspensions, lack of curriculum choices, lack of positive role models, lack of funding for schools, putdowns by teachers, lack of concern and respect from police, and poor media image.

When New Orleans' tax base was reduced in 1986, almost all youth services were cut back or eliminated. Public school budgets and services were also slashed at a time when crime, drugs, and violence were rapidly escalating. Large numbers of children began carrying weapons, perceiving that the city was not offering them adequate protection. Cries from female heads of households (whose numbers were growing) for help in raising their sons in a hostile urban environment increased. The Louis Armstrong Manhood Development Program (LAMDP) was one response to this crisis. LAMDP reestablishes the African tradition of male initiation rites whereby elders teach boys the art and science of becoming men. Despite its African focus, the program works with all urban males—Black, white, middle-class poor, delinquents, and non-delinquents.

LAMDP's name was inspired by Louis Armstrong, a native of New Orleans born on July 4, 1900. During his early adolescence he was charged with discharging a gun and was incarcerated at the New Orleans Colored Waifs' Home—owned, managed, and operated by an African American named Joseph Jones. Capt. Jones became the father Louis never had. His Waifs' Home was later merged into Milne Boys Home. Under the tutelage of Capt. Jones, Louis Armstrong was nurtured from boyhood to manhood, from a gun-carrying delinquent to a world ambassador of jazz. His transformation serves as proof of the good that can result from children being trained by elderly men who anchor them in values and self-discipline.

PROGRAM PURPOSE AND RATIONALE

In earlier, agrarian times, the rites of passage from boyhood to manhood were conducted directly through father to son. If father farmed, he taught his sons the art and science of farming and of relating to other men. These teachings always took place in the framework of the family. But times have changed. For many of today's urban Black males, what they learn comes from the streets, not from the family.

In *Home is a Dirty Street* (1975), Useni Perkins asserts that the street institution must be abolished as the sole source of nurture for urban male youths. He states that "though it stands as a necessary interim for survival, it fails to prepare a child for higher goals." Perkins argues that the street as a teaching institution must cease to be romanticized and valued as the epitome of ghetto survival. Otherwise our children "will never become motivated to seek out new alternatives which can help them change it [the ghetto]." LAMDP provides an alternative to the street by acting as a nurturing institution for urban male youth.

LAMDP is based on the premise that manhood does not just happen, but results from personal touch, guidance, caring, and patience. Growing up requires men to pass down their wisdom to the next generation. It requires hard work, discipline, and time, as well as rites and rituals to mark significant points along the way. LAMDP aims to increase a male child's capacity to be effective in all aspects of social life: religion, education, economics, politics, culture, recreation, and sex. The program nurtures the positive development of the mind, body, and soul through building up knowledge, self-esteem, and self-respect. LAMDP acts as an extended family and community that will provide positive male role models for boys between the ages of 8 and 17. It supports families and guides male youths to become responsible and productive citizens. Participants' accomplishments are manifested through each component of the program and are acknowledged and rewarded through participation in Rites of Passage ceremonies.

PROGRAM STRUCTURE

LAMDP is structured like the African continent, functionally divided into and named after African countries. Each nation is a self-contained teaching and learning module. The young men are required to learn about the unique aspects of the nation to which they are assigned (assignments are by age and grade level). These include name; geography; demography; flag and other national symbols; songs; ancestral and contemporary leaders and heroes; names of languages; history; economic, political, and social systems; and contributions the nation has made to world civilization.

In addition to knowledge about one specific African country, the young men are required to learn about broader indigenous African rituals, values, and social conduct such as eating, studying, playing, and solving problems together. They also learn proper male social demeanor, including how to greet adults. They must all learn the "Seven Rs" of the African family value system discussed above (see Appendix 5.A for "The Seven Rs Pledge"), as well as the "manhood pledge" (see Appendix 5.B); the "unity ritual" (see Appendix 5.C); African attire; manners; and chants, songs, and proverbs.

The program, which meets during after-school hours Monday through Thursday, begins with a meal prepared by the culinary staff. The first assignment after the meal is school homework and computer applications, the latter used for both boys' regular homework and personal skill development. Youths in each African nation are then assigned to one of the following sessions provided by program staff. These sessions generally last one hour when held on site:

- ☐ Anti-drug education;
- ☐ Anti-violence seminars;
- ☐ Cultural enrichment;
- ☐ Educational development skills;
- ☐ Group counseling;
- ☐ Mentorship/self-esteem;
- ☐ Recreation;
- ☐ Rites of passage;
- ☐ Teen parenting skills;
- ☐ Vocational education.

Within the framework of these sessions, there is time built in for storytelling and dialogue between youths and staff. Storytelling is a traditional African method of transmitting values, decision-making skills, and proper social conduct to children.

Manhood Development training is not held on Fridays, which are used to train staff in specific program skills. Some youths attend computer classes on Saturday. The program operates on a school-term basis. New participants can enter the program in August and January of each year.

In the spirit of two of the Seven Rs, responsibility and reciprocity, each youth is required to participate in community services. Boys are taught that responsibility means giving of yourself to make the place in which you live, work, and play better than you found it, and that reciprocity is the act of giving back in service and kindness that which you received from others. Another off-site component of the program is field trips, taken to broaden youths' exposure to social and cultural activities that build their self-esteem.

In the spirit of respect, responsibility, and reciprocity, LAMDP holds parent and guardian sessions throughout the year to develop external support systems for young participants. It is imperative that boys' primary caregivers be in concert with the program's values, concepts of social conduct, and discipline. LAMDP also has a strong Counsel of Elders comprised of local men from the community who help develop, refine, and sell the program to the public, as well as mentor the young men and evaluate their progress. Progress is measured on an individual basis, using an initial needs assessment on which to base later evaluations during the year.

LAMDP is predominantly staffed by men, based on the premise that only men can train boys to be men. However, one of the most outstanding components of the program is its African Dance Corps, which is staffed by a woman specializing in African dance. She is a strong team member who has been successful in teaching the youths traditional African dance and songs replete with drums, chants, and African salutations. (The African Dance Corps has performed at the National Association of Black Social Workers' National Conference in Atlanta, and is called upon to perform throughout New Orleans and Louisiana.)

The Rites of Passage. The primary objective of the Rites of Passage ceremony is to affirm the youth to move on to higher levels of challenge. Rites of Passage ceremonies are held three times a year at the end of each school semester and at the end of summer. The ceremony is a serious but joyous occasion attended by youths' immediate and extended families, the wider community, and specially invited guests and honorees. All the young men are asked to wear African attire. Not every youth is honored, only those who have mastered their designated assignments and have been marked by staff as worthy to ascend to the next higher level of study and application. Elders who are mentoring specific youths also have input into their evaluation prior to the Rites of Passage ceremony. Special assignments that youths must master before being eligible to participate in the Rites of Passage ceremony include self-knowledge, genealogy, self-discipline, community service, and self-reliance.

Based on excellence in social conduct and knowledge-building, and on peer recommendations, staff appoint youths to be "junior leaders." Junior leaders conduct the Rites of Passage ceremonies and execute special assignments for self-development and community enhancement throughout the year. They must earn the right to their status, which is acknowledged through a special ritual. The concept of junior leaders is an African one that allows peer group members to be chosen by one another to represent the group before the elder teachers. This tradition can be traced to the MAASAI tradition in Kenya, whereby young warriors choose a peer to represent their collective interests (Saitoti 1980).

MEASURING SUCCESS

In keeping with the Afrocentric method, which stresses conduct (Asante 1990), LAMDP's primary criterion for measuring success is the impact it is having on the social conduct of participating youths. The first stage of staff evaluation of youths concentrates on the Seven Rs listed above. Young men are judged on overt manifestations of the Seven-R value system that they display at home, school, church, community, and at the program site. The second stage of evaluation focuses on the areas developed by Madhubuti (1990) and Perkins (1991). Madhubuti's (1990) 12 "Secrets of Life" are as follows:

☐ Self-knowledge;
☐ Family;
☐ Community;
☐ Avoiding stress;
☐ Critical thinking;
☐ Discipline/motivation;
☐ Personal health plan;
☐ Spiritual search/reciprocity;
☐ Cultural interaction;

□ Self-reliance/ambition;
□ Creative production;
□ Adapting to change. (pp. 159–167)

Perkins' (1991) areas of growth, some of which overlap with Madhu-buti's, are also used by program staff to evaluate progress:

□ Manhood training;
□ Sex education;
□ Physical fitness and self-defense;
□ Survival training;
□ Health maintenance and hygiene;
□ Life management and values clarification;
□ Cultural enrichment;
□ Political awareness;
□ Educational reinforcement;
□ Racial awareness;
□ Financial management;
□ Spiritual enrichment.

LAMDP staff examine how youths have improved in the above areas and what positive impact the program has had on their social conduct.

PROGRAM EVALUATION

LAMDP conducts three process evaluations a year: one after each school term (following the fall and spring Rites of Passage ceremonies), and one after the summer camp experience. These evaluations assess the efficacy of the methods that program staff use to meet program goals, and are carried out by staff as a means of improving service delivery.

Evaluation results reveal that LAMDP's intervention methods are effective, and that the program has a positive impact on the social conduct of participating youths. Both parents and teachers attest to the dramatic behavioral changes they witness at home and school among program youths. These changes include more positive outlooks on life, and greater maturity and seriousness in the manner with which youths approach tasks. School administrators report that participants are more responsible and respectful, and that this is reflected in better grades and deportment. Single mothers say the program is "God sent." The program seems to have a greater impact on the behavior of younger males. In their evaluations of the program, participants who are 15 years and older are less complimentary because LAMDP requires them to engage in life changes that they are reluctant to make.

The process evaluation provides evidence that the Afrocentric approach is appropriate as well as cost-effective. LAMDP, which is a non-residential program, serves almost 15 times more youths and costs only 7.5 percent of the Milne Boys Home residential component. The key here is non-residential care. Maintaining young men in their own home reduces program costs by 90 percent.

However, the Louis Armstrong Manhood Development Program could reach more youths if it were decentralized and located in key areas around New Orleans. Increased program funds would increase the program's effectiveness by allowing it to increase its hours of operation. Ideally, LAMDP should be an all-day, five- or six-day-a-week program that includes a school component. The current three hours a day, four or five days a week do not allow sufficient time to adequately deprogram maladaptive behaviors among urban youths. Older teenagers, in particular, require more exposure to the rigors of the program.

CONCLUSION

Afrocentrism, as applied to social programs for young African-American males, is not merely an intellectual exercise or a reactionary protest to the Eurocentric world view. It is a practical, positive philosophy that strengthens the individual while respecting other perspectives. Afrocentric-based programs allow social agencies to use a culture-based model that is effective in transforming troubled African-American youths into productive citizens, because it gives them a foundation on which to grow and develop as principled, disciplined, strong, confident, compassionate, and responsible individuals. Below are several steps that need to be taken to spread the use of effective Afrocentric intervention strategies nationwide.

First, the translation of Afrocentric theory into social practice should be institutionalized by nationalizing and certifying Afrocentric programs, based on certain standards of quality and effectiveness. Doing so will guard against charlatans who make claims to offer African-based intervention strategies for youths but who do not understand the theory behind the Afrocentric approach. Certification could be carried out by universities and colleges with African studies programs. Certain elements of the Afrocentric model such as the Rites of Passage ceremony might also be incorporated into regular school settings.

Second, all practitioners need to know what works. Process and impact evaluations (and the funding to carry them out) should be included as part of any overall national or local Afrocentric youth project.

Third, corporations, foundations, and school districts might create and support coalitions linking schools and social service agencies, in order to improve community-based service efforts to nurture African-American youths.

Finally, funding should be found to support additional research on Afrocentric intervention strategies, in order to strengthen current theory and practice.

Notes

One of the tenets of Afrocentrism holds that the term "Black" replaces the anthropological term "Negro," and thus also begins with a capital letter. This chapter maintains that usage.

1. The Pan-Africa movement, whose members came from the African diaspora, had as its goal the liberation of African people around the world.

References

Asante, M. 1990. *Afrocentricity: The Theory of Social Change*. Trenton, N.J.: Africa World Press.

Asante, M. and Kariamu W. Asante. 1989. *African Culture: The Rhythms of Unity*. Trenton, N.J.: Africa World Press.

Barbour, Floyd, ed. 1968. *The Black Power Revolt*. Boston, Mass.: Extending Horizons Books.

City Welfare Department (New Orleans). 1987. *Annual Report*. New Orleans, La.

Clark, K. B. 1965. *Dark Ghetto*. New York: Harper and Row.

Coppock, Nsenga Warfield. 1990. "Afrocentric Theory and Application, Vol. 1: Adolescent Rites of Passage." Washington, D.C.: Basbab Associates.

Diop, C. A. 1959. *The Cultural Unity of Black Africa*. Chicago: Third World Press.

Harlan, Louis R. 1972. *Booker T. Washington*. New York: Oxford University Press.

Hill, Paul, Jr. 1992. *Coming of Age: African American Male Rites-of-Passage*. Chicago: African American Images.

Jeff, Morris F. X., Jr. 1988. "The Seven Rs of the African-American Family." Presented at the Black Family Conference, sponsored by the University of Louisville Department of African Studies, Louisville, Ky., March.

Kerner Commission. 1968. *Report of the National Advisory Commission on Civil Disorders*. New York: The New York Times.

Kunjufu, Jawanza. 1991. *Developing Positive Self-Images and Discipline in Black Children*. Chicago: African American Images.

Lewen, Arthur. 1990. *Africa Is Not a Country, It's a Continent*. Milltown, N.J.: Clarendon Publishing Co.

Madhubuti, H. 1990. *Black Men: Obsolete, Single, Dangerous*. Chicago: Third World Press.

Mbiti, J. S. 1969. *African Religion and Philosophy*. New York: Fredrick A. Praeger Publishers.

Nobles, W. W. 1982. "The Reclamation of Culture and the Right of Reconciliation." In *The Black Mentally Retarded Offender*. New York: United Church of Christ.

Orleans Parish School Board. 1988. "Educating Black Male Youth: A Moral and Civic Imperative." New Orleans Parish School Board.

Pasteur, A., and I. Toldson. 1982. *Roots of Soul*. Garden City, N.Y.: Anchor Press.

Perkins, Useni E. 1986. *Harvesting New Generations: The Positive Development of Black Youths*. Chicago: Third World Press.

————. 1975. *Home Is a Dirty Street: The Social Oppression of Black Children*. Chicago: Third World Press.

Redkey, Edwin. 1969. *Black Exodus*. New Haven, Conn.: Yale University Press.

Rowe, D. 1991. "Africentricity: A Multidimensional Paradigm." *Psych Discourse* 23, 2 (November/December).

Saitoti, Tepilit Ole. 1980. *MAASAI*. New York: Harry N. Abrams Publishers.

Sudarkasa, N. 1980. "African and Afro-American Family Structure: A Comparison." *The Black Scholar* (November/December): 37–60.

THE SEVEN Rs PLEDGE

I will honor my history by living by the social conduct of my foreparents.

I vow to make the place where I live and learn better than the way I found it.

I vow to live a *RELIGIOUS* life always seeking to do what is morally right and good.

I will *RESPECT* my parents, teachers, and other elders in the community and, in so doing, I will respect myself and my peers.

I will take *RESPONSIBILITY* for my conduct to give of my talents, my knowledge, and my skills to make the world a better place to live.

I will *RESTRAIN* myself from doing anything wrong that would embarrass my family, my school, my community, or myself.

I will live in *RECIPROCITY*. I will give back in kindness that which I have received because this is the only way to the good life.

I will live in the *RHYTHM* of oneness and wholeness with the universe, always creating oneness, joy, and peace in the environment in which I live.

I will live a life of *REDEMPTION*, recognizing that life always offers a second chance to redeem the mistakes of the past.

I will live the "Seven Rs" in my daily life because I will shape history, I will decide the future, and I will take my people to the victorious shores of our destiny.

MANHOOD PLEDGE

Prelude

We were born males not men.
We will become men when
we learn the art and
science of manhood.

Pledge

We vow to work to become men,
to leave childhood, boyhood behind us.
We vow to seek knowledge
of the best way to relate
to ourselves, to our Almighty,
to our families, and to the community.
We vow to know, to seek answers to
who we were, who we are, and know
where we are going.
We vow to be the positive example
of manhood and Brotherhood, to be a Brother
to Brothers, Brother to Sisters, and Brother
to the community and institutions to which
we belong.
We vow to work to make the place where we are
better than the way we found it.
We vow to develop ourselves to save lives not
take lives. We will provide, protect, and
secure life. We will be constructive, not
destructive.
We vow to live the "Seven Rs" of
Righteousness, Respect, Responsibility,
Restraint, Reciprocity, Rhythm, and Redemption.

Prologue

We know that life is hard work, but we accept that challenge for
ourselves, for you, for life, for the future. Because the future is open
and we shall decide!

UNITY RITUAL

We are comrades in arms
We raise our palms to the
Stars in honor of the God of Gods

We touch our fingers to Mother Earth to praise our
Creator's creative source in the universe

We reach out our hands to the world
The garden we must keep, nurture, and protect and

We center and focus our strength as African men
Black men because we know

I am because we are and because we are therefore I am

I am because we are and because we are therefore I am

I am because we are and because we are therefore I am.

Chapter Six

TRADITIONAL YOUTH SERVICE SYSTEMS AND THEIR WORK WITH YOUNG BLACK MALES

Jane Quinn

There is no single commonly accepted definition of the universe of youth organizations in America. Some of the best known organizations such as 4-H, Boy Scouts, and the YMCA are also the largest. In fact, the National Collaboration for Youth reports that its 15 member agencies serve an estimated 25 million young people a year.[1] But youth development work has traditionally been conducted by a vast network of other agencies—public and private, secular and religious, national and local. Below I analyze the programs and outreach of four types of U.S. youth service systems, and explore the role of these organizations in promoting the development of young black males age 10 to 15. The four systems examined are national youth agencies, religious youth groups, sports organizations, and municipal parks and recreation departments. I discuss the "ideal" youth program, based on input from youths themselves, elucidate principles of best practice for youth-serving programs, and outline recommendations for how our nation can better serve the needs of young black males.

Information for this chapter draws heavily on original research—interviews, literature reviews, youth focus groups, and commissioned papers and surveys—conducted as part of the Project on Youth Development and Community Programs of the Carnegie Council on Adolescent Development.

AMERICA'S YOUTH ORGANIZATIONS

Despite the great diversity inherent in this vast universe of services, many of these service systems share similar histories, overall goals, and challenges. On the historical side, several of these systems find their roots in the Progressive Era (approximately 1900 to 1930) that followed the American Industrial Revolution. The history of municipal recreation services is surprisingly parallel to that of the settlement house movement, the YMCA, and Boys Clubs of America, all of which were born from an urban reform agenda developed and activated by members of a "modernizing elite" (Eisenstadt 1966). Similarly, religious youth organizations grew out of a 150-year tradition and concern on the part of the church both for the moral development of young people and for increased church membership.

The spirit that guided the development of all of these systems was a sense of adults' responsibility to younger generations as well as a belief that collective action could contribute to the common good. In some cases, an additional factor was the desire of wealthy individuals to contribute to the well-being of those less fortunate. Much of the historical literature analyzing this period refers to the "deep social consciences" of individuals who provided leadership to the social movements of the Progressive Era (Richmond 1990, p. 2).

Present-day America shares many characteristics with turn-of-the-century society, including massive economic and social changes that have led to increasing disparities between rich and poor. Just as the social reformers of the late nineteenth and early twentieth centuries saw the need for new institutions to address the unmet needs of the poor, of immigrants, and of neglected and exploited children and youth, society today is seeking ways to respond to the crisis facing many of America's citizens, especially its approximately 1.5 million young black males.

Despite the similar histories of many of America's traditional services for youth, these services are not particularly well coordinated with one another, nor do they operate in the same ways. In fact, there are clear differences among these services in mission, structure, and audience.

Mission. Some American youth programs view their mission as comprehensive youth development, in that they consider the needs and strengths of young people in a holistic light, attending to all five of the basic areas of human development (these are cognitive, physical, emotional, social, and moral development). Other programs focus principally on one of these areas, while placing less or no emphasis on the other four. While few community-based youth development programs consider cognitive development to be their major purpose (based on the assumption that this is the principal role of schools), there is a decided trend among youth development organizations to define their work as "informal education."

Structure. Contemporary American youth organizations use five basic structures: 1) troop- or group-based; e.g., Boy Scouts, 4-H; 2) facility-based; e.g., Boys Clubs, YMCA; 3) team-based; e.g., sports; 4) relationship-based; e.g., Big Brothers; and 5) drop-in; e.g., recreation. These categories are not mutually exclusive. Relationships among youth themselves and between youth and adults are central to most of these structures, and small groups are utilized in many of them. But structure represents an important difference between organizations because it influences other features such as program intensity, content, process, and environment.

Audience. The service demographics of America's youth organizations reveal clear differences in factors such as geography (urban/rural/suburban), socio-economic status, and race and ethnicity. Consider, for example, table 6.1, taken from the 1988 National Education Longitudinal Study (U.S. Department of Education 1990). From this nationally representative sample of 25,000 American eighth graders, we can see, for example, that participation in Boy Scouts is tied directly to family income, with higher participation rates at the highest income levels and lowest participation among the poorest quartile. An inverse pattern appears for 4-H and Boys Club participants. Activity participation rates also differ by geographic location. Participation rates for Boys Clubs are highest in urban areas (14.6 percent) relative to suburban (9.1 percent) and rural (9.9 percent) areas, while participation rates for 4-H are highest in rural areas (14.9 percent) relative to urban (5.9 percent) and suburban (7.1 percent) areas.

Particularly relevant to this volume are the data about race. Race *per se* does not seem to be a determining factor in the decision to participate in out-of-school activities. While whites are somewhat more likely than youth of color to participate in out-of-school activities, these higher rates are reflected only in such activities as nonschool team sports and religious activities.

CURRENT YOUTH SERVICE EFFORTS
TO REACH YOUNG BLACK MALES

Appendix 6.A contains descriptive information concerning the history, mission, scope, and fiscal status of national youth organizations, religious youth groups sponsored by mainline churches, youth programs conducted by privately sponsored sports organizations, and

Table 6.1 PERCENTAGE OF EIGHTH GRADERS PARTICIPATING IN OUT-OF-SCHOOL ACTIVITIES, BY SELECTED BACKGROUND CHARACTERISTICS

Background Characteristics	Any Outside-School Activity	Scouts	Boys or Girls Clubs	'Y' or Other Youth Group	4-H	Religious Youth Groups	Hobby Clubs	Neighborhood Clubs	Summer Programs	Non-School Team Sports
Total	71.3	14.2	10.7	15.3	9.3	33.8	15.5	12.7	19.2	37.3
Sex										
Male	70.7	18.9	11.2	14.3	8.5	29.5	17.1	13.6	16.3	45.1
Female	71.8	9.8	10.2	16.2	10.0	37.9	13.9	11.7	22.0	29.9
Race/ethnicity										
Asian and Pacific Islander	67.9	13.1	9.1	12.7	4.7	27.4	16.7	11.8	24.2	32.0
Hispanic	60.3	10.9	13.2	13.9	6.1	24.6	15.5	13.3	19.5	31.3
Black	65.6	20.0	23.7	23.0	13.8	30.0	22.4	23.4	29.6	33.9
White	74.4	13.7	8.1	14.3	9.1	36.6	14.1	10.7	17.1	39.1
American Indian and Native Alaskan	60.9	17.3	18.0	15.7	10.0	27.5	20.6	17.6	22.0	34.1
Income quartile										
Lowest quartile	60.0	12.9	14.5	14.0	11.1	22.7	16.3	14.1	16.5	29.5
25–49%	68.5	13.6	11.1	15.5	10.0	30.1	15.0	13.3	16.6	35.6
50–74%	74.2	14.4	9.5	14.8	9.4	35.9	15.1	11.6	18.7	38.4
Highest quartile	82.6	16.0	8.0	16.7	6.7	45.6	15.5	11.7	24.7	45.2
Location										
Urban	69.1	15.2	14.6	17.9	5.9	29.6	17.7	16.7	23.7	35.6
Suburban	71.5	14.0	9.1	14.2	7.1	33.3	14.9	11.3	18.5	40.0
Rural	72.8	13.9	9.9	14.8	14.9	37.9	14.7	11.2	16.7	35.1

Source: U.S. Department of Education (1990), p. 55.

youth programs conducted by municipal parks and recreation departments. Below I briefly examine the efforts these organizations and others have made to target young black males. Note that included here are only those organizations for which such information is available.

National Youth Organizations

Boy Scouts of America (BSA), the second largest youth organization (after 4-H), served 4.3 million youth in 1990. BSA does not keep membership figures by race or income level, but a 1987 recruitment and retention study by the Stanford Research Institute indicated that approximately 18 percent of its membership are minority,[2] compared with approximately 34 percent of the youth population.[3] Other evidence (U.S. Department of Education 1990) confirms that BSA tends to serve more affluent youth. Membership dues, program fees, and uniform costs probably contribute to this pattern. Some Boy Scout Councils have attempted to address these issues by raising specific funds to conduct outreach efforts in low-income minority communities, including public housing projects and welfare hotels.

BSA hopes to reach more low-income, minority, and urban youth through its "Learning for Life" (in-school) initiative, launched in July 1991. An underlying premise of the program is young people's need for access to information and experiences that will promote the acquisition of pro-social values. The once-a-week sessions will be taught principally by classroom teachers. Many observers have criticized the design of the program for being too modest in intensity and for not tackling the tough service delivery issues, such as providing support and assistance to young people in their own communities during non-school hours.

Boys and Girls Clubs of America, through its network of some 1,200 neighborhood-based clubs, has a long history of service to low-income and minority youth. Currently some 51 percent of its 1.6 million constituents are from minority backgrounds and 66 percent are from low-income families. This history and tradition are regularly reaffirmed by the national organization's board of directors and its council (made up of member clubs).

Big Brothers/Big Sisters of America offers one-on-one matching between a youth and a volunteer adult. The organization currently has some 75,000 young people in "active matches" and another 35,000 youths on a waiting list. A disproportionate number of these waiting list youth are minority males, because recruitment of minority male adult volunteers has been a challenge. The national organization has addressed this issue directly in recent years through a variety of efforts: forming partnerships with minority organizations (National Urban League, COSSMHO); conducting public service announcement campaigns targeted at potential volunteers; and publishing a resource guide entitled *Pass It On*, which focuses on recruitment of minority males. This publication "takes its name from the concept that adults in the African-American, Latino, Asian-American, and Native American communities have important cultural values to 'pass on' to children and youths through programs like Big Brothers/ Big Sisters" (Big Brothers/Big Sisters of America 1992).

The country's largest youth organization, 4-H, is the youth development component of the U.S. Department of Agriculture's Cooperative Extension Service. It currently serves almost 5 million youths each year. Over half of 4-H participants are reached through school-based programs. Although there are no hard data to verify this assertion, many observers within and outside 4-H believe that a high proportion of the organization's service to minority youth, who constitute 24 percent of its current participants, occurs through school-based programs. A more recent endeavor, also designed to extend the reach of 4-H beyond its traditional service populations, is the organization's Youth-at-Risk Initiative. Funded by the W.K. Kellogg Foundation, this effort seeks to make 4-H program services available to more low-income and minority children, and to other young people living in high-risk environments. A significant staff development component (funded by the DeWitt Wallace-Reader's Digest Fund) has recently been added to the Youth-at-Risk Initiative.

Table 6.2 presents estimates of the number of young black males reached by the subset of youth organizations that offer the lion's share of such services. At best, this chart can provide only a hazy snapshot of current services by virtue of several factors: the lack of specificity in several of the data sources; the possibility that these figures reflect significant duplication of service, both within individual agencies and across organizations; and the fact that participation and membership carry a wide variety of meanings, from attending a single-session program or course to participating in facility-based programs 20 to 30 hours a week throughout adolescence. In the context of these caveats, a conservative estimate indicates that the country's major national youth organizations reach a large number of young black males each year; that much of this service is of short duration and modest intensity; and that little of it is evaluated in terms of its effectiveness in comparison to its own goals or in compari-

Table 6.2 ESTIMATES OF YOUNG BLACK MALES REACHED BY SUBSET OF
NATIONAL YOUTH ORGANIZATIONS THAT OFFER MOST OF
THESE SERVICES

Name of Org.	Total No. Served (1990)	% Young Adol.	% Male	% Black	Estimated Total Young Black Males
Boy Scouts of America	4,202,992	50 est.	97	12	250,000
Boys & Girls Clubs of America	1,580,000	50	70	35	200,000
Big Brothers/ Big Sisters of America	60,000	65	52	15	3,000
4-H	4,897,217	88	47	18 est.	375,000
YMCA	12,784,866	15 est.	52	15 est. (no data)	150,000
CWLA	2,000,000	33 est. (no data)	50 est. (no data)	35 est.	115,000
National Network	400,000	35 est.	47	20 est.	13,000
Girls Inc.	250,000	50	30	35	12,000
YWCA	2,000,000	10	26	15 est.	7,500

son to externally developed criteria such as those discussed by Ronald Ferguson (see chapter four of this volume).

Religious Groups

While national experts see considerable progress in recent years in the ability of churches to address the needs of young adolescents, they are not so sanguine about the efforts of religious youth organizations to respond to the youth development and primary prevention needs of young people living in at-risk environments (Dean 1991). These youth ministry specialists generally agree that the country's major denominations, for the most part, are not currently successful in reaching such young people; that many are beginning to seek ways to do so; and that if high-risk youth are being served by religious youth programs, these efforts are largely local and small, or through treatment and remediation initiatives (offered by such groups as Catholic Charities and Lutheran Social Services). Two notable exceptions are the work of Youth for Christ, a non-denominational religious organization that has targeted many of its services to teenagers living in high-risk environments, and the work of the Congress of National Black Churches, which has launched several innovative programs designed to provide educational and social enrichment to African-American youth.

The failure of many religious youth organizations to reach young people living at highest risk is particularly compelling in light of research indicating that religious participation and belief may serve as protective factors against high-risk behaviors. A host of studies has found consistently that high religiosity is inversely related to drug and alcohol use, sexual activity, and delinquency among adolescents (Amoateng and Bahr 1986; Cochran 1988; Forliti and Benson 1986; Hadaway, Elifson, and Petersen 1984; Jessor, Costa, Jessor, and Donovan 1983).

Sports Organizations

Table 6.3, taken from Seefeldt, Ewing, and Walk (1992), offers descriptive information about particular characteristics of selected national youth sports programs. Of note to the present inquiry is the apparent lack of emphasis in most programs on reaching out to youth in at-risk environments. Although representatives from each of the organizations indicated that there were no restrictions regarding race, creed, or socio-economic status, few of these groups compile data on the race and socio-economic status of participants. Fewer than half—only 7 of the 16—make special provisions to place programs in communities where they are accessible to low-income and minority youth. Also of note is the extent of the gender differences in current participation rates. Although all of these organizations provide programs for both boys and girls on either a single-gender or coeducational basis, boys are one-and-a-half times as likely to participate as girls.

Municipal Parks and Recreation Departments

Current fiscal constraints facing local governments (see appendix 6.A) will contribute to an already great disparity in the availability

Table 6.3 CHARACTERISTICS OF SELECTED NATIONAL YOUTH SPORTS
PROGRAMS

Organization	Age Range	Competition at National Level	Emphasize Fun, Social and Skill Dvlpt	Provision for Low-Income	Fee for Play
Amateur Athletic Union	N/A	yes	yes	yes	yes
American Youth Soccer Organization	5–19	yes	yes	yes	no
Dixie Youth Baseball	8–17	no	yes	yes	yes
Hershey Track and Field	N/A	yes	yes	no	no
Little League Baseball	6–18	yes	yes	no	yes
National Junior Tennis League	8–18	yes	yes	yes	yes
National Youth Sports Program	10–16	no	yes	yes	no
Police Athletic League	N/A	yes	yes	yes	N/A
Pony Baseball	5–18	yes	yes	no	yes
Pop Warner Football	6–16	yes	yes	no	yes
Soccer Association for Youth	6–18	yes	yes	no	yes
U.S. Ice Hockey Association	5–18	yes	yes	no	yes
U.S. Volleyball Association	6–adult	yes	yes	no	yes
U.S. Wrestling Association	8–adult	yes	no	no	yes
U.S. Youth Soccer Association	4–19	yes	yes	yes	yes
Young American Bowling Alliance	8–21	yes	yes	no	yes

Source: Seefeldt, Ewing, and Walk (1992).

of community recreation programs in upper and lower income areas.
Because of their reliance on the local tax base, publicly supported
recreation programs in America have evolved into a two-tier system,
with more and better services available in suburban areas than in
less affluent rural or urban areas. This disparity has been documented
in a number of studies, including a 1986 survey of major eastern
cities (U.S. Department of the Interior 1989) and a 1987 study of two
Chicago neighborhoods by staff from the Chapin Hall Center for
Children (Littell and Wynn 1989). Authors of the first survey—the
National Urban Recreation Study—observed the unfortunate irony
in this situation:

> While recreation opportunities for most inner-city residents are
> insufficient, city agencies and community leaders usually identify the
> needs of disadvantaged youth as their most pressing concern. The
> needs of inner-city youth are intensified not only by residence in
> recreation-deficient neighborhoods, but by other social and economic

disadvantages. In general, inner-city youth are members of low-income families, and thus more dependent on public recreation services; members of racial and ethnic minorities; less frequently exposed to a range of recreational opportunities, and therefore, possess fewer recreational skills.

ANALYSIS OF CURRENT SERVICES FOR YOUNG BLACK MALES

Below I turn to an analysis of the strengths and weaknesses of current services for young black males offered by a broad cross section of the country's traditional youth organizations. I will use national survey data, local community studies, and organizational statistics to estimate the number of young black males reached by current services. I will match the content and processes of these services against a set of research-based criteria that focus on the unmet needs of young black males. Finally, I will assess these organizations' current and future plans to serve young black males, and outline principles of best program practice.

Numbers Reached

The 1988 National Education Longitudinal Study (NELS) (U.S. Department of Education 1990) provides the best single database on young adolescent participation in non-school activities. As briefly discussed above and shown in table 6.1, according to this national survey, 65.6 percent of black eighth graders participated in some out-of-school activities, compared to 74.4 percent of whites and 71.3 percent overall. Although there was no separate analysis for black males, the study revealed clear gender differences in the types of activities preferred by boys, with higher participation reported in non-school team sports (45.1 percent for boys versus 29.9 percent for girls) and Scouting (18.9 percent for boys versus 9.8 percent for girls). An unexpected finding is the higher participation of blacks than whites in several specific types of activities: Scouting (20 percent for blacks versus 13.7 percent for whites); Boys or Girls Clubs (23.7 percent versus 8.1 percent); "Y" or other youth groups (23 percent versus 14.3 percent); 4-H (13.8 percent versus 9.1 percent); and summer programs (29.6 percent versus 17.1 percent).

A report on the first follow-up to the 1988 NELS data sheds additional light on these participation findings. A question that asked respondents to indicate the frequency of their participation in "youth groups or recreation programs" revealed the following: that fewer than 2 percent participated every day or almost every day; only 15 percent participated once or twice a week; another 15 percent reported participating less than once per week; and over half said they rarely or never engaged in these activities (U.S. Department of Education 1992).

Taken together, these findings would suggest that many young black males are being reached by traditional youth services. Some organizations and types of services are doing a far better job than others in this outreach. The data suggest that young black males from more affluent families appear to be better served than their less advantaged peers, that much of this participation seems to be conducted on a fee-for-service basis, and that much of this participation is of extremely modest intensity (one to two hours a week or less).

A related conclusion may be that young black males *want* to participate in organized out-of-school activities, given these relatively high participation rates. This conclusion, which can be drawn only on a very tentative basis from the data, is supported by other studies, which reveal that participation in community-based youth development programs is especially valued by minority youth and young people growing up in single-parent families (Brown and Conn 1990; Allen and Philliber 1991).

A comparison of the NELS data to the statistics provided by the national youth organizations themselves appears to corroborate the conclusions that large numbers of young black males are being reached, that they are somewhat underserved in comparison to whites and to the overall population, and that much of this participation is often in activities that are of modest intensity. The NELS data also appear to corroborate the conclusions of authors of the Carnegie papers on religious youth groups (Dean 1991) and sports programs (Seefeldt, Ewing, and Walk 1992)—that children of color and low-income youth tend to be underserved by these institutions and organizations.

One key finding of the NELS data—that participation in non-school extracurricular activities is correlated to family income level—is explained by a handful of other studies that used very different research methodologies. For example, Francis Ianni (1990) and his colleagues at Columbia Teachers College conducted in-depth ethnographic studies in 10 American cities and towns over a period of

13 years. They aimed to understand the interaction of the multiple influences (schools, families, peers, communities) on adolescent development. The findings of this analysis included the wide disparity between upper income and lower income communities in resources available to support youth development.

A similar conclusion was reached by researchers from the Chapin Hall Center for Children at the University of Chicago, who conducted an extensive study of services for young adolescents (age 11 to 14) in two Chicago area neighborhoods—one in the inner city, the other in a nearby suburb. The suburban community had nearly three times the number of secular organizations per 1,000 youth, and more than three times the number of activities per week per 1,000 youth. Furthermore, the surburban community offered a much greater range of program offerings, which included classes, sports, clubs or groups, social or civic events, and organized arts activities. The programs offered in the inner-city neighborhood were quite limited by comparison, tending to focus more on personal support and tutoring (Littell and Wynn 1989, p. ix).

Such studies can serve to elucidate the NELS finding that participation rates in out-of-school activities are associated with socio-economic status, with the highest participation rates (82.6 percent) among young people with family income in the highest quartile, and the lowest participation rates (60 percent) among youth whose family income was in the lowest quartile. The likely explanation for this difference is access and availability rather than interest, given that many studies show youth and parental support for increased services in low-income areas.

Current Program Content and Processes

The practices and techniques utilized by effective intervention programs for young black males, cited by Ferguson (chapter four of this volume), match nicely with lists developed by others including the Center for Early Adolescence (Scales 1990, pp. 13–14) and the Center for Youth Development and Policy Research (Pittman and Wright 1991). However, Ferguson's emphasis on non-destructive and pro-social choices, activities, and roles reflects the reality that young black males need experiences that protect them from and compensate for the violent, illegal, and anti-social influences that often exist in their environments.

The "Ideal" Youth Program

Ferguson's list also conforms with studies that have elicited the opinion of young people themselves about their needs and activity preferences. For example, as part of the Carnegie Project on Youth Development and Community Programs, the Task Force commissioned a series of youth focus groups in order to deepen the group's understanding of ways to make community programs more responsive to the needs of today's young adolescents. Sixteen groups were conducted, all composed of young people from lower socio-economic backgrounds. The groups involved equal numbers of "participants" and "non-participants" in an effort to learn from both sets of experiences. Girls and boys met separately, as did young people from different racial and ethnic backgrounds, and younger (age 10–12) and older (age 13–15) youth. Nine groups were conducted in urban settings, and seven in rural areas. Trained facilitators conducted the sessions, and older teens trained as peer educators served as co-facilitators of some of the groups.[4]

All groups responded to the same set of questions, which centered on such issues as: how they currently spend their time when they are not in school, activity preferences, content preferences, how young people learn about community programs, what young people like and don't like about the adult leadership of programs, and suggestions for improving the programs and services in their neighborhoods.

Key recommendations from this focus group study include the following:

1. *Develop Comprehensive Centers That Integrate Services.* While the focus group respondents offered an expensive and fairly grandiose vision of the "ideal" youth center, the features they most wanted were: staff who listened and respected them; a place that makes them feel safe and protected; a place where they can be themselves; and an interesting array of programs, including organized sports and classes on a variety of subjects.

2. *Train Program Leaders to be Truly Responsive to the Needs of Young People.* According to the focus group respondents, leaders of youth programs must possess a range of interpersonal skills. Above all, they must be kind, nurturing, consistent, trustworthy, and genuinely interested in young people. They should create a welcoming and supportive atmosphere in the organization or program. Many of these adolescent respondents expressed a dread of being singled

out, excluded, or embarrassed. Many minority youth also expressed concern that leaders not discriminate against them.

3. *Staff Programs with Individuals Who Can Address the Ethnic and Bilingual Needs of Specific Youth Populations.* Many non-native speakers of English expressed a desire for bilingual leaders who can help them to learn English. Although some black youth said that they would prefer black leaders, others felt that this was unimportant—they simply wanted good leaders.

4. *Recruit Leaders Who Represent All Ages.* The focus group respondents did not necessarily prefer adults as leaders of youth programs. On the one hand, they enjoyed programs led by young people (i.e., older high school and college-age students) because younger leaders were perceived as being energetic and more attuned to youth's interests. On the other hand, they perceived older adults (meaning anyone between the ages of 25 and 70) as having more experience and wisdom, and as being more dependable.

5. *Offer Programs That Address the Serious Concerns of Today's Youth.* Focus group respondents repeatedly expressed concern about social issues that might not have been of such immediate worry to previous generations of 11- or 13-year-olds: developing job skills, learning about birth control, handling sexual relationships, and coping with violence.

6. *Provide Programs That Are At Once Structured and Flexible.* These young adolescents were clearly interested in participating in organized activities. However, they frequently expressed a dislike of adults who are bossy and demanding, and who require youth to do things that they do not want to do or are not capable of doing. Similarly, young people wanted to be involved in programs, but they wanted to have a sense of ownership within those programs and to have a sense that the programs presented them with choices.

7. *Make Programs More Accessible.* Transportation difficulties in getting to and from organized activities were frequently cited as a reason for not participating. Thus, organizations should strive to establish programs in locations that are readily accessible to young adolescents and that do not require transportation by a parent or other adult. The majority of focus group youths expressed an interest in participating in organized programs; factors such as transportation,

proximity, and cost often created barriers to such participation. Groups should work to eliminate or reduce these barriers, and funders should recognize that transportation is an important cost of doing business.

8. Encourage Youth Not to Feel Intimidated When Learning New Skills or Developing Talents. Youth consistently expressed little interest in music, art, and dance courses, often because they believed they were not accomplished at these activities. They seemed to be intimidated when presented with an opportunity to learn a new skill or develop a talent. Organizations offering fine arts programming should recognize and address this misconception.

9. Offer Youth an Opportunity to "Show What They Know." Youth frequently said that they were not interested in a particular activity (such as dance lessons) because they already possessed a particular skill. An opportunity exists for program planners to parlay these skills into the foundations of community service. Young people who know how to dance might be encouraged to teach other youth. Talented athletes might serve as coaches for younger teams. In so doing, youth will develop leadership skills, as well as a certain level of confidence in their own abilities.

10. Clearly Define Community Service Within the Context of Youth Programs. When asked directly, young people in these groups were generally not interested in performing community service, which they believed to involve cleaning up after others. Nonetheless, many of these adolescents expressed a desire to help others. This altruistic spirit could be tapped and used to encourage young people to participate in a variety of community service and community action programs. Planners should clearly define community service within the context of their program, and should articulate the rewards and challenges to be attained in such work. They should also expect youth to play an active role in planning the types of community involvement efforts in which they will participate.

11. Acknowledge and Address Gender Differences. Although many of the respondents expressed a preference for coeducational programs, others clearly felt a need for at least some single-sex programming. Boys and girls were very interested in socializing with one another, but they were less interested in competing with one another, especially on the playing field. Thus, organized programs should offer activities that are both single-sex and coeducational. The same-sex programs, rather than encouraging sexist behavior or sexism, should be presented as opportunities for each sex to develop or acquire new skills in a non-threatening environment.

12. *Address Issues of Violence and Safety.* Many young people, especially those in urban areas, expressed a very real and serious concern for their personal safety. Programs must be perceived as—and must in fact be—a refuge from the violence that permeates many of America's metropolitan areas and so, too, the lives of many inner-city and urban youth.

The young black males in these groups were particularly insistent on several issues: their need for advice and skills related to violence; their need for safe places to congregate and participate in activities; their need for positive relationships, especially with adult male role models; and their need for assistance in securing gainful employment. The themes that emerged from all the focus groups, including those conducted with young black males, emphasized the needs that young people feel for people, places, and programs (choices of activities). These adolescents did not necessarily feel that they needed to receive all of these components from a single youth organization or program, but rather that they should have greater access to all three of these aspects of support in their neighborhoods and communities.

THE GAP BETWEEN THE REAL AND THE IDEAL

What these young people are describing is a system, network, or "web" of services at the local level. Such a service network would provide a rich array of people, places, and programs that are coordinated with one another, responsive to the needs and interests of youth, and easily accessible by all youth.

The reality that actually confronts American youth in many communities is quite the opposite. The handful of community-based studies that have addressed the issue of service delivery to young adolescents reveals three distinct themes. First, fragmentation rather than coordination characterizes the planning and delivery of youth development services in most communities. Second, communities vary widely in their ability to offer a full array of needed services. Third, low-income communities with high-density youth populations are the least likely to offer an adequate array of services. The need for community-wide planning and coordination of youth services is verified by our earlier description of the current services offered by the various sub-sectors of America's youth organizations. Few of these services are truly comprehensive in scope and content, and fewer still are intensive enough to meet the needs of young people, especially of young people whose families and schools may be less than supportive.

Reginald Clark (1988) argues that school achievement is influenced directly by how students spend their non-school time. Young people who have a chance to participate in what he calls "high-yield" activities do better in school. He notes:

I have discovered that we can more accurately predict a youngster's success or failure in school by finding out whether or not he or she typically spends approximately 20 to 35 hours a week (of the 60 to 70 waking hours a week that are available to a youngster) engaging in what I call constructive learning activity. In a given week, this would consist of 4 or 5 hours of leisure reading, 1 or 2 hours of writing of various types (whether writing grocery lists, writing in a diary, taking messages on the telephone, or writing letters), 5 or 6 hours of homework, several hours devoted to hobbies, 2 or 3 hours of chores, 4 or 5 hours of games . . . that require the player to read, spell, write, compute, solve problems, make decisions, and use other cognitive skills and talents transferable to school lessons. This constructive learning activity also includes exposure to cultural activities, theater, movies, and sports.

Clark further notes that these requisite learning opportunities are typically found in experiences that occur away from school in the home and community, and during evening hours, weekends, summer months, and school vacations. He outlines four factors that contribute to the value of a given activity: time spent on a particular learning activity; amount of opportunity afforded for active involvement in acts of cognition while engaged in the activity; the extent of input by knowledgeable adults; and the rules, standards, expectations, and goals that surround the activity as it occurs.

Clark's conclusions lend credence to the notion that young people, especially those from disadvantaged backgrounds, need access to a rich array of activities and services for a significant number of hours (20 to 35) each week over an extended period of time. Clark himself is currently engaged in a community-wide effort in Bakersfield, California, designed to extend the reach of current youth programs by ensuring that all young black males have access to at least 20 hours a week of constructive activities during non-school hours.

Current and Future Efforts to Expand Services for
Young Black Males

On the local level, the Bakersfield experiment is one of several interesting initiatives seeking to address the unmet needs of young black males. Another such effort is YouthNet in Kansas City, a service providers' group that focuses on the goal of increasing the quantity and quality of youth programs in low-income neighborhoods. Group members conduct joint fundraising as well as program development and implementation, which has resulted in significant improvements in local service delivery, particularly to young black males.

A promising new collaboration between the New York City Board of Education and United Way of New York City, called CAPS (Community Achievement Project in the Schools), has combined funding from both sources to support a variety of community-based programs designed to prevent school failure and promote healthy adolescent development. In 1991, the first full year of implementation, CAPS involved 96 schools and 108 community-based organizations. The program seeks to match young people at risk of dropping out of school with agencies that offer needed supportive services such as counseling, tutoring, and sports programs.

The Chicago Cluster Initiative is using a different model to coordinate and expand both public- and private-sector youth services. The Initiative is a cooperative partnership among nine municipal and nonprofit agencies that are committed to taking a comprehensive approach to promoting educational achievement and life success among disadvantaged youth. Plans call for the Cluster Initiative to be implemented in four sites in Chicago over the next five years, then to be replicated citywide. To date, the Cluster has begun implementation of this coordinated approach in one of its four designated sites, DuSable High School, and in DuSable's local feeder schools at both the elementary and middle school levels.

On the national level, there appears to be little coordinated attention on the part of traditional youth service systems to the issue of strengthening and expanding services to young black males. In fact, interagency vehicles for cooperative action such as the National Collaboration for Youth have been noticeably silent on this issue. However, individual agencies have undertaken a variety of activities, including expansion of outreach efforts; enactment of specific strategies to recruit minority staff and volunteers; initiation of programmatic changes designed to make program content more relevant to the interests and responsive to the needs of young black males; and experimentation with changes in program settings (locating programs in housing projects and detention centers). While few of these efforts are targeted specifically at young black males, several of them, if successful, would have the effect of expanding services to this population. For example, there is a decided trend among the national youth agencies toward expansion of services to at-risk youth. And nearly every national youth organization is experimenting with new delivery systems. However, the most popular technique—bringing youth organization programming into schools during the school day—does little to address the documented needs of young people for more constructive alternatives during their discretionary time, or to reach out to youth who no longer attend school. Another trend among the national youth organizations is related to staff development. Many of these groups are retooling their existing staffs through concerted training efforts, and many are also recruiting minority staff and volunteers.

Principles of Best Practice

Both research and experience support the adoption of the following principles of best practice for reaching and serving young black males through traditional service systems.

□ *On both the national and local levels, youth service organizations and institutions should work together to create systems of support for young black males.*

The current uncoordinated and fragmented array of programs and services should be replaced by a creative and responsive network of services provided by agencies and organizations that see themselves as sharing common goals. Youth needs, rather than organizational concerns, should be the focal point of such networks.

□ *On both the national and local levels, organizational leadership— for example, boards of directors of nonprofit organizations, community boards of municipal services—should make an informed, long-term commitment to addressing the needs of young black males.*

Many traditional organizations act as if they are not aware of the crisis facing young black males in America. Others are aware, but appear unconcerned or do not know how to respond. There is a tendency for organizations to use their current programs and delivery systems as their starting point and to attempt to reach out to the young people who are easiest to serve or whose needs match most closely an organization's current practices. On the other hand, organizations that are successful in reaching and serving young black males (for example, Boys and Girls Clubs of America and the Police Athletic League) have made an explicit and long-term commitment to this work. This commitment is initiated at the national level by the organization's highest governing structures and is regularly reexamined and reaffirmed. A host of organizational structures can be used to infuse the entire system with the commitment and to support implementation over the long term.

□ *On both the national and local levels, organizational leaders must be able and willing to allocate or generate the financial resources needed to carry out their commitments to serve young black males.*

A few organizations are in the enviable position of having more resources than they need to support current operations. The Boy Scouts of America, for example, has enjoyed multimillion dollar surpluses annually in recent years. Other organizations have substantial fundraising mechanisms in place and are able to secure the resources they need to implement their long-term plans. As individual agencies and institutions seek to expand their programs for young black males, they will face key questions such as whether current funds could be reallocated for the purpose, and what sources might be tapped to generate new resources to support program modification and outreach. Because of their strategic and policy implications, these questions should be discussed by organizational leaders such as boards of directors, not just by agency administrators. Similarly, the leadership of adult service clubs such as the Kiwanis and Lions Clubs—which have traditionally provided support for many of America's mainline youth groups—should hold policy-level discussions about how to target their substantial human and financial resources.

□ *On both the national and local levels, organizations should base their program interventions on the best available knowledge of the needs of young black males and of effective program design.*

Program developers should draw on the growing body of national information about young black males and on specific knowledge of young people in their communities. Young black males themselves should be asked for their opinions and suggestions, and these ideas should be considered an important part of the knowledge base on which interventions are designed. Like all sound youth development programs, those for young black males should have a strong theoretical framework for the methodologies they employ, and a solid grounding in research on high-risk behaviors and environments. The experience of staff and volunteers in working with youth should also be considered part of the knowledge base used by the programs.

□ *Programs for young black males should be intense enough to make a difference in their lives.*

The frequency and duration of program activities should be adequate relative to program goals and objectives and to the needs of the young people served. These programs should recognize and address individual needs. If a program is building-based, the facility that houses the program should be open long hours, and at times that are convenient for young people. Effective community programs for young black males should actively seek ways to intensify contact with young people—for example, by providing camping or retreat experiences, particularly when youth have more discretionary time (weekends and summers). The need for change in this direction is supported by a growing body of literature (Walker and Vilella-Velez 1992; Girls Incorporated 1991) indicating that sustained and comprehensive interventions are needed in order to effect real change in the lives of disadvantaged youth.

□ *Programs for young black males should offer content that is relevant to their current and future needs and that is appealing to their interests.*

Effective programs will deal with issues that deeply concern young black males as they move through adolescence and prepare for adulthood. These programs do not shy away from issues that some adults might perceive as controversial, such as reproductive health or interpersonal violence. These programs recognize that when young people say they want community programs to be "fun," they often mean that they want relevant, often serious content to be offered in interesting and meaningful ways. Sports and recreation can be used as "hooks" to attract young black males, and as a vehicle for promoting academic achievement and the acquisition of life skills and prosocial values. Program content should also address the desire of young black males to learn job skills and obtain access to gainful employment. Last but hardly least, programs should determine if the basic needs of young people (for food, safety, and shelter) are being adequately met, and do what they can to address these issues if necessary.

☐ *Effective programs for young black males should use active educational and social support processes.*

Experiential learning and hands-on activities are the primary vehicles for service delivery in effective youth development programs. Young people should be offered many opportunities to develop new skills, and programs should emphasize skill development through practice and reflection. Recognition of accomplishments should be built into the educational process. This active learning mode should be implemented in the context of supportive relationships, in recognition of young adolescents' needs for positive connections with both peers and adults. Programs should deliberately seek to provide opportunities for peer leadership, through which young people have an opportunity to teach same-age or younger peers.

☐ *Effective community programs for young black males should offer sustained individual attention from skilled and committed adult leaders.*

These adults (paid and unpaid staff) should share the program's philosophy; understand its goals and have the skills to implement them; be willing to share leadership with young people and have the requisite knowledge and skills to do so; and be consistent and reliable in their work with youths.

In order to ensure consistency in adult leadership, staff and volunteers should be carefully recruited, well trained, and consistently supported and recognized by the sponsoring organizations. Special efforts should be made to recruit older black males as staff and volunteers. Mainline organizations may find it effective to develop solid working relationships with minority organizations such as the NAACP, the National Urban League, Concerned Black Men, and black fraternities and other adult service groups. This can help such youth organizations establish credibility in minority communities and secure adult volunteers as board members, mentors, role models, and program leaders.

□ *Effective community programs for young black males offer a strong sense of place and a strong sense of belonging.*

These programs should provide a comfortable atmosphere that allows young people to feel welcome and encourages them to participate actively. Programs should be accessible, safe, and intimate, and should encourage all members to have a stake in what happens within the program or agency. They should have clear expectations and predictable environments, and may provide symbols of membership such as t-shirts, membership cards, and certificates of accomplishment. They should recognize that identity formation in adolescence is fostered by group membership and participation.

□ *Effective programs for young black males should be well rooted in, and reach out into, the communities they serve.*

Such programs should seek to help young black males develop satisfying relationships and make useful connections throughout the community; foster positive and meaningful relationships with the families of participants; and work collaboratively with other agencies including schools. The programs should see themselves as part of the community, and work to be fully integrated into the life of that community. They can do this by being responsive to community needs, and willing to modify their approaches as the needs of communities change. Programs must recognize that the young people who could benefit from their services most may be those who are least likely to knock on their door. Therefore, programs must be proactive, creative, and persistent in recruiting participants.

GENERAL RECOMMENDATIONS

Traditional youth organizations have the advantages of stability, durability, and credibility. They also have the disadvantages of a defined constituency that frequently resists change. Traditional organizations face the challenge of needing to overcome the tendency to say, "But we've always done it this way." When traditional organizations become large organizations, there is the additional tendency of needing a significant amount of advance planning to implement changes through the multiple levels of the system. While innovation may not be the long suit of many traditional youth organizations, real change is possible; in fact, change has been necessary in order for these organizations and systems to survive. Harnessing the untapped potential of America's traditional youth service systems in a focused effort to address the contemporary needs of young black males will require a multifaceted effort involving many sectors of society. Yet all of society has a stake in the outcomes—diminished or productive futures for 1.5 million of our youth.

At minimum, national youth organizations should seek to have their service demographics match national demographics. Some of the largest service systems fall short in this regard, while others do not keep the most basic data that would allow them to track the demographics of the youths they serve. An added accountability problem is that few organizations or institutions conduct systematic outcome evaluations that permit them to assess the effectiveness of their services for any of their constituents—young black males or others.

Much could be done to harness the potential of America's traditional youth service systems in order to make them more responsive to the current needs of young black males. The recommendations below are grouped by specific youth organization sectors and supportive structures.

National Youth Organizations. On a collective level, the national youth organizations should use the National Collaboration for Youth structure to conduct a systematic assessment and planning effort directed at the needs of young black males. As part of this effort, the Collaboration should actively recruit other national organizations, especially minority organizations and minority-serving organizations, into membership. Working together, these national organizations should use national census and social indicator data to assess the needs of young black males; match these needs to their current services and resources, identifying gaps in service; and develop joint plans that might include working partnerships between two or more Collaboration agencies, as well as individual organizational plans that are part of a larger national plan. Outside funding, both public and private, could be sought for such an initiative.

Local Communities. National studies can provide a broad overview of critical issues, and national organizations can play a significant role in unifying and improving the work of their member agencies. However, it is at the local level—the point of direct service delivery— that young people receive or fail to receive the support they need on the road to adulthood. American communities vary widely in the types of protection and support they are able to offer youth. But they share one common characteristic: precious few American communities engage in comprehensive community-wide planning around youth services. Yet it is this very process that ensures that services for youth are adequate and coordinated. When viewed as a unit of planning, "community" may be defined as a neighborhood in a large urban area; an entire town; a small city; or even a county. More important than the boundaries of any given community is the sense of shared responsibility and interdependence that this concept implies.

Communities that want to plan an effective system of services for young people need to engage in a five-step process on an ongoing basis: 1) establish permanent planning structures; 2) conduct a thorough needs analysis; 3) assess current services and match these services to identified needs; 4) develop and implement a plan to improve the actual delivery of services; and 5) evaluate the results of the strengthened system of services. There are many good resources that can help communities to undertake this process in a thorough and tested manner (United Way of America 1982). Youth bureaus, mayoral coordinating boards, and United Way planning councils are three effective planning infrastructure models that share several common features: responsibility, accountability, visibility, relative stability, and financial and political clout.

Schools. In the abstract, few would argue against the proposition that young people would be better served by systems in which schools and other community institutions work together. Yet there are many barriers to school–community collaboration, including logistical, financial, legal, and bureaucratic problems. Despite the presence and persistence of such barriers, known solutions do exist, and range from the simple to the complex.

At the simplest level, schools and community-based agencies can work together to share information about individual students and effect appropriate referrals from one institution to another. A second level of cooperation would see community agencies delivering program services in school facilities, either during the school day or before and after school. A third level involves joint planning that focuses not just on individual students but on the delivery of services for all students. A fourth level, one that has been realized in few communities, is a unified system of educational and human services. This system views its role as youth development, and recognizes the common goals of schools and community agencies while respecting their inherent differences and strengths. Schools and community agencies may find it useful to work from one stage to the next, with the goal of achieving this fourth level of service integration.

Policymakers. Local, state, and federal policies all play a critical role in supporting or failing to support healthy adolescent development. An ideal set of public policies would be integrated at the local, state, and federal levels. It would be firmly rooted in the philosophical notion of youth as resources, would focus on increasing support for basic youth development services (as opposed to treatment and remediation), would target services to areas of greatest need, and would give priority to locally generated solutions.

Even in this time of fiscal austerity, some local communities have taken the lead in improving their services for children and youth. While successful models vary in strategy and approach, they share many common features. All are directed toward service delivery improvement; have the leadership and blessing of top-level government officials; build on existing systems while recognizing the need to plan, coordinate, and organize these services differently; and have generated or allocated new financial resources as part of their efforts.

Other exemplary features of successful approaches include efforts to: coordinate all municipal services through sharing of publicly owned facilities (for example, coordinated use of recreation facilities by both the education and recreation departments); effect better coordination between public and private agencies serving children; and involve youth directly in community-wide planning. In addition, local service delivery improvement efforts are generally rooted in effective public policy. In some communities—San Diego, for example—child advocates have worked with municipal officials to craft a statement that articulates the city's commitment and responsibility to all its children and youth.

A highly significant recent trend has been the establishment of a variety of state-level approaches to improvement in the coordination of education, health, and social services. Many of these approaches are directed toward children, youth, and families living in high-risk environments. Nonetheless, according to one national expert, "No state has realized the goal of developing comprehensive and statewide programs that move beyond the planning and demonstration stage" (Dryfoos 1991).

Many observers believe that the strongest model at the state level for strengthening community-based services for all youth is the youth bureau/commission approach, which has a long history in New York State and which has been implemented in Oregon since 1989. The Oregon system is rooted in a legislative mandate that assures the right of every child in the state to opportunities to graduate from high school healthy, literate, and skilled. The State Commission seeks to coordinate all community efforts aimed at children from birth through age 18. Under the new law, each county has a youth commission charged with planning local services, and these commissions receive state support for some of their efforts. Since their inception, many of these commissions have engaged in a community action planning process that has involved both public and private services providers. The Oregon experiment is noteworthy on several fronts: it quickly translated a state-level mandate to needed action on the local level; it provides financial support and incentives to local actors; it has built on the experiences of earlier reform initiatives; and it has survived a change in administration.

On the federal level, both macro-level public policies (concerning employment, poverty, housing, education, and civil rights) and specific youth development policies contribute to the climate of improvement or decline in adolescent outcomes. Three specific youth development policies would strengthen support for all American teens. The first is full funding of the Young Americans Act, recent federal legislation designed to establish a basic national youth policy and to build the infrastructure needed to plan, coordinate, and implement effective youth development services at the national level. This legislation was passed in 1989 but was never funded. The second policy is federal legislation that would allocate new financial resources to youth development services delivery at the local level and would complement the national- and state-level planning mechanisms established by the Young Americans Act. In this regard, current proposals for Youth Development Block Grants, for the Youth Development Act of 1992, and for the Comprehensive Services for Youth Act of 1992 deserve serious attention.

The third policy is the provision of adequate support (through the annual appropriation to the Cooperative Extension Service) for the Youth Development Information Center, which would actively disseminate information about youth development programs, curricula, professional contacts, funding, research, evaluation, and advocacy. In addition, a specific federal activity that would strengthen services to young black males would be significant funding of the Minority Male Initiative in the U.S. Department of Health and Human Services.

Funders. Key funding strategies that would strengthen community-based youth development services, including services for young black males, include: strengthening and stabilizing the funding base for these services' basic operations; moving from categorical (problem-specific) funding to core support for youth development; adding public dollars to the already substantial amount of private monies that support youth development services; reallocating some existing resources from upper- and middle-income to low-income areas; targeting new mcnies to low-income neighborhoods; and establishing funding priorities for professional development of youth workers, outcome evaluation of youth development programs, and advocacy on behalf of youth. United Ways, community and national foundations, corporations, individual contributors, and government at all levels should play a role in this strengthened and reconfigured funding system.

Researchers. Researchers and practitioners have much to gain by forging partnerships around program design and evaluation. Researchers can witness and participate in the increased application of their ideas, while practitioners can strengthen the efficacy of their interventions. Both have opportunities to enrich their own perspectives by sharing their expertise and learning from one another. Strengthening the ties between the research and practice communities will require: improved outreach activities by both parties; increased incentives, especially on the part of universities, for participation in community-based initiatives; additional funding supports for research–practice collaborations; and increased attention to non-school issues and to the needs of youth of color in large-scale national surveys.

Notes

1. As of June 1, 1992, the 15 member agencies of the National Collaboration for Youth included the following: American Red Cross, Association of Junior Leagues, Big Brothers/Big Sisters of America, Boy Scouts of America, Boys and Girls Clubs of America, Camp Fire Boys and Girls, Child Welfare League of America, 4-H, Girl Scouts of the USA, Girls Incorporated, the National Network of Runaway and Youth Services, the Salvation Army, WAVE, Inc., YMCA of the USA, and YWCA of the USA.

2. Personal interview with BSA Board President Richard Leet and Chief Scout Executive Ben Love, June 12, 1991.

3. According to 1990 U.S. Census Bureau figures, 34 percent of the population age 5 to 17 is either black, Hispanic, Asian, or Native American. If the category of "other" is included, that figure rises to 39 percent.

4. These teens, age 16 to 18, were members of the Center for Population Option's Teen Council, through which they had participated in 60 hours of peer leadership training. In addition, they received special training in focus group facilitation conducted by staff from S.W. Morris & Co. of Chevy Chase, Md., the firm that conducted the focus group study for the Carnegie project.

References

Allen, J. P., and S. Philliber. 1991. "Process Evaluation of the Teen Outreach Program: Characteristics Related to Program Success in Preventing School Dropout and Teen Pregnancy in Year 5 (1988–89 School Year)." New York: Association of Junior Leagues International.

Amoateng, A. Y., and S. J. Bahr. 1986. "Religion, Family, and Adolescent Drug Use." *Sociological Perspectives* 29: 256–63.

Benson, P. L. 1990. "The Troubled Journey: A Portrait of 6th–12th Grade Youth." Minneapolis, Minn.: Lutheran Brotherhood.

Big Brothers/Big Sisters of America. 1992. *Pass It On Volunteer Recruitment Manual: Outreach to African-American, Latino/a and Other Diverse Populations.* Philadelphia, Pa.: Big Brothers/Big Sisters of America.

Boys and Girls Clubs of America. 1991. "The Effects of Boys and Girls Clubs on Alcohol and Other Drug Use and Related Problems in Public Housing Projects." A demonstration study sponsored by the Office for Substance Abuse Prevention, New York, March.

Boys Town Center for the Study of Youth Development. No date. "A Profile of Participants in Religious Youth Activities—1980: From the High School and Beyond Study of the National Center for Education Statistics." Boys Town, Nebr., 6.

Brown, S. J., and M. Conn. 1990. "Girl Scouts: Who We Are, What We Think." Study conducted for the Girl Scouts of the USA, New York.

Clark, Reginald M. 1988. "Critical Factors in Why Disadvantaged Students Succeed or Fail in School." New York: Academy for Educational Development.

Cochran, J.K. 1988. "The Effects of Religiosity on Secular and Ascetic Deviance." *Sociological Focus* 21: 293–306.

Dean, K. C. 1991. "A Synthesis of Research on, and a Descriptive Overview of, Protestant, Catholic, and Jewish Religious Youth Programs in the United States." Unpublished manuscript prepared for the Carnegie Council on Adolescent Development, Washington, D.C.

Dryfoos, J. G. 1991. "States' Response to Youth-At-Risk Issues: Preliminary Report to the Carnegie Corporation on Work in Progress in 1990." Unpublished manuscript, January.

Eisenstadt, S. N. 1966. *Modernization, Protest, and Change.* Englewood Cliffs, N.J.: Prentice Hall.

Erickson, J. B. 1991. *1992–93 Directory of American Youth Organizations.* Minneapolis, Minn.: Free Spirit Publishing.

Ewing, M. E., and V. Seefeldt. 1989. "Participation and Attrition Patterns in American Agency-Sponsored and Interscholastic Sports: An Executive Summary." Final report to the Athletic Footwear Council of the Sporting Goods Manufacturers Association, Ann Arbor, Mich.

Forliti, J., and P. L. Benson. 1986. "Young Adolescents: A National Survey." *Religious Education* 81: 199–224.

Girls Incorporated. 1991. "Truth, Trust and Technology: New Research on Preventing Adolescent Pregnancy." New York: Girls Incorporated.

Hadaway, C. K., K. W. Elifson, and D. M. Petersen. 1984. "Religious Involvement and Drug Use Among Urban Adolescents." *Journal for the Scientific Study of Religion* 23: 109–28.

Ianni, F. A. J. 1990. *The Search for Structure.* New York: The Free Press.

Jessor, R., F. Costa, L. Jessor, and J. E. Donovan. 1983. "Time of First Intercourse: A Prospective Study." *Journal of Personality and Social Psychology* 44: 600–26.

Littell, J., and J. Wynn. 1989. "The Availability and Use of Community Resources for Young Adolescents in an Inner-City and Suburban Community." Chicago: University of Chicago, The Chapin Hall Center for Children.

Martens, R. 1986. "Youth Sport in the U.S.A." In *Sport for Children and Youth: Vol. 10,* eds. M. Weiss and D. Gould. Champaign, Ill.: Human Kinetics Press.

Office of Technology Assessment. 1991. *Adolescent Health, Volume I: Summary and Policy Options.* OTA-H-468. Washington, D.C.: U.S. Government Printing Office.

Pittman, K., and M. Wright. 1991. "A Rationale for Enhancing the Role of the Non-School Voluntary Sector in Youth Development." Paper commissioned by the Carnegie Council on Adolescent Development, Washington, D.C.

Richmond, J. B. 1990. "The Hull-House Years: Vintage Years for Children." Unpublished manuscript.

Scales, P. C. 1990. "A Portrait of Young Adolescents in the 1990s: Implications for Promoting Healthy Growth and Development." Carrboro, N.C.: University of North Carolina at Carrboro.

Seefeldt, V., M. Ewing, and S. Walk. 1992. "An Overview of Youth Sports Programs in the United States." Unpublished manuscript prepared for the Carnegie Council on Adolescent Development, Washington, D.C.

Smith, C. 1991. "Overview of Youth Recreation Programs in the United States." Unpublished manuscript prepared for the Carnegie Council on Adolescent Development, Washington, D.C.

U.S. Department of Education, National Center for Education Statistics. 1992. *User's Manual, National Education Longitudinal Study of 1988, First Follow-Up: Student Component Data File User's Manual, Vol. I.* Washington, D.C.

————. 1990. *National Education Longitudinal Study of 1988: The Profile of the American Eighth Grader.* Washington, D.C.: U.S. Government Printing Office.

U.S. Department of the Interior, President's Commission on Outdoors. 1989. "National Urban Recreation Study: An Executive Report." Washington, D.C.

United Way of America. 1982. "Needs Assessment: The State of the Art— A Guide For Planners, Managers, and Funders of Health and Human Care Services." Alexandria, Va.

Walker, G., and F. Vilella-Velez. 1992. "Anatomy of a Demonstration." Philadelphia, Pa.: Public/Private Ventures.

DESCRIPTION OF CURRENT SERVICES

National Youth Organizations

Material presented here focuses on five mainline youth organizations: Boy Scouts of America, Boys and Girls Clubs of America, Big Brothers/Big Sisters of America, 4-H, and the YMCA of the USA. Services to young black males provided by other traditional youth organizations (for example, through the school-age child care programs of Girls Incorporated and the YWCA) and by other National Collaboration for Youth agencies (Child Welfare League of America, National Network of Runaway and Youth Services, Salvation Army, and WAVE, Inc.) will be briefly described. These descriptions are based on reviews of organizational documents (annual reports, program materials including handbooks and curricula, newsletters and magazines, and research reports) and on in-depth personal interviews with the staff and board leadership of each organization.

Boy Scouts of America. The second-largest (after 4-H) of America's youth organizations, Boy Scouts of America (BSA) served 4.3 million youth in 1990. Of all the traditionally male-serving organizations, BSA has held closest to its history in this regard. While no longer exclusively boy-serving (the organization's Explorer Program for adolescents has been coeducational since 1972 and its new in-school "Learning for Life" program also serves both genders), at present some 98.6 percent of BSA's members are boys and young men, age 6 to 17.

On the national level, BSA appears to be the wealthiest of America's youth organizations, with an annual national budget of approximately $80 million, assets in excess of $230 million, and annual operating surpluses of over $11 million in 1989 and 1990.

BSA's emphasis on character development has remained constant throughout its 82-year history. The organization stresses "traditional values," including service to others, through troop-based activities led by volunteer leaders. In recent years, BSA has sought to update its programming and its image through programmatic attention to such contemporary issues as drug abuse and sexual abuse. Its "Five Unacceptables" campaign encourages Boy Scout members to engage in community service related to current social problems such as hunger and homelessness. A central issue facing BSA at present is a series of legal challenges concerning membership and leadership.

Boys and Girls Clubs of America. A short answer to the frequently asked question, "What is the difference between Boy Scouts and Boys Clubs?" might be "Almost everything." Boys Clubs, which became Boys and Girls Clubs of America (B/GCA) in 1991, emphasizes facility-based services to low-income and minority youth through its network of some 1,200 neighborhood-level clubs. In contrast to Boy Scouts and other troop-based organizations, which provide an average of one to two hours of programming a week, the average Boys and Girls Club is open about 30 hours a week for program activities. Staffed by trained professionals whose work is supplemented by volunteers, the clubs use a combination of large groups, small groups, and individual modalities in program delivery. The B/GCA program is intended to be comprehensive. The organization's "core program" focuses on six areas: health and physical education; citizenship and leadership development; cultural enrichment; social recreation; personal and educational development; and outdoor and environmental education. Since clubs retain considerable autonomy in actual program delivery, the extent to which individual clubs achieve this holistic balance varies tremendously, with some clubs emphasizing sports and recreation far more than the other areas.

On the national level, B/GCA has developed a number of national programs that deal with youth employment, health, sports and fitness, youth leadership, community service, and the arts. A recent outside evaluation of B/GCA's "SMART Moves" (substance abuse prevention) program revealed that the organization's comprehensive youth development program, with or without interventions targeted toward specific risks, both reduces problem behavior and promotes pro-social behavior. In order to evaluate five Boys and Girls Clubs that had implemented the "SMART Moves" intervention, each of these clubs was assigned two control sites: one public housing site with a Boys and Girls Club but without "SMART Moves," and one public housing site without a Boys and Girls Club. These control sites were geographically and demographically matched with the sites having clubs with "SMART Moves." The evaluators found that, while the differences in impact between the clubs without "SMART Moves" and clubs with the targeted intervention were not great, there were substantial differences between the housing projects that had clubs and those that did not in relation to positive outcomes for youth, for parents, and for the surrounding community (Boys and Girls Clubs of America 1991).

Big Brothers/Big Sisters of America. A third delivery system, that of one-to-one matching between a young person and a volunteer adult, is offered by Big Brothers/Big Sisters of America (BB/BSA). The basic BB/BSA program is supported on the local level by professional casework services. The national office sets standards for its 500 plus local affiliates, provides training for staff and volunteers, and develops national programs and other support materials. One recent national program, "Empower," focuses on prevention of sexual abuse, an especially thorny issue for this organization, as well as for several of the other boy-serving agencies. BB/BSA is working with Public/Private Ventures, a Philadelphia-based firm, on a comprehensive five-year evaluation of its basic mentoring program. When completed the evaluation promises to offer valuable information about four sets of issues: the effects of the mentoring relationship on the lives of participating youth; volunteer recruitment and screening; administrative and operational practices that constitute the BB/BSA program model; and a qualitative examination of the interactions that take place between adults and the youths with whom they are paired. The evaluation, which was begun in 1990, is being conducted at 15 sites around the country.

4-H. The country's largest youth organization is also the only major national youth organization that receives the bulk of its financial support from government sources. On the national level, 4-H is part of the U.S. Department of Agriculture, reflecting the organization's deep roots in this country's rural economy. As the youth development component of USDA's Cooperative Extension Service, 4-H is tied to the land grant college system, founded in 1862. At its inception, the land grant college system represented an innovative step in bridging the gap between research and practice. The 4-H system itself, founded in 1914, currently serves nearly 5 million young people (age 9 to 19) each year. Although the traditional 4-H program follows a small-group (club) model with an adult volunteer leader, today over half of 4-H participants are reached through school-based programs (often in-class courses conducted during school hours). Many of these courses focus on science and nutrition education, and are not very different in content and approach from traditional school programs. Others are oriented more toward youth development and life skills, and incorporate experiential education methods.

It is difficult to calculate the total amount of the 4-H annual budget, either on the national level or in the aggregate, because support is provided by national, state, and local public dollars, as well as by some private monies. USDA's Cooperative Extension Service estimates that approximately one-fourth of its $361 million annual budget is allocated to 4-H.

The formal relationship between 4-H and land grant colleges and universities provides the organization with access to the research and evaluation capacity of those institutions. Many doctoral dissertations have evaluated the impact of participation in various aspects of 4-H programs. The Youth Development Information Center in Greenbelt, Maryland, has an almost complete collection of these dissertations. Because there is really no national 4-H program, it is difficult to apply the findings of these studies to the entire system. However, these evaluations underscore the value of participation in 4-H programs, and are often cited as support for participation in other kinds of non-formal education.

YMCA of the USA. Many multiservice organizations provide some programming for youth, but for most, the amount of youth programming is small in the context of the organization's total priorities, and the focus is on problem treatment rather than youth development. However, in some national multiservice organizations, youth programs represent a substantial and increasing priority. The YMCA is one such organization.

Although its members no longer need be young, male, or Christian, the YMCA currently serves a large number of boys and young men through its network of 2,069 neighborhood-based centers. Thirty-seven percent of the 12,784,886 people served by the YMCA in 1990 were children and youth, age 6 to 17, and 55 percent of these were male. These statistics reflect the fact that the YMCA is currently the largest provider of school-age child care in the country, and much of this programming is provided on a fee-for-service basis. The YMCA keeps no statistics on the race or ethnicity of its members or program participants; hence, it is difficult to know how many young black males are currently reached by one or more of its many programs.

The YMCA shares many structural features with Boys and Girls Clubs, in that it offers a building-based program conducted by a combination of paid professional staff and program volunteers, utilizing large- and small-group formats supplemented by some individual counseling. Another similarity is the extent to which local affiliates enjoy a high degree of autonomy from the organization's national headquarters. Although there are some nationally developed YMCA programs, the organization's local affiliates are not required to implement them. Unlike B/GCA, which has retained its longstanding commitment to serve disadvantaged and minority youth, the YMCA in many communities has come to rely on fees for service, and has therefore marketed its programs to more affluent audiences. A round of lawsuits concerning how the YMCA reports and uses its unrelated business income, combined with external criticism and internal debates on mission, have resulted in the recent decision by the YMCA's national board to recommit itself to youth work, with some focus on services to disadvantaged populations. Plans include a return to group work and to outreach activities, with a particular focus on young adolescents age 9 to 14.

Other National Youth Organizations. As indicated in table 6.A.1, there are a number of other national youth organizations and multiservice agencies that reach large numbers of young people each year. This table presents an overview of the service demographics of 15 member agencies of the National Collaboration for Youth and of 5 other organizations (American Camping Association, ASPIRA, COSSMHO, NAACP, and the National Urban League) that were interviewed by the Carnegie Task Force on Youth Development and Community Programs. Several features of this table are relevant to the present analysis. First, some of these organizations know very little about the people currently served by their organizations. Second, only one organization (Girl Scouts of the USA) remains totally single-sex, and all of the traditionally male-serving organizations now serve some girls, young women, and in some cases adults. Last, young adolescents represent a small proportion of the service populations of some of these groups (Girl Scouts, YMCA, YWCA) and a large proportion of others.

The Child Welfare League of America serves a high proportion of minority youth (49 percent of 2 million total youth served), but the organization has no data on gender or age, making it difficult to

Table 6.A.1 CHARACTERISTICS OF YOUTH SERVED BY SELECTED NATIONAL ORGANIZATIONS

Organization	Total Youth Served	Percentage Young Adolescents[a]	Percentage Female	Percentage Minority[b]
American Camping Association	5,300,000 youth and adults	N/A	N/A	N/A
American Red Cross	1,025,756 youth	N/A	N/A	N/A
ASPIRA Association, Inc.	17,000 age 3 to 20	N/A	N/A	100 (Hispanic)
Big Brothers/Big Sisters	90,073[c]	67.2 (10 to 15 years)	49	31.3
Boy Scouts of America	4,292,992 age 6 to 20	25 (11 to 13 years)	3	18
Boys & Girls Clubs	1,700,000 age 6 to 18	44 (11 to 16 years)	30	51
COSSMHO	20,000	N/A	N/A	mostly Hispanic
Camp Fire Boys and Girls	600,000 age 5 to 18	50 (10 to 15 years)	62	26
Child Welfare League of America	2,000,000 18 and under	N/A	N/A	49
4-H Clubs	5,657,657 age 9 to 19	68 (9 to 14 years)	52	23.5
Girl Scouts of the USA	2,560,718 age 5 to 18	6 (11 to 14 years)	100	14.1
Girls Incorporated	250,000 age 6 to 18	63 (9 to 18 years)	71	51
Junior Achievement	1,300,000 age 9 to 18	68 (9 to 14 years)	45	31.5
NAACP	40,000 20 and under	N/A	N/A	primarily black
National Network of Runaway and Youth Services	404,279	38 (14 and under)	53	36
National Urban League	150,000 age 12 to 14	N/A	N/A	85 (black)
Salvation Army	349,541 age 3 to 19	N/A	N/A	N/A
WAVE, Inc.	10,068 age 14 to 21	N/A	49	N/A
YMCA of the USA	5,800,000 18 and under	26 (12 to 17 years)	46	N/A
YWCA of the USA	700,000 18 and under	26 (12 to 17 years)	74	29

Source: Information presented in this table was drawn from each group's most recent annual report as of Spring 1992 and organizational interviews conducted by the Carnegie Task Force on Youth Development and Community Programs. These figures reflect the fact that methods of counting or estimating numbers served vary from agency to agency. As indicated (N/A), many organizations do not have information in some of these categories.

a. These figures reflect the fact that methods of age grouping vary from agency to agency.

b. These figures reflect the fact that some of the studied organizations serve primarily one racial or ethnic group, others serve a more diverse population, and some do not have data available on this aspect of their service demographics.

c. Of these 90,073, 77 percent have been matched with a volunteer, while 23 percent are on a waiting list to be matched.

Table 6.A.2 FINANCIAL STATUS OF SELECTED NATIONAL YOUTH
             DEVELOPMENT ORGANIZATIONS

Organization	Annual Expenses	Surplus/ Deficit[a]	Total Assets
American Camping Association	$2,958,574	$83,398	$1,549,418
ASPIRA Association, Inc.	1,187,408	103,308	677,132
Big Brothers/Big Sisters of America	3,995,088	(205,929)	1,946,030
Boy Scouts of America	75,491,000	9,723,000	255,639,000
Boys and Girls Clubs of America	16,097,026	(532,407)	31,819,100
Camp Fire Boys and Girls	4,116,579	(298,150)	3,111,430
Child Welfare League of America	6,269,838	154,156	10,635,220
Girl Scouts of the USA	32,631,000	3,529,000	90,492,000
Girls Incorporated	3,670,248	(22,998)	5,953,420
Junior Achievement	8,440,405	805,834	10,365,625
WAVE, Inc.	5,880,455	48,873	1,623,075
National Network of Runaway and Youth Services	783,748	(1,501)	124,172

Source: Most recent annual reports available from each organization as of spring 1992.
a. Because of generally accepted principles of not-for-profit accounting, surplus and deficit figures may include both unrestricted and restricted funds as well as land, property, and equipment.

ascertain how many young black males are reached by its member agencies. The work of these agencies tends to be directed toward young people who are "in risk" (in foster care, group homes, or under court supervision), as opposed to "at risk."

Similarly, member agencies of the National Network of Runaway and Youth Services often see young people who are already experiencing serious problems, although these agencies frequently offer a wide range of services in addition to providing shelter and crisis intervention counseling.

Some young black males receive youth development services through the school-age child care programs of local YWCA and Girls Incorporated centers, and through the club programs, camps, and self-reliance courses of Camp Fire Boys and Girls.

As shown in table 6.A.2, in all of these organizations, the finances of the national offices are largely separate from the finances of their local affiliates, with a few exceptions. Local affiliates frequently pay dues or fees to the national office in exchange for a range of services, and the national operations may pass some funds to local affiliates as part of national demonstration programs. The table provides information not only on the relative size of each organization's operation but also on the aggregate level of resources that these organizations are able to generate annually on the national level.

Religious Youth Groups Sponsored by Mainline Churches

In a paper prepared for the Carnegie Task Force on Youth Development and Community Programs, the Reverend Kenda Dean (1991) provided a synthesis of the research on, and a descriptive overview of, Protestant, Catholic, and Jewish youth programs in America. Her paper is based on personal interviews with 53 national leaders in religious work, including the youth ministry heads of all major branches of Protestantism, Catholicism, and Judaism, and on printed research and program literature. The following description and analysis draws heavily on Dean's work.

Participation Data and Trends. The autonomous nature of most local congregations, even of those affiliated with national denominations, complicates the task of presenting a nationwide overview of religious youth programs. But there is substantial evidence of the sizable number of these programs and organizations, of their extensive reach, and of their current and potential influence on positive youth development. Fully one-third of the organizations listed in the *Directory of American Youth Organizations* (Erickson 1991) are religiously affiliated, and this resource does not list the many local organizations and denominational programs that are known to exist. With few exceptions, religious youth programs share an uncertainty about the numbers of youth they serve. A handful of national studies have offered estimates on the percentage of youth who participate in religious youth organizations. For example, the 1988 National Education Longitudinal Study found that 34 percent of eighth graders reported such participation, with girls participating at a higher rate than boys (U.S. Department of Education 1990). The 1980 High School and Beyond survey reported that 36.5 percent of sophomores participated in church activities, including youth groups (Boys Town Center, no date); and the Search Institute's 1990 study of more than 46,000 Midwest teenagers found that 57 percent of respondents claimed involvement in a church or synagogue, which predicts but does not imply participation in a religious youth organization (Benson 1990).

Participation trends show a mixed picture across denominations. Most of the Protestant denominations surveyed by Dean reported that participation in their youth programs had declined over the past three decades for a variety of reasons, including the diminishing amount of financial resources allocated to such work. Youth ministry enjoyed a resurgence within the Catholic Church during the 1980s, due in part to increased resources and national leadership, including the publication of national program guidelines in 1976. Conservative evangelical youth ministry reportedly experienced moderate growth during this same period, while funding for and participation in Jewish youth work remained relatively stable.

Religious youth work has traditionally placed emphasis on older adolescents, particularly high school-age students, although there has been a recent trend (beginning about a decade ago) toward greater focus on young adolescents. The work of the Search Institute in Minneapolis, the Center for Early Adolescence in Chapel Hill, North Carolina, and Group Publishing in Loveland, Colorado, has contributed greatly to the design and implementation of these recent efforts by helping program planners to understand the developmental needs of young adolescents and to build programs that are responsive to those needs. Religious youth leaders have recently reported higher involvement among 10- to 15-year-olds than among older teenagers, estimating that between 50 and 75 percent of youth involved in their denominations' youth programs were under 15. The age of 13 appears to be a critical juncture for many young adolescents in deciding whether or not to continue participation; formal programs for teenagers such as Hebrew school and confirmation classes are stressed during early adolescence. But once these rites of passage are completed, many young people find there is nothing to "graduate into" or that the new program does not meet their needs.

Youth Programs Conducted by Privately Sponsored Sports Organizations

Youth sports programs can generally be categorized according to six types: 1) agency-sponsored programs; 2) club sports; 3) recreation programs; 4) programs sponsored by national youth organizations; 5) intramural programs; and 6) interscholastic programs (Seefeldt, Ewing, and Walk 1992). Of particular relevance to the topic of this chapter are the agency- and organization-sponsored efforts and the programs run by municipal parks and recreation departments, since club sports generally operate on a for-profit and fee-for-service basis, and since intramural and interscholastic programs are sponsored by schools.

The term "agency-sponsored" is used to describe local sports programs sponsored by adult service clubs such as Lions Clubs, Kiwanis Clubs, and Police Athletic Leagues. A distinguishing feature of agency-sponsored programs is that one agency within a community often assumes responsibility for one sport, to the exclusion of all other sports. In this model, numerous sports may be sponsored and administered by various community agencies, resulting in a variety of sponsorships without a common structure or philosophy among the offerings within a given community. Local agencies often affiliate with national sports-specific organizations, thereby increasing the competitive opportunities for their participants by exposing them to district, regional, or national-level competitions. Agency-sponsored athletic programs are therefore greatly influenced by the rules of their respective national governing bodies, whose regulations are mandated in all competitions beyond the intracity level. Examples of such national programs are Little League Baseball, Pop Warner Football, U.S.A. Hockey, and the American Youth Soccer Association.

Included in the youth organization-sponsored category are the sports programs offered by such groups as Boys and Girls Clubs, Boy Scouts of America (Varsity Scouts), and the YMCA. The model followed by these groups differs from that of sporting agencies in that their programs are more likely to provide opportunities to participate in a variety of sports, in activities developed by the national organization (such as Boys and Girls Clubs' "Olympic Sports" and "Super-Fit All Stars" programs), and in competitions organized through some of these national organizations. In addition, individual local chapters of these organizations may also coordinate leagues and have some affiliation with sports-specific national governing bodies.

Of the six types of youth sports programs, agency-sponsored and recreation programs have by far the highest rates of participation. By one reliable estimate, 35 million children and adolescents (age 6 to 18) participate in youth sports programs per year and, of these, approximately 6 million are involved in school-sponsored programs (Martens 1986). Far fewer are involved in club sports programs.

While these estimates provide some insight into the scope of youth sports programs, they provide only limited information about the nature of participants' involvement. A 1989 nationwide study of the participation and attrition patterns of young people age 10 to 18 provides insight into the reasons why youth join, stay in, and drop out of agency-sponsored and school-based sports programs (Ewing and Seefeldt 1989). Of the approximately 8,000 youth surveyed in the study, 55 percent reported having participated in agency-sponsored sports. The vast majority of these youth report participating on a sports team and, in fact, most youth reported involvement on more than one team. Participation rates by race varied widely: white, black, and Hispanic youth participated similarly in baseball and basketball, but blacks and Hispanics were under-represented in soccer, volleyball, and individual sports such as tennis and swimming.

This study further reveals that the highest rates of participation occur at age 10, then steadily decline from age 10 to 18. The study's authors offer three reasons for this decline: it may reflect a lack of emphasis in these programs on components that meet the needs of adolescents; it may be a result of the increased popularity of scholastic sports programs, which frequently offer greater opportunities for advanced competition; and it may be tied to inadequate coaching.

Youth Programs Conducted by Municipal Parks and Recreation Departments

Community recreation is most frequently a service of local municipal governments. However, services may also be delivered by a county agency, an unincorporated community, a special taxing district, or another geographic area with a definable population. Recreation services are generally offered by a combined recreation and parks department, with the functions of both services merged into a single unit of the local government.

While community recreation services are provided in nearly every American community, national statistics on the number of individuals (youth or adults) participating in these services or on the total dollars allocated to them are not available. Children and youth are known to be major users of these services, although recreation departments report that youth participation tends to drop off at about age 13.

Recreation agencies operate a variety of facilities including community centers, parks, pools and other aquatic facilities, athletic fields, golf courses, playgrounds, play fields, winter sports facilities, outdoor nature centers, stadiums, camps, beaches, and zoos. Agencies also provide leadership for a diverse program of sports and games, arts and crafts, dance, drama, music, social recreation, outdoor recreation, special events, and other activities.

Community recreation agencies are managed by professional staff, with the assistance of a large number of volunteers, and normally operate under the direction of a citizen board or commission. The board or commission may be elected or appointed, and may have policy-setting or advisory functions. The local network of services is supported by several national professional associations, and by federal and state government agencies. The two major professional associations are the American Association for Leisure and Recreation, and the National Recreation and Parks Association. In addition, an organization called Roundtable Associates increases attention to the needs of disadvantaged minorities within municipal parks and recreation systems.

Organized recreation programs were developed to provide children and youth with safe places to play and as an alternative to involvement in delinquent behaviors. As these services evolved, many recreation departments greatly expanded their purview, seeking to provide a full range of athletic and social opportunities for all citizens— young and old, wealthy and lower income. This level of service was sustained during certain periods—after World War I, in the 1930s, and again from the mid-1960s through the mid-1970s. However, the past 15 years have brought a steady decline in the availability of funding for municipal recreation services. This decline appears to be continuing as local governments face significant budget shortfalls. The current fiscal crisis has resulted in reduced staffing, decreased hours of facility operation, and the elimination of some programs that are not self-supporting or funded by outside sources. All current projections indicate that these funding cuts will be a long-term phenomenon.

Community leaders at all levels seem to agree on the value of participation in recreation programs, particularly for youth. The Office of Technology Assessment's (1991, p. I-81) report on adolescent health, for example, called for the expansion of community recreation services, noting that youth participation in organized recreation programs can result in appropriate use of discretionary time; potential for adult guidance; possible reduction of anxious or depressed feelings; opportunities for learning life skills and social competence; opportunities for work; and possible reduction in substance abuse, especially among disadvantaged youth.

Although there is much agreement in the professional literature on the need to expand organized recreation opportunities for young people, especially those living in low-income neighborhoods, nowhere is there a suggestion that the problem rests on a lack of good program models. Several recreation departments have experimented successfully with innovative after-school care programs, midnight basketball leagues, summertime urban camping initiatives (some in public housing projects), and a variety of outreach efforts that include the use of mobile vans and collaborations with school systems (Smith 1991, p. i).

Current challenges facing municipal parks and recreation departments include how to: become more responsive to the needs of young adolescents and young people living in high-risk neighborhoods; cope with budget cutbacks; secure alternative funding sources; lobby for increased resources and greater equity of service; recruit, train, and retain qualified staff, particularly staff who are skilled in working with youth; increase cooperation and collaboration with other community agencies; and improve documentation and evaluation of services.

Part Three

POLICY CONTEXT:
BARRIERS AND OPPORTUNITIES

Chapter Seven

TOWARD A NATIONAL YOUTH DEVELOPMENT POLICY FOR YOUNG AFRICAN-AMERICAN MALES: THE CHOICES POLICYMAKERS FACE

Andrew B. Hahn

INTRODUCTION

The United States has no national youth policy per se. We certainly do not have a national policy for early adolescents in the age range of 10 to 15 years old. And we do not have a special national policy earmarked for African-American youth.[1] What we typically have are "self-sufficiency" policies at the national level for older teens (age 15 to 21) that trickle down to local vendors who may or may not represent particular demographic groups in the community. For youth in the younger group, age 10 to 15 years old, appropriate programming mostly means involvement in school-based extracurricular activities and involvement in voluntary associations such as the Boys' Club, scouting, or sports teams (see chapter 6 of this volume). Most young people are enrolled in public schools, but the federal role in public education is modest and federal funds earmarked for early adolescents are even more so. Youth involvement in voluntary organizations is largely separate from national policy except for the general way that government treats nonprofits through tax exemptions, rules on charitable giving, and the occasional demonstration project. Initiatives for early adolescents are preparatory and preventive, that is, they serve as feeders into subsequent public-funded training and education services.

This chapter provides information about the national policy system that gives support to the programs for older teens. By understanding the public policy context for programs for 15- to 21-year-olds, the author hopes to contribute to a better understanding of the environment our younger teens will enter.

Although this chapter does not deal directly or exclusively with young black males, my approach is relevant to program issues affecting African-American youths. Are young black males a challenge to programs and policymakers, as documented by the dire statistics reviewed in this volume? In this chapter I turn this question around by documenting how the nation's policies and programs, particularly employment and training policies for the poor, are frequently a challenge for young people, by making participation and success difficult for program participants.

I start by examining youth policy in this country, including what is meant by "policy" and the choices government makes about its policies. I look at current private job training and the public Jobs Training Partnership Act, and the extent to which they reach the young black men who need these services. I show how government policy tends to favor programs for older rather than younger teens, who stand to benefit most from early attention, and I ask whether a public policy emphasis on age rather than race would be a useful way to gain support for addressing the needs of young black men. I define several problems in current policy thinking regarding programs for young adolescents (age 10 to 15). Finally, I argue for the kind of policies that I believe would help the nation respond more affirmatively to young people's needs, especially the needs of young minority males.

Both advocates and researchers agree that policies must support age-appropriate, developmentally sound, comprehensive, long-term, effective programs. There is considerable agreement on these principles and, in fact, these elements constitute a sort of mantra in the "youth-at-risk" field.[2]

How close are we as a nation to developing and implementing public policies that support these principles? To answer this question I use as a case study "second chance" youth employment and training programs, that is, those funded outside the mainstream of public education. These are the primary mechanism by which the national government shows its concern for promoting the self-sufficiency of minority youth. Job training policy in the "second chance" system invites questions about education policy in the "first chance" system, as well as the many challenges of social service delivery and related assistance. These other issues will be brought into the discussion but only as they relate to employment and training.

DEFINING AND EXAMINING AMERICAN YOUTH POLICY

I begin by defining the term "policy" and tracing what is known about the Jobs Training Partnership Act (JTPA) as a policy system.

Some readers may wonder why I devote so much attention to this particular public policy approach. There are two reasons. First, JTPA is the only federally funded game in town. At the national level, outside of public education (including vocational education), there is no other official policy system that defines itself as being in the business of promoting the self-sufficiency of economically disadvantaged and minority youth. Second, JTPA is a fascinating case study that offers lessons relevant to a variety of social policy fields affecting young people.

"Policy" is a rather elastic term that means something different to policymakers than to the public. For the public, thinking about job training policies for young black males most likely means thinking about targeting, that is, who gets what services and under what eligibility criteria and justification. But to the policymaker, "policy" is broader than decisions about targeting and services. It may be useful to consider the broader definition of the term "policy" from the policymaker's perspective.

A Framework for Understanding "Policy"

Political scientists have devised frameworks for defining and studying policy. One particular framework (Heidenheimer 1983) involves four factors, each reflecting the choices governments make with respect to: 1) the *scope* of particular policies; 2) the *distribution* of services; 3) the *policy instruments* used by government; and 4) the degree to which the government *balances restraint with a willingness to innovate.*

SCOPE AND DISTRIBUTION

We can illustrate the issue of policy scope by asking how governments define public and private responsibilities. In the field of programs that help prepare young people for the labor market, I have argued that the nation has chosen happily, as a public responsibility, the provision of a broad range of services to assist largely low-income youth get ready for the workplace, with an important caveat: public involvement is limited to ways that minimize interference with labor markets (Hahn, Ganzglass, and Nagel 1992). The American approach to youth job training is interventionist on the side of upgrading and changing people but timid when it comes to changing institutions and markets. Thus it is likely that, in regard to urban minorities, policy in support of human capital upgrading will continue to dominate the field, while anti-discrimination measures, affirmative action, mandated on-the-job training, wage subsidies, and payroll taxes for training are likely to meet with more resistance in policy circles. This is an illustration of the policy choice the nation has made about scope of effort in the job training field.

DISTRIBUTION

Choices of distribution concern eligibility and targeting. Forty percent of all federal spending for JTPA must be spent on youth,[3] referring to services for economically disadvantaged youth between 15 and 21. Younger teens, as noted previously, are not covered in this legislation. What about race and ethnicity? Close to 50 percent of youth training opportunities for older teens are filled by racial/ethnic minorities. But choices concerning targeting actually begin at an earlier stage.

JTPA starts with a targeting requirement that it must serve 90 percent of people who meet government definitions of economic hardship. Eligibility is determined when program staff consult local tables of family income that are supplied by the Bureau of Labor Statistics; the enrollment decision is based on income rather than race. The amount of funds available to a local community is determined by the JTPA funding formula, which is based mostly on local unemployment levels. These targeting provisions shape who is served in local programs. Other criteria then kick in, such as requirements to serve dropouts or other disadvantaged groups. Finally, local funding agencies such as private industry councils select vendors who can meet the above criteria. Most vendors specialize in a particular kind of training (e.g., GED services, clerical trades training, English as a second language) or in serving a particular kind of group. Community-based organizations may specialize in serving males or African-American youth or Mexican Americans. The choice of vendors is the most significant decision a community can make in terms of targeting by race or ethnicity. The legislative provisions of the JTPA are silent in this respect.

Many questions have been raised about these official distribution criteria. When young blacks are crowded in neighborhoods of persistent poverty, is it sensible or efficient to target job training opportunities in such complex and round-about ways? Some have argued that this is the price minorities must pay for a program that is truly national in scope, with objective criteria that provide an equal chance for service to whites, Hispanics, and blacks. Others have asked how income testing works in school settings—the single largest provider of youth services under JTPA—where there is reluctance among many educators to determine income eligibility among students. There are further questions about distribution. For example, what happens when many youth come from families just over the "notch" of eligibility? And how tolerant should federal and state officials be when a young male with close ties to his natural family claims that he is a "family of one" to qualify for federal job training? Other people have raised questions about whether there are enough vendors representing the interests of "at-risk" youth such as urban minority men.

POLICY INSTRUMENTS

Governments choose from a variety of instruments and tools for their policy interventions. In the United States, we rely on a complex set of relationships among federal authorities, governors, state job training coordinating councils, local private industry councils, service delivery areas, and vendors such as schools, community-based organizations, and private firms that actually deliver services. We use financial set-asides, mandates, performance standards, and other policy instruments to make the partnerships work.

McDonnell and Elmore (1987) describe four general categories of policy instruments. Mandates are "rules governing the action of individuals and agencies, intended to produce compliance." Inducements are the "transfer of money to individuals or agencies in return for certain actions." All layers of government have discretionary and demonstration funds available to them to induce certain behaviors, promote certain approaches, and build knowledge. The third element in the McDonnell–Elmore scheme is capacity-building instruments or the transfer of funds for the purpose of upgrading intellectual capital, human resources, and materials. National, state, and local investment in technical assistance and practitioner-oriented dissemination of research are elements of the "capacity building" agenda.

The last category of policy instruments is system-changing activities, or the "transfer of authority among individuals and agencies to alter the system by which public goods and services are delivered." This factor lies at the heart of what policymakers and private philanthropy try to do by supporting comprehensive youth initiatives at the local level, or when they promote coordination among the various strands of the employment/training system.

RESTRAINT VERSUS INNOVATION

The fourth factor in Heidenheimer's framework concerns choices of restraint and innovation. What is the balance between enforcing

compliance of rules/regulations (restraint) and loosening requirements for the sake of innovation and experimentation? What is the
government's balance between cheerleader and tough cop? In the
decentralized JTPA system, for example, federal–state relationships
are often touchy issues. The balance between innovation and restraint
often turns on issues of authority and interpretation of the federal–state role. These interpretations shift with different administra-
tions and appointments. One administration will be proactive, while
another will be reactive to states and local communities.

   The four-element policy framework illustrates that policy is a complicated matter. It is not simply a question of having a vision of a
"good" policy, choosing a target group, and funding the initiative.
Policymakers have many tools, perhaps too many, in their arsenal.
Tools associated with the same policy often push and pull programs
in conflicting directions. One task of the policymaker is to try to
assure consistency of outcomes stemming from the use of different
policy tools. This isn't always easy, as shown below.

ARE PRIVATE JOB TRAINING AND GOVERNMENT
PROGRAMS REACHING THE YOUNG BLACK MEN WHO
NEED THEM?

Young minority males in the early teen years will not "age" into a
policy system with nearly enough opportunities. Both the public
and private sides of the youth self-sufficiency enterprise are small.
Moreover, most older youth training in the United States is not government-supported and therefore is not subject to explicit policy
control. Since private training is tied to the employment sector, many
minority youth currently do not benefit much from it. As for the
public side, in absolute terms, opportunities are few and far between
for urban minority youth.

The Private Side

Unsubsidized, private employer-based training activities account for
the bulk of the training of the existing workforce in this country,
with estimates as high as $210 billion devoted to private training,
$25 billion of which is spent on young workers. Despite these broad
estimates, not much is known about the actual scale of youth training

in the regular economy or the motivations of firms providing the training.

Lynch (1989) tried to come up with some figures on the numbers of young people who receive private training of one sort or another in the United States. Distinguishing between private and public training is itself difficult, since many proprietary schools enjoy public subsidies primarily through federal financial support. She found that between 1978 and 1983 only one in four young Americans had been involved in some sort of private sector training. Race and sex influenced the probability of receiving different types of training. Women and nonwhites were "much less likely to receive training within a firm, either through an apprenticeship or other forms of on-the-job training" (Lynch 1989, p. 22). Only 2 percent of all nonwhite older youth studied were in on-site private sector training compared to 4 percent of white youth.

The Public Side

Though the scope of private training is small, the extent of government-supported training is tiny. The public side of the American youth training system is marginal in terms of the amount of federal funding and the ability of the system to reach a healthy share of the "universe of need." In fiscal year 1989, the Department of Labor operated nine programs, most of them under JTPA, with total funding of $3.8 billion (U.S. General Accounting Office 1989). This represents not even one-quarter of one percent of the federal budget. It is altogether insignificant in terms of GNP. The under-investment results in a very significant unmet need in the populations designated as eligible for service.

How many older teens are actually served by the JTPA "second chance" system? The total estimated number of youth of all characteristics in JTPA is approximately 1,117,300. Most (54 percent) are enrolled in short summer job training programs (Hahn, Ganzglass, and Nagel 1992). These figures reveal that JTPA is a very small youth system. In fact, the program is a good example of social policy trying to wring the most performance out of an extremely small enterprise.

Consider the figures for young black males who terminated the year-round (non-summer and non-residential) portion of JTPA in program year 1989. The number of young black men age 21 and under was 43,619. The residential Job Corps program (another part of JTPA) serves about 25,000 additional black males (Hahn, Ganzglass, and Nagel 1992).

How do these enrollments match the universe of need? Dryfoos (1990) provides evidence suggesting that nationwide about 15 percent of 15- to 21-year-olds are at very high risk, 62 percent are at moderate risk, and only 25 percent are not at risk. Since the population in this age range numbers approximately 20 million people, the JTPA program is serving only 5 percent of the total. This is far short of the 15 percent Dryfoos estimates to be very high risk, that is, youth in need of JTPA programs.

It is useful to consider the population of African Americans in the age range generally covered by self-sufficiency programs—14 to 21 years old. In 1990 there were roughly 1.6 million blacks between 15 and 17 years old, and 1.6 million between 18 and 20 years old. Assuming that two-thirds were in need of services, the universe of need was roughly 2.1 million young African Americans, or 1 million young black males. This figure can be compared to the 68,000 young black males enrolled in non-summer JTPA components (including Job Corps). The proportion served is less than 7 percent of the total group needing services. Other studies have looked at the national share of income-eligible individuals that JTPA serves and have concluded that it reaches only 5 percent of all such persons (U.S. Department of Labor 1989).

By any of these standards, the JTPA program is small for all youth and also for young black males. Such a small program, even if 100 percent effective, cannot be expected to have an impact on aggregate social and economic indicators such as illiteracy, school completion rates, or the national jobless rate among black teens.

As noted earlier, there are explicit income guidelines governing participation in JTPA. Although JTPA programs have official income guidelines that set conditions for program eligibility, informal targeting goes on as well. For example, JTPA often makes use of discretionary funds at the federal, state, and local levels to target services to African-American teens and others who fare poorly in the labor market or are thought to be "at risk." This kind of informal targeting in American youth programs is a distinctive feature that stands in contrast to many European and Asian countries (Skocpol 1989; Osterman 1988).

In America, older youth policy has developed as a subset of American labor market/manpower policy rather than as a component of education policy. American youth programs were placed under the jurisdiction of the Department of Labor to serve as second chance programs outside the education system. Grubb (1989, p. 70) points out that the "existence of parallel systems for job-related training extends back at least to the 1930s. The Roosevelt administration, believing that public schools were unsympathetic to the poorest children, established job training programs outside the educational system, both to reach the poorest individuals who might not accept school-based training and to establish a more flexible and shorter-term job training program than were conventional within high schools . . ."

One might think that a policy of targeted services would avoid the inefficiencies usually associated with universalistic approaches. However, the American strategy has come under attack by critics who have raised the specter of "creaming" or the phenomenon of programs choosing to serve the most able of the group of eligible economically disadvantaged (Grinker Associates, Inc. 1986; Walker, Feldstein, and Solow 1985).

Advocates for expanded services for young black males often argue that even if race-based targeting proves too contentious for American policymakers, why not accomplish the same goal by funneling resources to communities where the most urban black males live? This certainly makes sense but does not conform to current JTPA funding formulas.

The Labor Department allocates two-thirds of state and local JTPA funds based on the distribution of unemployment. The rest is disseminated according to the distribution of low-income populations. Concentrations of low-income people count a lot in the formula, although they are not always a prerequisite for program assistance. Areas with high unemployment (e.g., some suburbs) may receive a disproportionate share of funds even if their share of the low-income population is low. These formulas also mean that central cities or particular neighborhoods with high concentrations of minority populations often do not get the share of funding needed to meet the needs of their citizens.

THE ROLE THAT AGE PLAYS IN PUBLIC POLICY FOR TEENS

Below I review what is known and unknown about the age factor in self-sufficiency policies for early adolescents. Much less is understood about public policies for early adolescents (age 10 to 15) than about those for older youth (age 16 to 24).

The role of age is often overlooked in the debates over targeting children and youth services. Scales (1991) writes that an "ever-sharpening appreciation must be cultivated of the special issues present for different age groups of children and youth." This sharpening is underway. But it has occurred largely in a general context rather than through a hard-nosed comparative analysis of the virtues and limitations of directing national resources to particular age segments, such as early adolescents versus older teens.

Since the 1970s much has been written about early adolescents as a distinct and identifiable group. Philanthropic programs have sprung up (e.g., Lilly, Edna McConnell Clark, Carnegie, and others), think tanks have been established (e.g., the Center for Early Adolescence), and national commissions have been organized around the theme of early adolescents (Carnegie Council on Adolescent Development 1989). Much of this important work can be viewed as consciousness raising, fact finding, and context setting. Through these activities, the case has been effectively made that early adolescents are different than older adolescents, that middle schools need to be improved, and that after-school enrichments are needed in every community. What has not occurred, however, is a systematic review of the appropriateness, feasibility, and viability of targeting—by age—a variety of policy-supported programs and incentive structures that promote the ability of young people to achieve and to aspire. The stage has been set, but policymaking for this group continues to be largely ad hoc and incoherent. This challenge is as important and complex as thinking about the significance of race in youth policies.

Many of the authors in the present book are representative of the positive movement among advocates for better and more services for early adolescents. The emerging literature from this field reveals that a mismatch often exists between the program offerings of young teen projects (and even middle schools) and the intellectual and emotional needs of students. When it comes to helping young adolescents with their futures, we have found that many school-based and community programs are indeed unable to offer the high content, high support, and high expectations that society and the labor force will require (Hahn and Kingsley 1991.) This is a general problem made worse for young black males by curricula and programming approaches that are insensitive to the group membership and gender realities described by other writers in this volume.

Building on the emerging consensus that young adolescents, age 10 to 15, comprise a distinct and identifiable group by virtue of developmental maturation, many advocates would like to see new national and local policies in support of this group. But there is little serious work that discusses the benefits and costs of targeting employment and training services to this or other age groups. In the tangible world of policy choices, current enthusiasm for "early adolescents" is based more on folk wisdom than solid research.[4]

For example, advocates invoke customized programming for young adolescents as a self-evident good. Yet neither the inherent efficacy of such an approach nor the tradeoffs involved have been subjected to sustained investigation. Service gaps for young adolescents are obvious (JTPA being a prime case in point; it begins at age 15). Yet few age-oriented surveys have been undertaken of the existing policy terrain. Because the policy research community has not adequately mapped out the contours of this environment, debate about its characteristics (i.e., the degree to which the specific needs of young adolescents are being addressed in national public policies) relies more on anecdote than evidence. It remains unclear what a more sensitive policy for young adolescents would look like in practice, and how policymakers could be persuaded to focus in on this demographic niche.

Why, without a firm knowledge base, do I suspect that age targeting should be examined in greater detail? First, by the time youth reach secondary school age, the period in which most employment/training services begin, many youth are already in serious difficulty. Here the analogy is to the early childhood movement and Head Start. Reformers have initiated policies in the preschool period to avoid costly remedial strategies in the early grades of public education. The same argument could be made about the importance of intervening early in the late elementary school and middle school years. Second, by the secondary school years, the difficulties teens face often interfere with their ability to benefit from the programs offered to them. Programs at an earlier age may produce more success. Third, there is growing evidence that many of the services we used to think were only appropriate for older youth are in fact more appropriate for younger youth. A good example is higher education awareness programs. Most of these programs now begin when youths are juniors in high school. Yet sixth graders need to understand the benefits and requirements associated with post-secondary education so they can make informed course selections starting in junior high school.

Evidence that we need to intervene earlier is seen in some sample statistics assembled for this book by the author from a large national survey of American school children. Special unpublished tabulations on urban, low-income (under $15,000 family income) African-American male public school eighth graders in the 1988 National Education Longitudinal Study (NELS), conducted by the U.S. Department of

Education, reveal some startling facts about the well-being of one of
the poorest segments of youth in America:

☐ Nearly one-third have been held back a grade by eighth grade, a
reliable precursor of future dropout behavior;
☐ Eleven percent report that their fathers are dead and only 19 percent report living in a household in which a father is present;
☐ Forty-four percent of the group have no specific place to study
and do homework; 16 percent report that their parents or guardians
rarely or never check on their homework;
☐ Nearly half have not talked to a counselor about planning their
high school program or about jobs or careers after high school;
☐ Twenty-two percent report that their parents have received a warning about school attendance problems and 53 percent indicate that
their parents have received a warning about their poor grades;
☐ Sixty percent have been sent to "the office" at least once for misbe-
having and half indicated that their parents received warnings about
their behavior.

The author also looked at these youngsters' involvement in non-
school activities, the kind of experience that can contribute to their
development and that is the subject of this book. The NELS data
show that about half of these poor African-American young males
are not involved in *any* out-of-school activities. By eighth grade these
youth are unattached and disconnected. These are national data from
one of the largest American surveys ever undertaken of young teens.
The numbers speak to a group of young black teens who, by age 14
to 15, face serious challenges. Yet, we have reported that much of
our national youth policy begins when youth are older. We have also
argued that we know too little about how our other national policies
affect younger teens, if at all.

I end this discussion of age targeting in youth policy by raising a
question related to public policy targeted at young black men. In
response to public antipathy for race- and class-based social welfare
programs, scholar Theda Skocpol (1989) suggests that, whenever
possible, policymakers try to embed targeted services within a rubric
of universal services. She argues that this might help secure popular
support for programs and remove the stigma often associated with
participation in racially segregated services.

In regards to young black men, we might ask whether a public
policy emphasis on age rather than race would be an appropriate
way to gain support for attention to this group's program needs.

Shifting the policy focus in this volume from "young black males" to "young" might help build public support and provide a way to "target within universalism," as suggested by Skocpol.[5] Ultimately, this is a question of political strategy but given the tiny scope of the present array of policies, it is an approach, in this author's opinion, worth pursuing.

PROBLEMS IN CURRENT POLICY THINKING

Government policymakers could improve the number and quality of programs for young adolescents, including young black men, by reevaluating how government pays for program services, how it invests (or does not invest) in training youth development professionals, how it tends to consumer needs, and how many resources it devotes to demonstration projects for youth age 10 to 14.

Paying For Services

The U.S. government approach to financing job training for youth affects the kinds of services delivered at the grassroots level. Consider again the case of JTPA in which contractors are paid only if they achieve certain performance goals such as placing a target share of trainees in jobs, arranging alternative education, or helping youth achieve approved competencies believed by community leaders to be useful for entering the labor market.

In contrast, most public programs are funded on the basis of inputs. Public education is a good example. Once education funds are collected on the basis of local property tax assessments, they are distributed by a formula that builds on average daily attendance, an example of inputs. At the federal level, elementary and secondary education is earmarked to meet certain broad purposes established by Congress. These funds are also distributed on the basis of inputs such as the number of needy students in eligible school districts.

The results-oriented performance standards have been seen in many quarters as a positive social policy development, worthy of replication. Thus, when the Perkins Vocational Education Act (1990) and the Family Support Act of 1988 were considered by Congress, policymakers adapted some of JTPA's performance standards approach. This outcome-driven approach is likely to influence future public policymaking and will probably be debated in the context of new youth development policies.

But an equally strong chorus of critics has emerged to challenge the performance-based system of payments used in national youth policy. These critics argue that JTPA youth programs are too short in length (often 24 weeks) because the programs are rewarded for rapidly placing young people in meaningless jobs. From a practitioner's perspective, achieving volume in enrollments pays more than providing quality, long-term services for very "at-risk" youth.

The evaluation literature is clear: program payment methods have profound impacts on the nature and quality of services provided. Yet in the case of new youth development programs for early adolescents described throughout this book, policymakers will find it very difficult to identify appropriate measures of outcomes. What kind of outcome measures should we devise for programs for African-American 11-year-olds who are learning about their heritage or about public safety or about the value of community service? The goals of youth development—basic safety, self-esteem, ethnic/racial pride, and so on are difficult to measure and even harder to tie to to payment/ reimbursement structures. The present generation of "deficit"-driven programs (aimed at reducing school leaving, drug use, and teenage pregnancy) yield more suitable goals for outcome-driven performance measures than tomorrow's youth development programs. For these reasons, if youth policies were to evolve toward an "asset-based" model (aimed at healthy youth development), I would favor cost reimbursement techniques or variations of other input arrangements. These alternatives are, of course, not without their own problems including poor cost controls, over-spending, and an emphasis on inputs with uncertain knowledge of outcomes. But *the key point is that linking program payments to outcomes in comprehensive "soft" programs for young teens is likely to distort what these programs really do. This may be especially the case with the grassroots programs described throughout this volume.*

Investing in Youth Development Workers

One central element in the implementation of youth programs is the staffing function. It is a truism in the field that effective staff development leads to better program performance. Yet public policy tends to de-emphasize this fact, as evidenced by various technical requirements. For example, JTPA rules restrict the percentage of a youth program's budget that can be used for administration. By setting this figure low, policymakers are trying to make sure that their funds support services rather than agency overhead. But without staff training, young people cannot be well served.

Although staffing is the kind of variable given lip service in the youth program literature, human resource upgrading or training for staff rarely appears high on anyone's list of policy innovations. Attention in policy reform circles continues to be riveted on program design issues, largely ignoring the people who make the designs work or fail. Meanwhile, the challenges practitioners face are growing, not only in terms of the multiple problems that at-risk youth bring to programs, but also in terms of staff's need to adapt to the funding environment, meet rules and regulations, cope with deteriorating physical infrastructures, and so on.

Since 1977, Brandeis University's Center for Human Resources has conducted surveys of hundreds of youth program staff. Workers now report more problems and more stress related to their inability to find workable solutions to these challenges than ever before. Good staff is also getting harder to find and retain. This may be especially true for those who are interested in and committed to working with young minority males in distressed neighborhoods.

None of this is surprising in light of the lack of professional standards for most frontline jobs in youth agencies. Except for a generic college degree (often waived), staff are typically not required to have significant professional counseling or teaching experience with at-risk youth prior to being hired. Many program staff, in fact, are former clients of the same programs. This is not necessarily a bad thing; youth programs, like other neighborhood initiatives, have provided an important route out of poverty for staff as well as clients. The problem is that the field has never engaged in a serious discussion of what the prerequisite qualifications of youth workers should be. To what extent, for example, should "community" qualifications (same background, ethnicity, neighborhood as clients) serve as a substitute for formal, credentialed backgrounds? How often are these in conflict, where, why, and when? What qualifications, in fact, do youth workers need?

Contrast the attention given to human resource issues in the youth development field to how these issues are treated in the private sector. Tens of thousands of private managers participate in executive seminars, graduate training programs, and other upgrading forums and benefit from numerous journals, books, and tapes. Consider, for example, Burger King. This corporation, one of the largest employers of disadvantaged youth, requires prospective franchise managers to attend an 80-hour program before they are even offered a franchise. Owners are then required to attend a 10-day intensive course on the technical aspects of the business. In addition, training, technical assistance, and strong quality control are regularly provided by Burger King. According to a New Jersey franchise owner, employee retention is a major problem. "These are the [teenagers'] first jobs and you have to really relate to them . . . I recently took a course on counseling teenagers so I could do this better" (cited in DeLone 1990, p. 21). This Burger King manager might have had more training in counseling youth than the average not-for-profit youth development worker.

Levin and Sanger (1991) suggest that it is managers at the program level who generally come up with innovative strategies:

> Innovation rarely springs from analysis of all the options, although that is the approach of the policy analysis whose thinking dominates so many of our schools of government and public administration . . . To the contrary, we found that management matters most. Innovative success most often results from a sequence of steps that Robert D. Behn of Duke University has described as "Ready, Fire, Aim." First, what appears to be a good idea is implemented. Then it is evaluated by observation in the field. Then, corrected and refined. This is the messy and imperfect process, repeated over and over, that produces effective management and successful program development . . .
>
> . . . innovation is not the sole domain of charismatic leaders. The message is that the skills and approaches necessary to launch innovative initiatives can be taught and learned. Some innovators may be born that way, but others can be trained . . .

The youth development field is very small. The share of resources in this tiny system devoted to upgrading staff is even more limited. Professional development strategies are not high on the national policy agenda. Yet we believe that, given the other limitations of public policy described in this chapter, investing in youth development workers may be the single most effective strategy for national policymakers.

Tuning in to Consumers' Needs

Public policies regarding issues such as consumer protection, drug and health care, children's television, and car safety have been reshaped and reformulated to meet the consumer revolution, yet a consumer perspective has not yet reached the youth development field.

Elsman (1989) attacks youth policy planners for virtually ignoring a consumer/customer approach. He argues that:

> At its simplest, marketing is concerned with only a single question, "What does this person want and what is he or she willing to do in exchange for it?" Only the "customer," not the "seller," can answer this question. Consciously or not, the customer will base the answer on two considerations:
>
> (1) Price: The time, trouble and expense of acquiring a product or service; and
> (2) Value: The customer's perception of whether it is worth the price...

Elsman calls these concepts commonplace in the private sector but foreign as "Sanskrit" in the social services arena. He describes how youth programs concentrate on the "needs" of clients rather than on their "desires" when designing programs. He suggests that program managers spend more time doing market research by talking with potential customers to discover what they want and what they are willing to do to get it.

Based on interviews with young black males, Elsman suggests some customer-centered steps to help reach young people. These include:

☐ Sequencing services so clients get what they want when they want it. Educational services, for example, are a hard sell for newly enrolled older youth, so Elsman calls for work experience and income-generating activities in the early stages of program participation.

☐ Focusing not so much on jobs or income but on what these assets can buy such as an apartment or the ability to "get Mom out of the projects." Some programs have responded to this challenge by offering a variety of financial incentives and social supports for participants.

A good example of how programs for youth might better be tailored to consumer desires stems from a study of urban black youth commissioned by the Robert Wood Johnson Foundation to help prepare for an educational campaign. According to a *St. Louis Dispatch* (May 29, 1992) article about the study, these youth would rather risk death than be blackballed by peers for raising issues of safe sex, drug use, or similar ems. The study's authors report that messages must be crafted in ways that address the concerns of peer groups and each young person's fear of being left out of the group. According to one of the authors, "if you come up with arguments kids can use within the peer setting without losing face, then, bang, you've got a winner." This is a successful approach because it gives kids what they want, as any consumer service would. In the policy community, however, a "consumer" perspective is seen as a local choice by service providers, largely outside the realm of public policy. Clearly, this is an area where policymakers could experiment with innovative approaches.

Learning About Program Effectiveness from Demonstration Projects

Program activity and evaluation since 1983 has been initiated mostly by private foundations through a number of highly visible national demonstration projects. These projects have resulted in carefully crafted evaluations that help to inform both policies and programs. Most demonstration projects over the last decade have begun with youths 14 years old or older. I do not know of a single large scale, rigorously evaluated, multisite demonstration project whose aim was the promotion of self-sufficiency among minority adolescents age 10 to 14 years old. This is not to suggest that the country does not have many interesting programs that are helping youth age 10 to 15 to become aware of their career and post-secondary school options. Some of these programs are described in this book. However, such programs have not been part of structured demonstration projects with careful evaluation components. One obvious implication for national policymakers and philanthropists is to devote more resources to demonstration projects for youth in the 10- to 14-year-old range.

What can be done at the policy level to help the community programs described in this book that work with and nurture young minority males? What can be done to make the role of "age" a more explicit part of federal policymaking?

TOWARD A NATIONAL YOUTH DEVELOPMENT BLOCK GRANT ACT

A new Consolidated National Youth Development Block Grant Act starting with early adolescents, age 10 to 15, and going up through age 19, would build on the recommendations presented in this chapter.[6] The Consolidated National Youth Development Block Grant Act would serve a broad base of youth, but the technical targeting procedures would earmark funds to young African-American youth, and others residing in cities with the highest concentrations of persistent poverty. In this way, Skocpol's (1989) admonition to "target within universalism" could be met. The Act would consolidate several youth-related public policies, bringing them into the fold at the time of their re-authorization.

The aim of the Act would be to promote healthy development among a broad base of youth (not necessarily and literally "universal," but coverage would appear so in the authorizing language of the Act). The Act would give primacy to problem prevention through the development of healthy young people (see chapter 3 of this volume for Pittman's definition of healthy development).

The Act would have four titles. Unlike traditional "deficit-driven" legislation in which policymakers have established particular outcomes as their measure of performance (and only pay if those outcomes are reached), the youth development strategy would represent a return to the social programs of the past. Funders would pay programs for "reasonable" and allowable costs associated with programming, yet within ceilings established for this purpose.

Title 1, the early adolescent "prevention" component, would be placed under the direction of large community and voluntary institutions such as Boys'/Girls' Clubs, Scouts, and the YMCA/YWCAs, as well as the many small grassroots organizations that have pioneered special curricula or neighborhood-based initiatives. Title 1 would focus exclusively on young teens in the 10- to 14-year-old range. With special financial aid, community groups of all sizes would have the potential of reaching many more poor youth in after-school and weekend programs than current practices allow. The service providers would have to demonstrate the capacity for serving young teens and the ability to reach youth generally regarded as "hard to serve." The self-sufficiency goals of the programs would be promoted through expanded higher education awareness initiatives, community service, entrepreneurship, mentoring, teenage suicide prevention, and anti-violence initiatives. Additional services would encourage recreation, participation in arts and culture, training in basic health and safety, interpersonal skill and leadership development, preparation for further education and training, and participation in a host of group identity and racial/ethnic education initiatives. The legislation would not prohibit or promote any specific curricula, as long as the youth development goals of the programs were consistent with the authorizing legislation and the programs promoted self-sufficiency for young teens and their families.

Title 2, the school-to-school and school-to-work components for older teens (age 15 to 21), would be integrated with the emerging apprenticeship legislation from the Clinton administration along with the other federal "trio" programs such as Upward Bound. It would connect to much of what is presently done in the Jobs Training Partnership Act, but with new resources for dropouts and others with potential labor market barriers. *Title 2* would preserve a strong role for local private industry councils. Its services would include job search assistance, counseling, vocational exploration, try-out employment, work experience, public works, and work crew activities tied to the community service movement.

This new block grant approach would emphasize professional development of program personnel (*Title 3*) through expanded spending on technical assistance, certification requirements, credentialing, and management training.

Title 4 would call for a continuation and expansion of community-based initiatives begun by private foundations shown to have particularly positive benefits for young teens. These initiatives include creation of community-wide youth-serving systems involving urban collaborative board structures, community planning/research activities, community mobilization with youth empowerment, integrated case management systems and referral networks, and peer program-to-program technical assistance.

How would these block grants tie into existing or other proposed revenue streams? Should block grants bypass or bolster the state government role? What entities at the local level should receive the funds to distribute to local programs? These are the kinds of questions youth advocates must turn to in the next few years.

In this chapter I have argued that thinking about youth development policies for young African-American males should mean, first, thinking about age differences among youth. Public policies for 10-year-olds will not resemble public policies for 19-year-olds. This is a strikingly simple point, but one that has largely eluded the field.

Choosing among the proposals suggested in this chapter and funding the right policy tools to implement them should not be left to professional policymakers alone. These are choices we should make as a nation. Our deliberations reflect what kind of society we will have and what kinds of programs we will put in place to help our youth develop and prepare for a complex new century. Youth development programs alone will not remedy all the problems faced by young African-American males. But with good public policies, our young people and our society are likely to have a better future.

Notes

Additional support for this chapter comes from a Lilly Endowment grant supporting investigations into the role of age in American youth policy.

1. There are exceptions. For example, there is a Minority Male Initiative Office within the Department of Health and Human Services. Generally, however, federal policy is not organized around particular racial/ethnic groups.

2. These are the conclusions reached by a large-scale review of youth programming conducted by authors invited to write papers published by Brandeis University's Center for Human Resources and (Philadelphia-based) Public/Private Ventures for the U.S. Department of Labor in 1992. Portions of the present chapter draw on my chapter in that publication (Hahn, Ganzglass, and Nagel 1992). A small section of the present chapter also draws on Hahn (1992).

3. Recent amendments to JTPA create a specific youth title within the broad Act. My description of JTPA covers how it operated in 1992 before enactment of the amendments.

4. The author is involved in a Lilly Endowment-supported project to examine the role of age in youth policy. The Carnegie Council on Early Adolescence also has examined these issues. Leonard Stern (1992) writes in a background paper for the Council that "rarely is it possible to isolate funds for programs which target young adolescents, ages 10 to 15. Most of the data either bifurcates this age group or includes it within a range of adolescents."

5. Among those who argue against this approach are Greenstein (1991) and Willie (1991). Greenstein suggests that to speak of universal programs during an era of severe budget deficits is highly unrealistic. Willie cites studies of Title III of the Higher Education Act that have shown that racial minorities receive fewer opportunities and less financial aid in universal programs than might be expected.

6. The proposal here for a Consolidated National Youth Development Block Grant Act should not be confused with real proposals with similar sounding names that have been prepared by public interest groups.

References

Carnegie Council on Adolescent Development. 1989. *Turning Points: Preparing American Youth for the 21st Century.* New York: Carnegie Council on Adolescent Development.

DeLone, Richard H. 1990. "Replication." Paper prepared for Public/Private Ventures, Philadelphia, Pa.; summer.

Dryfoos, Joy G. 1990. *Adolescents At Risk: Prevalence and Prevention.* New York: Oxford University Press.

Elsman, Max. 1989. "Frankie and his Friends: An Adventure in Social Marketing." Paper prepared for the Manpower Demonstration Research Corporation, New York.

Greenstein, Robert. 1991. "Universal and Targeted Approaches to Relieving Poverty." In *The Urban Underclass*, eds. Christopher Jencks and Paul Peterson. Washington, D.C.: The Brookings Institution.

Grinker Associates, Inc. 1986. "An Independent Sector Assessment of the Job Training Partnership Act. Final Report." New York: Grinker Associates, Inc.

Grubb, W. Norton. 1989. "Innovation Versus Turf: Coordination Between Vocational Education and Job Training Partnership Act Programs." Berkeley, Calif.: National Center for Research in Vocational Education.

Hahn, Andrew. 1992. "Managing Youth Development Programs for At-Risk Youth: Lessons from Research and Practical Experience." New York: (ERIC) Center for Urban and Minority Education, Teachers College, Columbia University.

Hahn, Andrew, Evelyn Ganzglass, and Gloria Nagel. 1992. "National Human Resource Policy for Poor Youth." In *Dilemmas in Youth Employment: Findings From the Youth Research and Technical Assistance Project*, Volume 1-2. U.S. Department of Labor. Washington, D.C.: U.S. Government Printing Office.

Hahn, Andrew, and Chris Kingsley. 1991. "Future Options Education." Brandeis University, Center for Human Resources, Heller Graduate School, Waltham, Mass.

Heidenheimer, Arnold J. 1983. *Comparative Public Policy: The Politics of Social Choice in Europe and America*. New York: T. Martin's Press, Inc.

Levin, Marty, and Bryna Sanger. 1991. "Commentary." In *Governing* [a newsletter of the Congressional Quarterly Inc.] (February).

Lynch, Lisa M. 1989. "Private Sector Training and Its Impact on the Earnings of Young Workers." NBER Working Paper Series #2872. Washington, D.C.: National Bureau of Economic Research.

McDonnell, Lorraine M., and Richard F. Elmore. 1987. "Alternative Policy Instruments." Center for Policy Research in Education, the RAND Corporation, Santa Monica, Calif.

Osterman, Paul. 1988. *Employment Futures*. New York: Oxford University Press.

Scales, Peter C. 1991. "A Portrait of Young Adolescents in the 1990s." Center for Early Adolescents, University of North Carolina, Carrboro, N.C.

Skocpol, Theda. 1989. "Targeting Within Universalism: Politically Viable Policies to Combat Poverty in the United States." Paper prepared for the Conference on the Truly Disadvantaged, sponsored by the Committee for Research on the Urban Underclass, Social Science Research Council.

Stern, Leonard W. 1992. "Funding Patterns of Nonprofit Organizations that Provide Youth Development Services: An Exploratory Study." Paper commissioned by the Carnegie Council on Adolescent Development for its Task Force on Youth Development and Community Programs, Washington, D.C.

U.S. Department of Labor. 1989. "Working Capital: JTPA Investments for the '90s." A Report of the Job Training Partnership Act (JTPA) Advisory Committee. Washington, D.C.

U.S. General Accounting Office. 1989. "Job Training Partnership Act: Services and Outcomes for Participants with Differing Needs." GAO/HRD-89-52, Washington, D.C.

Walker, Gary, Hilary Feldstein, and Katherine Solow. 1985. "An Independent Sector Assessment of the Job Training Partnership Act." Washington, D.C.: National Commission for Employment Policy.

Willie, Charles V. 1991. "Universal Programs in Education Are Unfair to Minority Groups—Opinion." *Chronicle of Higher Education*, Dec. 4.

Chapter Eight

CONCLUSIONS AND IMPLICATIONS

Ronald B. Mincy

While the claim that young black males are an endangered species may be overstated, there can be no doubt that there is a crisis among those who become high school dropouts. Because society bears high health care, criminal justice, and welfare costs, this crisis calls for immediate attention. The evidence suggests that the number of black males in crisis can be substantially reduced, if we help black males age 10 to 15 in high-risk family and neighborhood environments develop the competencies they need to make successful transitions to adulthood. Put differently, it may be possible to avoid some of the crisis as a by-product of preparation for adulthood. This suggests that Youth Development Programs Serving Young Black Males (YDBM) should be considered as alternatives to treatment and prevention programs. At present we put all of our service dollars into treatment, prevention, and incarceration, without knowing how effectively such programs work. Instead, we should invest some of our service dollars to develop and test youth development programs.

Unfortunately, the structure of youth-serving agencies and funding agencies is not up to the task. Youth service in America has developed along two separate tracks. Private programs are supported and maintained by middle and upper class parents—of all race and ethnic groups—with the will, means, and knowledge to engage non-family resources on behalf of their children. These programs emphasize preparation for adulthood. In contrast, publicly funded programs emphasize prevention and treatment for troubled youth. For youth from families and communities that cannot support private youth development programs, there are, at best, programs to prevent specific delinquent behavior. The other developmental needs of these youth go substantially unmet. American society has left disadvantaged youths on their own to discover who they are and how they should relate to others.

To move from here, we need individual resourcefulness and social vision. Some youth-serving agencies must make new commitments to young black males from high-risk environments, while other youth-serving agencies must build the capacity to match their stated commitment. Youth-serving agencies and the philanthropic agencies that support them must change their procedures for seeking and granting funds to overcome structural barriers to the financing of YDBM programs. Finally, policymakers who are looking at the crisis with the fragmented lenses resulting from their categorical programs must be willing to support the development, demonstration, and evaluation of youth development programs. If these programs prove more successful than current approaches, policymakers must reform social policy affecting youth accordingly.

Three general conclusions emerge from the material presented in this volume. First, there is an enormous amount of programming activity underway. Policymakers therefore have a wealth of raw material from which to construct an effective structure of interventions to promote healthy development among young black males. Second, this activity is fragmented, and collaboration among agencies developing programs is not likely to occur naturally. Third, there are specific policy, programming, and funding obstacles that impede progress, but there are several options for removing these obstacles.

Below I emphasize the overlapping, corroborating, and supporting findings presented in the previous chapters and in two conferences that helped to shape this volume. The narrative below follows the order of the themes in the volume, stressing needs, responses, and barriers/opportunities to YDBM programs.

NEEDS

Young black males require specialized adaptations of the youth development programs that, according to Pittman and Zeldin (chapter 3), all youth need. The most fundamental goals of youth development programs are to help early adolescents meet their basic needs, master competencies critical for successful transitions to adulthood, and establish critical connections to others.

Several contributors discuss how practitioners adapt general youth development guidelines to the unique circumstances of young black males from high-risk backgrounds. Lee (chapter 2) argues that YDBM programs should provide opportunities for youth to develop ongoing relationships with successful adult black males. These programs also should allow young black males to learn and practice skills for over-coming developmental obstacles that are common to youth in low-income black neighborhoods such as pervasive crime, violence, drug use and sales, and early sexual encounters. The teaching of such skills is a common feature of the programs reviewed by Ferguson (chapter 4). To be culturally appropriate, Lee and Quinn (chapter 6) argue that YDBM programs should accept and apply African/African-American cultural principles in the same way that programs targeting majority youth routinely incorporate Eurocentric cultural principles. Jeff (chapter 5) reviews programs that have an African worldview at their core. Since religiosity and spirituality are important features of this world view, he argues that YDBM programs should emphasize these values.

There are also aspects of the developmental needs of young black males that were lacking in the programs reviewed by the authors here. Quinn suggests that in order to be effective, YDBM programs need to be intense. Programs that last only a few hours per week just cannot compete with the many hours during which young black males are idle or are exposed to negative peer pressure. Jeff would like to see manhood training programs serve young black males seven days a week. However, currently resources are not available to pro-vide for such an expansion.

No single program should be expected to meet all the needs of young black males. In fact, these youths may benefit even more from services and opportunities in a variety of settings and from a variety of service providers. For instance, agencies normally providing youth development programs only a few hours a week (e.g., the Boy Scouts) might well extend their program models to young black males. How-ever, none of the agencies sponsoring programs reviewed by the contributors appeared to coordinate with other agencies to provide services to young black males. This fragmentation is one of the weak-est aspects of current YDBM programs.

RESPONSES

Despite the array of public and private youth-serving agencies and programs, our nation is a long way from meeting the YDBM service needs described in this book, at least for young black males from high-risk environments. Quinn shows that few of the oldest and best financed youth-serving agencies have made effective outreach efforts to black male youth from high-risk environments. Those that have done so rely heavily on categorical public funding, and thus specialize in treatment and prevention programs. The result is that YDBM service deficiencies are quantitative in that not enough YDBM programs exist, and qualitative in that those that do exist aim at treating specific problems (such as drug abuse) rather than nurturing youth development more generally.

National Youth-Serving Agencies

Efforts to reach young black males by the large national youth-serving agencies affiliated with the National Collaboration for Youth seem modest when compared to the combined resources of these agencies and the number of young black males who need services. As Quinn's work suggests, these agencies rarely serve young black males from high-risk environments. This point is confirmed by Ferguson, who sampled programs in twenty cities for his chapter. None of the programs identified by local informants as making a difference in the lives of young black males was a local affiliate of a member of the National Collaboration for Youth. This is troubling not only because of the potential resources that these affiliate members could marshall, but also because of the potential they are overlooking of providing young black males with opportunities to achieve, develop character, contribute to their communities, and form positive associations with their peers. These opportunities are the stock and trade of the large national organizations.

A few well-established national youth-serving agencies do have specific programs targeted to low-income, minority communities. For example, through its outreach to housing projects and its efforts to address substance abuse, the Boys' and Girls' Clubs of America is attacking important developmental obstacles that face young black males. And through its advertising campaigns and collaboration with black fraternities and other institutions, Big Brothers/Sisters of America may be able to provide same-race and same-gender role models to thousands of young black males now waiting to receive mentors. However, we do not know to what extent programming by these agencies attempts to connect young black males to their families and communities, nor do we know if these programs accept and apply African/African-American principles. Clearly much more could be done.

Independent Agencies

The independent sector, consisting of community-based agencies not affiliated with national youth-serving agencies, does appear to be reaching young black males in high-risk environments. However, this sector relies heavily on government funding, which tends to be categorical and focused on preventing specific behaviors, especially substance abuse and violence. Independent agencies have several other handicaps in comparison to affiliates of national youth-serving organizations. Independents are understaffed and lack the personnel needed to recruit, screen, orient, and train enough volunteers to mount large programs. Independents have budgets too small to provide for much training and development of staff, or to regularly evaluate their programs. A supportive funding and policy environment is needed to build a capacity among independent agencies.

Minority Community Agencies

Agencies based in the minority community offer a variety of programs that are reaching young black males from high-risk environments. Churches, fraternities, independent community-based agencies, and civil rights groups provide culturally sensitive programs but have few resources. Minority agencies without national affiliations are limited by the same capacity constraints that other independents face. Although minority agencies affiliated with national fraternities, church denominations, and civil rights groups address a variety of minority concerns, the needs of high-risk youth are given a low priority.

The major national foundations have provided funding to the Congress of National Black Churches and the National Urban League for programs, program evaluations, program development, and media campaigns related to young black males. But other agencies based in the minority community seem beyond the reach of the major foundations. The problem could be that these agencies are new, their fiduciary responsibility is weak or unproven, or they are local agencies with no national umbrella organization providing technical, fundraising and other kinds of assistance.[1]

BARRIERS AND OPPORTUNITIES

The most important barriers to the development of YDBM programs are barriers of knowledge, funding, and policy. These obstacles also represent the most important opportunities for those working to develop YDBM programs. Because of the growth of research on young black males, policymakers and practitioners have a much stronger knowledge base from which to develop programs. The development of new institutional research capacity should allow this to continue. Besides new studies of the status of black males, ways to understand their behavior, and evaluations of prevention and treatment programs serving young black males, researchers should develop the details of YDBM programs and develop constructs to measure their effectiveness.

Knowledge

Fortunately, the volume of research and advocacy relating to black males has increased dramatically in the past few years (Majors, forthcoming). This activity has not only increased our current understanding of the conditions and needs of young black males, but also has stimulated new research programs and two new journals, which will organize and disseminate new knowledge and encourage additional research.[2]

There is and will continue to be a wealth of general knowledge about the developmental needs of young black males. However, as Hahn (chapter 7) points out, policymakers and practitioners lack specific knowledge about what constitutes a youth development program and how such programs can be evaluated. To answer these questions, new funding for research on program models must become available.

Funding

As long as government remains committed to narrowly focused prevention and treatment programs, private funding is critical to the development of YDBM programs. Therefore, private philanthropies should provide additional support for YDBM programs. Such support could occur only if these sources assign a higher priority to youth development in general and to young black males in particular. Evidence of such support would also help to counteract the perception among the public and among some youth-service providers themselves that young black males from high-risk environments are unsalvageable.

How To Strengthen Independent Agencies. As discussed in this volume, independent YDBM programs have the most effective outreach to young black males of any youth programs in the country, but they are out of the loop as far as gaining mainstream funding is concerned. To place themselves within the reach of national foundations that may be willing to increase support for YDBM programs, independents may have to affiliate themselves with some kind of national structure, as suggested by Wiener in appendix A. National affiliation also could help independents to obtain support for certain general operating costs that public and private funders seem unwilling to cover in program grants.

An example of such an affiliation is occurring among Afrikan-centric (also known as Afrocentric) Rights of Passage programs such as those described in Jeff's chapter. These programs represent a truly promising intervention, but they and their associated curricula need to be evaluated and refined. To be sure, many programs fall under the Afrikan-centric label and service providers vary in their interpretations of this programming. However, since the 1960s there has been a core of researchers, social workers, and practitioners working— with little support from mainstream institutions—to define an Afrikan-centric value system and a curriculum that can serve as the guiding principles for YDBM programs. The Afrikan-Centric National Rights of Passage Kollective (ANROPK), formed to help local groups around the country develop and replicate Afrikan-centric program models, is developing curricula, setting minimal standards, and producing material to help standardize programs and maintain the credibility of the program model. Its members are also establishing by-laws and undertaking other steps necessary to become a nonprofit agency eligible for tax-exempt contributions. ANROPK could well become a conduit for resources for rites-of-passage programs throughout the country.[3]

How National and Indirect Service Agencies Can Help. Organizing coalitions among themselves is one way that YDBM programs can gain credibility and attract attention from national foundations. For their part, national foundations interested in supporting independent YDBM programs could change the structure of grantmaking to reach independent agencies. Matching-fund grants are one creative way to do this. A national foundation could agree to match grants by community and corporate foundations for YDBM demonstration projects operated by independent agencies.[4]

Independents should be allowed to use some portion of any new funding to develop the capacity to expand YDBM programs. One way to build this capacity is to hire, train, and develop staff. The chapters by Hahn and by Pittman and Zeldin point out that staff training and development is a neglected area in many independent community-based agencies. Staff members need to be trained to seek funds from a wide variety of possible funding sources. Wiener (see appendix A) argues that independents need to expand their staff so that some can specialize in fundraising activities. Staff members also need training to work with 10- to 15-year-old males from high-risk environments, and to adapt their programs to the urban, African-American, and youth cultures. Finally, staff members need training to gather and analyze data on the effectiveness of their programs.

"Indirect" service agencies can also be helpful to independent agencies running programs for young black males. During our research we discovered a few agencies, which we call indirect service agencies, that do not serve youth directly. Instead, these indirect service agencies provide staff training and technical assistance to several independent agencies that serve youth in a given community. By exploiting economies of scale now available to affiliates of national youth-serving agencies, indirect service agencies lower training and administrative costs for independent youth-serving agencies. Project Raise in Baltimore, Maryland, and The Mentoring Center in Oakland, California, are two good examples of indirect service agencies. On the national scale, we uncovered only one agency, the National Urban League, that provided such services to independents serving young black males. With the support of national foundations, notably the Carnegie Corporation of New York, the National Urban League operates the Adolescent Male Development Center (AMDC). AMDC serves National Urban League affiliates, independents, and local affiliates of national youth-serving agencies. AMDC has held annual conferences for YDBM affiliate and non-affiliate service providers since 1989; developed information and media campaigns to bring national focus to the need for YDBM programs and to increase the number of volunteers available for affiliate and non-affiliate programs; and provided culturally sensitive training to local affiliates of national youth-serving agencies with YDBM programs. The National Urban League's leadership in this area is not surprising because it is a civil rights agency primarily serving the black community. Nevertheless, AMDC is the best example of what might be accomplished if other national agencies would marshall some of their resources and experience to build YDBM programs.

Finally, federated campaigns, modeled after the United Way, are another potential source of indirect support for independent YDBM programs. As Wiener points out in appendix A, the United Way collects millions of dollars annually from workers throughout the country through employer-sponsored campaigns and distributes revenues to the nonprofit organizations for a variety of programs. Employer campaigns operated by several other agencies (such as the United Black Fund) target their revenues to nonprofit agencies in the black community, because in their view, these agencies have been neglected by the United Way. Independents offering YDBM programs should affiliate with these federated campaigns so they can receive disbursements.

What Private Funders Can Do. Private funders can give national youth-serving agencies incentives to offer more YDBM programs in high-risk communities. Incentives are necessary to help these agencies cover the costs of serving youth in families that cannot afford to pay fees for services or youth in communities that cannot afford to support local affiliates. According to Quinn, these agencies would have to create special programs designed to work effectively with young black males. Program staff would have to become culturally sensitive, would have to provide intensive services, and would probably have to recruit more minority volunteers.

Private funders could also give national youth-serving agencies incentives to offer physical space or technical assistance to independent YDBM programs in high-risk environments. For example, agencies that operate facility-based programs such as the YMCA or the Boys' and Girls' Clubs of America could rent their facilities to independents operating YDBM programs. National youth-serving agencies could train independent staffers in proposal writing; program evaluation; volunteer recruitment, screening, training, orientation, and retention; and so on. In this way, independents would develop the capacity to build larger programs that might achieve the scale needed to attract substantial foundation funding.

What Corporate Officers Can Do. The corporate sector can play an important role in the development of YDBM programs beyond the funding this sector now provides. Corporate officers sit on the boards of the United Way and other federated campaigns, on the boards of national youth-serving agencies, and on the boards of national, corporate, and community foundations. As Wiener points out, youth-serving agencies seek corporate officers for their boards because these officers can bring in contributions and other resources. Since minorities are underrepresented among corporate officers (and among other segments of the population with control of financial resources), there are few minorities who sit on the boards of national youth-serving agencies. National foundations have heavily recruited and promoted minorities to senior-level positions, but other foundations and national youth-serving organizations have not. Without minority board members, the foundations that fund independents and national youth-serving agencies may be unaware of the needs of minority communities and youth. Even if national youth-serving agencies were aware of these needs, they may not know how to respond in culturally sensitive ways and they may not be trusted by members of minority communities.

Corporate officers, therefore, are in a unique position to help make YDBM programs more available. As influential insiders, they can encourage corporate and community foundations and national youth-serving agencies to diversify the race and ethnic composition of their boards and senior staff. Corporate officers can also encourage these agencies to target young black males in high-risk environments, and can lobby foundations to fund these efforts. These steps could increase the volume of services that reach young black males in high-risk environments and increase the likelihood that such services meet the unique needs of young black males.

Policy

Shifting public funds to YDBM programs will require a major shift in policy. As shown in chapter 1, young black men are disproportionately represented among labor force non-participants, victims and perpetrators of violence, general assistance recipients, and inmates of prisons and mental health institutions. These trends already are forcing policymakers in several service areas to focus on black males as a distinct population. For instance, in the area of criminal justice, the policy shift is moving beyond sentencing issues. The Justice Department is funding programs to promote nonviolent conflict resolution, mostly targeting young black males, and the Office for Substance Abuse Prevention is actively funding programs intended to reduce drug use, especially among young black males.

General policy discussions involving black males also are underway. A 1990 Sentencing Project report, showing alarming rates of incarceration among young adult black males, touched off hearings by the Senate Banking and Urban Affairs Committee on the status of African-American males (Mauer 1990). Following these hearings, the 21st century Commission on African American Males was appointed to hold additional hearings and issue a commission report. Similar commissions have been formed by the executive or legislative branches in at least six state or local governments including Ohio, Illinois, Maryland, California, New York, and Indiana. Among other concerns, each of these commissions has had to focus on crime and labor force non-participation among poorly educated black males.

However, as long as these efforts remain fragmented and focused on the problems of adults and older teenagers, there is little hope for progress. Real progress requires health, labor, criminal justice, and other policymakers to recognize the need to reach black males at a younger age. Data presented in this volume and elsewhere suggest that the health, employment, and criminal justice problems of older black males are often the results of choices they made when they were 10 to 15 years old. Despite this evidence of the long-term consequences of problems that emerge in early adolescence, our nation has no coordinated policy to help young black males in high-risk environments to prepare for adulthood.

Policymakers must begin to view the youth development competencies defined by Pittman and Zeldin as essential to the future success of young people. These competencies may be as important as the academic competencies taught in schools. But if the home, school, and neighborhood environments of young black males provide little opportunity for them to acquire these competencies, some other institution must fill the void. From this perspective, community-based agencies operating YDBM programs are not luxuries that our society can ill afford in lean fiscal times. Instead, they are necessary supplements to the resources available to help parents in high-risk neighborhoods to prepare their boys for adulthood. Put bluntly, we can pay now to develop YDBM programs, or we can pay later to maintain jails, morgues, hospitals, mental institutions, and modestly effective employment and training programs.

If we decide to pay now, we must reform services for young black males in high-risk environments in three ways. First, more formal arrangements must be made among categorical programs to integrate services. Young clients (and their families) often have needs that single-problem programs cannot meet. By formalizing the connections among such programs, these clients can be referred to other programs that provide needed services. Such service integration will require some centralization of authority across categorical programs (Kusserow 1991). Second, services must become more comprehensive. This will require relaxing categorical funding guidelines and changing eligibility criteria. Currently, most publicly funded programs determine eligibility for youth services using the present behavior or problem status of youth. Instead, eligibility must be based on the presence in early adolescence of antecedents and markers for later problem behavior. This brings us to the third change needed: programs serving young black males in high-risk environments must move from deterrence to youth development. This will involve helping youth meet a variety of basic needs and acquire a variety of competencies described by Pittman and Zeldin.

This developmental perspective suggests that policymakers can reduce delinquent behavior as a by-product of YDBM programs. But the more ambitious goal is to help the larger universe of young black males prepare to assume legitimate roles in families, workplace, and communities. I agree with Pittman, Zeldin, and Hahn that policymakers must support research and program evaluations to find out if YDBM programs serve youth better than programs designed to help youth avoid specific delinquent behaviors. But this means that policymakers must be open to evaluations that include, but go beyond, measures of reduced delinquency. It also means that partnerships involving education, criminal justice, health and human service, and perhaps labor departments should continue to support demonstrations and evaluations that cross categorical funding lines.

SUMMARY OF RELEVANT LEGISLATION

I am sympathetic to Hahn's (chapter 7) recommendation for a new National Consolidated Youth Development Block Grant Act. Through such an Act, the federal government could help to establish and promote early adolescence as a critical intervention point, and forge new relationships between government and community-based agencies that sponsor youth development programs. Further, the federal government could support efforts to define the basic competencies that early adolescents should achieve, similar to federally supported efforts to establish goals for the health and education of children and youth (U.S. Department of Health and Human Services 1991; The White House 1990). This exercise could have two important benefits. First, it could articulate the broad outlines of a youth policy. Various federal departments could organize their youth programs around these broad outlines and attention could be given to youth needs (and service integration issues) that available programs leave unmet. Without such a broad outline, youth policy might not evolve from the universe of currently fragmented programs that now exist. The present arrangement makes it difficult to identify and tackle unmet needs and service integration issues. Second, the public resources used to provide YDBM would be universally available to help all early adolescents develop the competencies that fully functioning adult citizens should master.

Much of the framework for this Act and related reforms already has been laid out in existing, pending, and proposed legislation. The most important examples include: the Young Americans Act (H.R. 1492) passed in 1989, but never fully funded; the Youth Development Act (H.R. 4544) introduced in 1991, but not passed; the Comprehensive Services for Youth Act introduced in 1992, but not passed; and a proposal for Youth Development Block Grants being developed by the National Collaboration for Youth. Most legislation places the responsibility for such programs within the Department of Health and Human Services (DHHS).

The Young Americans Act required coordination of the activities of approximately 60 federal programs serving children, youth, and families with the Commissioner of the Administration for Children, Youth, and Families (ACYF) in DHHS. The Act also authorized grants for state and community programs to coordinate resources; develop and implement comprehensive, coordinated state and community services; and demonstrate successful program approaches that fill service gaps. As part of the coordination effort, and perhaps to draw attention to youth policy issues, a White House "Conference on Young Americans" was to be convened by the president in 1990.

The Comprehensive Services for Youth Act would authorize the Public Health Service in DHHS to provide grants to promote the coordination and delivery of comprehensive education, health, and social services to youth (10 to 21 years old) in high-risk communities and their families. Services would be provided through a system of school-based, school-linked, or community-based locations. Besides service integration, service providers also could use grant funds for programs to promote health, career education, social competency, school completion, and life skills training to youth.

Both the Young Americans Act and the Comprehensive Services for Youth Act only speak to the need for service integration. The Youth Development Act and the Youth Development Block Grant Act would create vehicles for government to reach beyond its historical deficit focus to support community-based programs like those described by Pittman and Zeldin. Such programs help youth develop physical, social, and educational competencies and life skills. The Youth Development Act targets youth (10 to 15 years old) and would support programs that gave youth opportunities to develop these skills and competencies through community service. These programs would be funded by grants to community-based public or private nonprofit agencies. The grants would be administered by the Commissioner of the Administration for Children, Youth, and Families of DHHS. The Youth Development Block Grant Act targets youth (age 6 to 19) and would be administered by a hierarchy of youth development commissions and boards appointed by public officials. There would be substantial local autonomy to define local youth development needs, which would serve as guidelines for grants to local programs.

This legislative framework includes a full range of choices that target services at youth in poor or high-risk environments. The Young Americans Act attempts to lay the groundwork for a national youth policy.[5] Therefore, it does not specify any formula for targeting services at youth in poor or high-risk communities. Similarly, the Youth Development Act is not targeted, reflecting the view of its proponents that all early adolescents need to develop health, social, and vocational competencies. In contrast, the Youth Development Block Grant proposal allocates funding using a formula that favors counties with high poverty rates among children and youth between 6 and 19 years old. Within any county, the allocation rule favors programs that use strong outreach efforts to low-income youth and their families. Going a step further, the Comprehensive Services for Youth Act would provide services exclusively for youth in high-risk environments.

There are arguments for and against explicit targeting in legislation. Legislation without targeting would leave intact the current disparities in access to youth development programs between youth in high-risk environments and other youth. Such legislation also could affect the kinds of agencies that provide youth development services. Many independent and minority agencies that are serving young black males lack the administrative staff to compete with the national youth-serving organizations for grants. Therefore, a bill lacking a targeting mechanism could underutilize the very agencies that over the last few years have gained the trust of young black males and have acquired experience working with them. On the other hand, Hahn argues that because targeting within universalism is necessary for wide public support, explicit targeting within the language of the legislation might be unnecessary. Instead, targeting could be accomplished through regulations and other policy devices that Hahn suggests. I believe such explicit targeting, within a universal program, is needed.

Finally, except for the Young Americans Act, the current legislative framework locates services for youth in community-based organizations and recognizes the need to build the capacity of these organizations through staff training, culturally sensitive programming, and so on. These are features emphasized by several authors, including Quinn, Hahn, and Pittman and Zeldin. For example, recipients of Youth Development Block Grants must devote between 5 and 10 percent of grant funds to training and educational materials for staff members. The Youth Development Act requires that eligible grantees spend at least a quarter of grant funds to train staff, especially in adolescent development. Grantees also must adapt to the experience, interests, family background, gender, and race or ethnicity of participating youth.

The Comprehensive Services for Youth Act has very specific capacity requirements. First, grantees must use at least 10 percent of grant funds for staff training and technical assistance. Second, the Act would emphasize school-based and school-linked programs, presumably because most youth can be found in the public schools. However, the high rates of suspension and expulsion among young black males suggest that the public schools may represent inhospitable places for many black males. Unless explicit steps are taken to distinguish such a program from the school, young black males who encounter disciplinary problems in school might not voluntarily participate in school-based, school-linked programs. One step would be to employ teachers and school administrators in the program selectively, or not at all. Finally, the Comprehensive Services for Youth Act would require service providers to coordinate services and provide programs in ways that demonstrate cultural sensitivity and linguistic appropriateness.

In sum, the current legislative framework includes alternative ways to coordinate existing categorical programs; to provide new funding for comprehensive and youth development programs; to target these programs to youth in high-risk environments; and to build the capacity of community-based programs to expand and improve these programs.

WE CANNOT AFFORD TO WAIT

Increased public funding of Youth Development Programs Serving Young Black Males should not await passage of proposed legislation such as the National Youth Development Act, which will not happen overnight or even in the next few years. These kinds of proposals simply do not enjoy the same public support as other legislation affecting children and youth such as expansion of Head Start, youth apprenticeship programs, expansion of the National Community Service Act, and reauthorization of chapter 1.

Government can no longer afford to overlook the needs of young black men in this country; federal and state taxpayers are already sinking significant sums into the treatment of troubled male adolescents after the problem behavior has occurred. There are available at our finger tips more effective ways of spending funds already devoted to young black males. We need not wait until national youth policy is reformed; as the contributors here have shown, there are concrete steps that can be taken now. We need only listen to what our youth are telling us about what they need to develop into healthy, productive contributors to our society.

Notes

1. I am grateful to Richard Brown and Keith Fulton of the National Urban League's Adolescent Male Development Center for sharing data on foundation support of programs serving black male adolescents.

2. The new research programs include the Albany (NY) State Center for the Study of the Black Male, and the Morehouse Research Institute (MRI), in Atlanta. The new journals are MRI's *Challenge: A Journal of Research on Black Men,* and the *Journal of African American Male Studies,* published by the National Council of African American Men.

3. Interview with Paul Hill by telephone May 1992; and interview with Darryl Kennon by telephone May 1992.

4. I wish to thank my colleague James Gibson, former executive director of the Equal Opportunity Program at the Rockefeller Foundation, for this suggestion.

5. It follows the model of the Older Americans Act, which laid the groundwork for the expansion of elderly entitlements beginning in the mid-1960s.

References

Kusserow, R. 1991. *Services Integration: A Twenty-Year Retrospective.* Washington, D.C.: U.S. Department of Health and Human Services, Office of the Inspector General.

Majors, Richard G. Forthcoming. "A Reason for Hope: An Overview of the New Black Male Movement in the United States." In *The American Black Male: His Present Status and His Future,* eds. R. G. Majors and J. Gordon. Chicago: Nelson-Hall, Inc.

Mauer, Marc. 1990. *Young Black Men and the Criminal Justice System: A Growing National Problem.* Washington, D.C.: The Sentencing Project.

U.S. Department of Health and Human Services, Public Health Service. 1991. *Healthy Children 2000: National Health Promotion and Disease Prevention Objectives Related to Mothers, Infants, Children, Adolescents, and Youth.* DHHS Publication No. HRSA-M-CH-91-2, September.

The White House, Office of the Press Secretary. 1990. "National Goals For Education." Statement released Feb. 26.

FUNDING YOUTH DEVELOPMENT PROGRAMS FOR YOUNG BLACK MALES: THE LITTLE WE KNOW

Susan J. Wiener

How are the resources in our society being allocated to help community-based youth programs that serve young black males? Here I investigate the magnitude and sources of financial assistance being made to nonprofit community-based agencies that provide general youth development services to young African-American males. I also review some of the organizations that solicit funding for youth programs and discuss obstacles to fundraising faced by youth-serving programs. Finally, I suggest ways to address the mismatch between available funding and the needs of programs that support black male youth development.

Many programs that provide general development services for young black males are small, independent, community-based programs such as those discussed by Ferguson and Jeff in chapters 4 and 5, respectively. While these community-based programs sometimes offer the only youth services available to young black males in high-risk environments, they rely on government funding, which tends to focus on problem behavior and remediation. There is little or no government money available for general youth development programming.

The large, nationally affiliated youth development agencies discussed by Quinn in chapter 6 such as the Boys' and Girls' Clubs and Big Brothers/Big Sisters of America provide a variety of general development programs and activities for youth. These agencies are primarily supported by private sector funding from foundations, corporations, local United Ways, and individuals. Unfortunately, these national agencies are not equipped to (or simply do not) serve the numbers of young black males that could benefit from their services. The few national agencies that are black focused, such as the National Urban League, devote only a small portion of their overall programming to youth services.

GENERAL YOUTH DEVELOPMENT FUNDING: HOW MUCH MONEY ARE WE TALKING ABOUT?

Calculating the amount of funds supporting programs for young black boys is extremely problematic. The array of programs and funding sources and the lack of any unified database make allocations difficult to trace. Furthermore, grants are typically broadly inclusive, going to all youth or all minority programming as opposed to minority youth programming. Because it is impossible to obtain data on how much money goes exclusively to programming for young black males, I discuss data on youth development in general and present some approximate figures representing support for black male youth development. Despite the rough nature of these latter figures, we can say with certainty that the total amount reaching 10- to 15-year-old African-American boys is only a small fraction of the total going to youth development in general. As shown below, total allocations to youth development are quite small relative to federal and private sector outlays in this country.

In 1989, the youth development and human service organizations providing children and youth services that filed tax returns, together received $2.4 billion in public support. This included gifts, grants, and contributions from private and government sources. Expenses for these same organizations were $4.7 billion. Most likely the difference between expenses and public support was made up for by service fees, dues, and other assets. These figures do not account for a great number of organizations whose revenue was less than $25,000 in 1989 and thus did not file with the IRS (Hodgkinson et al. 1992).

Federal government support for these organizations comes from a variety of government agencies and programs which provide an estimated $15 billion to youth services that potentially reach young black males. Private sector contributions are made primarily by foundations, corporations, and individuals.

States and localities also allocate funds for schools and community youth services. States use additional funds received from federal agencies to provide grants to schools and community-based organizations for youth services. These grants are administered under regulations and bureaucracies that vary from state to state. Estimating the outlays of state and local governments is difficult because of inconsistencies across states and the lack of centralized information.

The funding our nation dedicates to youth development is a small fraction of both federal and private sector outlays. Approximately 4 percent of discretionary domestic outlays of $182.5 billion in 1990 was dedicated to youth services, and another 4 percent to human service programs that could have benefited youth. In 1990 the $300 billion national defense budget was 20 times greater than youth spending. And in 1992, U.S. taxpayers paid $8.9 billion to incarcerate adult black men (Mauer 1992), illustrating the significant amount of money spent on punitive measures imposed against African-American men rather than helping youth develop positive and healthy skills. Of the potential $15 billion of federal outlays spent on youth services, only a fraction was likely to have reached teenage black males and very little was spent on youth development (Office of Management and Budget 1991 and 1993).

The private sector similarly contributes only a small portion of its total outlays to youth development programs. Since 1955, philanthropic giving has grown dramatically from $7.7 billion to $122.6 billion in 1990 (in current dollars). In 1990, individuals provided the lion's share of charitable contributions—83.1 percent. The remainder of philanthropic giving in 1990 was provided by bequests—$7.8 billion (6.4 percent of the total), foundations—$7.1 billion (5.7 percent of the total), and corporations—$5.9 billion (4.8 percent of the total). However, these resources support an immense variety of purposes ranging from the arts to wildlife preservation to religion. In 1990 religious activities received the largest portion of philanthropic donations—over 50 percent—while human service nonprofits received just under 10 percent (American Association of Fund-Raising Council Trust for Philanthropy 1991). The percentage of total philanthropic funds given to youth development organizations, a subset of human services, has never been estimated. However, the Foundation Center (1992) reports that in 1991 youth development organizations received 2 percent of large foundation grants, which represented over 50 percent of all grants that year; and a survey of 330 companies in 1990 reported that national youth organizations were the beneficiaries of 0.7 percent of corporate giving (Klepper 1992).

It is clear that existing funding levels for youth development are too low to provide substantial assistance to black youth. Even assuming that the $2.4 billion of public support going to youth development and human service organizations were evenly distributed, each American child would receive $53 of services. However, these resources are not evenly distributed between suburban and inner-city youth (Carnegie Corporation of New York 1992, p. 71). The small proportion of funds available to young black males is clearly not enough to provide the level of youth development services required to overcome mounting obstacles of inner-city life faced by many youths in low- and moderate-income families. If youth development programs are to have a significant influence on black youth, additional resources are needed.

WHO IS CONTRIBUTING? BREAKDOWN BY TYPE OF FUNDING SOURCE

The diversity of youth-serving organizations described in this volume is matched by the diversity of their funding sources. The public sector funds black male youth development programs primarily through federal agencies, but also through state and local agencies. Private sector contributions come from foundations, corporations, local United Ways and United Black Funds, churches, community institutions, and private individuals. Each of these sources is discussed in turn below.

The Federal Government

Historically, the federal government has played an important role in supporting the field of youth development. Many independent community-based programs for youth began during the 1960s and 1970s in part due to generous federal funding (Weber 1992). The government has long recognized and relied upon the service delivery capacities of nonprofits. Although President Reagan sharply reduced federal funding for nonprofits in the early 1980s, government funding sources continue to provide a majority of the support for non-affiliated community-based organizations serving adolescents and youth in high-risk situations[1] (Abramson and Salamon 1986).

Table A.1 shows the sources of federal grants for youth services categorized by agency. The table was compiled using published resources about government expenditures on programs that serve youth. The majority of these grants were targeted at homeless and runaway youth, were allocated to satisfy goals of juvenile justice, were provided directly to school systems, or were budgeted to fight the "War on Drugs." Most of these government programs focus on youth's deficits and problem behaviors, as opposed to general development activities. Some initiatives have specifically been targeted at young black males. These include the High-Risk Youth Demonstra-

Table A.1. FEDERAL EXPENDITURES FOR YOUTH EDUCATION, PREVENTION, AND TREATMENT PROGRAMS, FY 1990

Agency	Spending in FY 90[a] (in $ millions)
ACTION	
Drug Alliance Demonstration Program	4.5
Volunteers in Service to America	2.7
Foster Grandparent Program	1.9
Retired Senior Volunteer Program	0.4
Total ACTION	9.5
Department of Education	
Education for the Disadvantaged—LEA Grants	4,358.0
Education Block Grants for States	519.3
Education for Homeless Children and Youth	7.2
Drug-Free Schools and Communities Program	287.7
School Dropout Demonstration Assistance Program	19.9
State Agency Neglected and Delinquent Education Program	31.6 FY 89
Even Start (ages 1–7)	24.4
Follow Through (ages 12–18)	7.2
Special Programs for Students from Disadvantaged Backgrounds (TRIO)	118.2 FY 89
Basic State Grant—Opportunities Program	850.7
Fund for Innovation in Education	18.8
Fund for Improvement and Reform of Schools & Teaching	8.4
Eisenhower Math and Science Education Act	153.3
Allen J. Ellender Fellowships	3.7
Gifted and Talented Children	17.8
Arts in Education Program	3.9
Law Related Education Program	4.9
Innovative Projects for Student Community Service	1.5
Vocational Education: Basic State Grants	845.9
Vocational Education: Consumer and Homemaking Services	34.2
Vocational Education: Programs for CBOs	10.9
Other programs	427.3
TOTAL to education agencies	7,754.9
Department of Health and Human Services (HHS)	
Social Services Block Grant	2,767.0
Dependent Care State Grants	13.2
Office of Minority Health	2.4
Administration for Children, Youth and Families: Youth Gang Drug Prevention Program	14.8
Runaway and Homeless Youth Program	28.8

Table A.1. FEDERAL EXPENDITURES FOR YOUTH EDUCATION, PREVENTION,
AND TREATMENT PROGRAMS, FY 1990, Continued

Drug Abuse Prevention among Runaway and Homeless Youth	14.8
Targeted Outreach Program—Boys' Club	0.1
Independent Living Program (foster care)	50.0
Transitional Living Grant Program (ages 16–21)	9.5
Child Welfare Services	252.6
Indian Child Welfare Services	8.7 FY 89
Adolescent Family Life	9.4
VISTA and Related Volunteer Programs	25.7 FY 89
Office of Community Services:	
Community Services Block Grant	380.6 FY 89
Demonstration Partnership Program	3.5
National Youth Sports Program, NCAA	9.7
Family Violence Programs	8.3
National Institute on Drug Abuse:	
AIDS Outreach Demonstration Grants	70.0
Alcohol, Drug Abuse, and Mental Health Block Grant	1,192.9
Preventative Health and Health Services Block Grant	84.1
Family Planning	135.7
Indian Health Service Substance Abuse Services for Youth	18.7 FY 89
Office for Substance Abuse Prevention:	
Community Partnership Demonstration Grant Program	50.0
Community Youth Activities Program	13.5
High-Risk Youth Demonstration Grant	26.4
Gang Community Reclamation Project	0.5
Minority Substance Abuse Prevention Project	0.5
National Institute of Mental Health:	9.8
Child and Adolescent Service System Program	
Office for Treatment Improvement (ADAMHA):	29.7
Treatment Grants to Crisis Areas/Target Cities	
Treatment Improvement in Critical Populations	38.1 FY 91
Treatment Campus	18.0 FY 91
Other programs	14.6
TOTAL Department of Health and Human Services	5,301.6
Department of Justice	
Office of Juvenile Justice and Delinquency Prevention:	0.6
Alternative School Program	
Reaching At-Risk Youth in Public Housing	0.1
Targeted Outreach Gang Prevention/Intervention for Public Housing Residents (Boys' Club)	0.4
Special Education and Rehabilitation of Serious Juvenile Offenders	0.3
Boy Scouts	0.1

Table A.1. FEDERAL EXPENDITURES FOR YOUTH EDUCATION, PREVENTION,
AND TREATMENT PROGRAMS, FY 1990, Continued

American Indian/Alaska Native Youth Study	0.7
Proyecto Esperanza/Project Hope	0.1 FY 88
Students Mobilized Against Drugs	0.3
National Congress of Black Churches' Drug Abuse Prevention	0.2
Formula Grants Program (Funds for courts, detention, correction, etc.)	45.8
DOJ Intermediate Sanctions, Boot Camp	3.2
Other programs	31.3
TOTAL Department of Justice	82.9
Department of Labor	
JTPA, Title IIA—	
Training for Economically Disadvantaged Adults and Youth	605.0
JTPA, Title IIB—	709.4
Summer Youth Employment Project (ages 14–21)	
JTPA, Title IVB—Job Corps for 16–21 year olds	742.0
Youth Opportunity Unlimited	1.1
Cities in Schools	0.6
TOTAL Department of Labor	2,058.1
Department of Housing and Urban Development	
Public Housing Drug Elimination Grant Program	8.2
Youth Sports Program	0.3
TOTAL Department of Housing and Urban Development	8.5
Department of Transportation	0.4
Total Federal Outlays for Youth	15,215.8

Sources: Office of Management and Budget (1991); Office of National Drug Control
Policy (1991); U.S. Department of Justice (1992); National Network of Runaway and
Youth Services (1991); and Select Committee on Children, Youth and Families (1990).
[a]Amounts are for FY 1990, unless otherwise noted. Figures for FY 1989 or 1991 were
used in cases where FY 1990 figures were not available.

Note: Totals may not add due to rounding.

tion Grant from HHS's Office for Substance Abuse Prevention, the
National Youth Sports Program sponsored by HHS's Office of Community Services, and the Summer Youth Employment Program
administered by the Department of Labor through JTPA.

The Private Sector

Relative to the public sector, the private sector funds a smaller but
growing portion of youth development programs. In the past few

years private donors have increased funding of initiatives serving minority causes (Smith and Martin 1992a; American Association of Fund-Raising Council Trust for Philanthropy 1991; The Foundation Center 1993). Private sector funders can be divided into four categories, analyzed separately below: foundations; corporations; federated campaigns such as the United Way; and other contributors such as churches, service groups, and private individuals.

FOUNDATIONS

Foundations play a critical role in supporting youth development agencies. As entities whose raison d'être is to provide financial backing to services meeting their own goals, foundations have unique freedom to support new and experimental ideas. Such flexibility is particularly important for programs designed to serve young black males, which often differ in focus and methods from the national youth-serving organizations.

Over the past decade, foundation support for agencies serving young black males has increased. In 1991, the largest foundations granted funds totaling $1.8 million to organizations for youth development services to young black males. This represented more than a 700 percent increase over large foundation contributions seven years before.[2] Approximately 4 percent (or $69 million) of all foundation grants of $5,000 or more were made to youth development organizations and other human service organizations serving children and youth in 1990 and 1991 (measured from September to September of each year). Of the 1,815 grants made to youth through these two types of organizations, 41 were targeted specifically at black youth, and 70 were targeted at services for minority youth, which could include black youth (Stern 1992).

This funding, however, has been used exclusively to finance a handful of programs. Between 1983 and 1991, 46 percent of large foundation money granted to programs for black boys went to National Urban League affiliates. An earlier study of funding patterns among programs serving at-risk youths age 10 to 15 found that one-third of all 1990 foundation support was given to affiliates of five national youth agencies: Boys' and Girls' Clubs, Boy Scouts, Girl Scouts, Junior Achievement, and Big Brothers/Big Sisters. These figures are based on computer database searches of The Foundation Center's (1993) *Foundation Grants Index*, which includes only 2 percent of grant-making foundatons (i.e., those issuing grants over $5,000). However, these foundations account for 44 percent of foundation giving (Stern 1992).

The ten largest U.S. foundations account for almost one-quarter of all foundation assets (Salamon 1992). Typically their grant-making guidelines are nationally focused, an orientation that leads the larger independent foundations to finance research (which can be conducted on a national scale) over service delivery (which is predominantly regionally or locally based). With the exception of demonstration programs, large national foundations typically base grant awards on evidence of effectiveness before supporting program services. Thus, they prefer to finance well-known programs such as affiliates of the national agencies listed above.

All foundations, including the national ones, designate at least a portion of their grants for initiatives in their local community. For example, the John D. and Catherine T. MacArthur Foundation, the sixth largest foundation in the country, has a special grants program for projects in Chicago. Private foundations that are not nationally oriented, such as the Lilly Endowment in Indiana, devote most of their funding to local programs. Foundations even grant special exceptions from their stated interests for projects located in their communities. In 1989, W. K. Kellogg Foundation made 42 of its 109 grants to programs in Michigan that it would unlikely fund if in another state (Olson, Kovacs, and Haile 1990).

The size and specification of a foundation's grants vary according to its assets, geographic scope, and self-determined fields of interest. There are three types of foundations that fund youth development: community, independent, and corporate foundations. This last category of funding source will be treated further below under corporate giving more generally.

Community Foundations. Community foundations provide funding almost exclusively to programs and initiatives in their community or region; their endowments come from many individual donors and other foundations (Kovacs 1992). Community foundations place a great emphasis on human services, demonstrated by the 27 percent of their grants directed to this sector. This amount equals what community foundations give to education (26 percent), and is greater than their amount of support for arts (13 percent), health (14 percent), or public/society benefit organizations (14 percent) (Council on Foundations 1992). Community foundations seem well-suited to fund unproven or independent programs because of their proximity to and detailed knowledge of community needs and resources.

In fact, several community foundations are at the forefront of financing experimental programs in their cities. For example, the

Cleveland Foundation created the Cleveland Commission on Poverty to design an innovative plan to turn poor neighborhoods into healthy communities by using strategies developed by residents. In Baltimore the Abell Foundation provides grants to several local programs serving black youth. These include the Morgan State Center for Educating Black Males, and Project RAISE—a community-based program that combines private and public sector resources to help improve the academic achievement of inner-city school children. Philadelphia Futures receives continuing support from the Commonwealth Fund for a model mentoring program being considered for replication in other cities. The program—Sponsor-A-Scholar—matches low-income high school freshmen with mentors from the community. Each sponsoring adult or couple mentors a student through high school and into college while donating $1,500 per year for college tuition (Philadelphia Futures 1991/1992).

Although grants from national foundations are usually larger, community-based foundations seem less prone to shy away from the service delivery focus and experimental nature of many local youth development initiatives for young black males.

Independent Foundations. Independent foundations, formed by an individual, family, or group of individuals, also provide some funding for programs serving young black males. These foundations do not necessarily limit grants to programs in the community in which they are located. It is difficult to describe the funding patterns of independent foundations because they vary widely depending on assets and the goals of the foundations' founders. In 1989, 29,000 independent foundations gave a total of $6 billion (Renz 1991).

CORPORATIONS

Corporation-sponsored giving represents an increasingly significant portion of funding for nonprofit organizations and has almost reached the level of foundation support for same. O'Connell (1987) reports a 250 percent increase in corporate philanthropy between 1975 and 1985. The growth in corporate philanthropy is attributed to the awareness that "Corporations understand that neither the public nor the private can solve basic problems alone. There has to be a partnership" (Winthrop Knowlton as quoted in Armbrister 1988).

Although corporate-giving programs are sometimes modeled after foundations, they employ a greater variety of giving methods. There is no such thing as a model of corporate giving; every corporation is different. Some businesses sponsor philanthropic activity by establishing an independent corporate foundation. Others provide philanthropic grants directly, as a company or from internal departments such as marketing, advertising, or personnel. Or a sales representative of a firm may sponsor an event in his market community. In-kind gifts and donations are a large part of corporate giving and may very well equal or surpass the corporate dollar contribution to nonprofit efforts. In-kind gifts include donations of office equipment such as computers and furniture, as well as the allocation of employee time to activities such as tutoring in neighboring schools or training nonprofits in management and other executive skills.

The matching grant programs offered by many companies allow employees to direct a portion of their company's philanthropic activity. With matching grants, employees contribute to the organization of their choice and the corporation matches individual employee donations dollar-for-dollar. Some corporations place restrictions on the types of organizations that qualify for matching gifts. United Ways and other federated campaigns increasingly rely on the cooperation of private sector companies to participate in campaign drives that raise money through employee payroll deductions.[3] Another corporate innovation is a program that allows employees to request grants from their company for the nonprofit organizations in which they volunteer.

Corporations and their affiliated foundations often target grant making to areas where the company has a plant, subsidiary, or other important operation (for example, ARCO in Los Angeles, Coca-Cola in Atlanta, Prudential in Newark, and Amoco in Chicago). In many cases businesses choose to support programs that can directly or indirectly benefit their products. For example, B. Dalton's nationwide chain of bookstores is committed to literacy and provides financial support to programs that teach reading skills (O'Connell 1987). The most likely candidates to support programs for young black males are companies that produce goods consumed by young black males, and companies based in large cities with large black populations— for example, Nike, Colgate-Palmolive, the GAP, Levi Strauss, and Coca-Cola.

Corporations have become increasingly interested in financing initiatives for minorities. A 1992 study found that corporate funding of minority causes has grown substantially (Smith and Martin 1992a). This survey of the top 500 U.S. companies found a 50 percent rise between 1985 and 1990 in the number of companies that explicitly fund minority concerns. The findings indicate that these companies are motivated by the changing demographics of their workforce. The growing purchasing power of minority consumers also has led companies to expand into these markets. However, corporate funding of minority causes does not necessarily reach the hands of minority service providers. Many organizations that provide services to minorities but whose leaders and staff are not minorities themselves are successfully vying for minority funding (Smith and Martin 1992b).

The most significant corporate initiative directly serving minority youth today is the National Urban League, formed partially as a result of corporate-supported networks of organizations in the black community (Smith and Martin 1992a). A recent nationwide Urban League initiative called the Male Responsibility Project, intended as a catalyst in the creation of culturally sensitive pregnancy prevention programs for males, directly targeted black male teenagers to help them prevent premature fatherhood.

There now appears to be significant interest among the business community in helping nonprofit programs that serve young black males, but channeling the resources of the business sector may be difficult without consensus on the best way to support minority causes (Smith and Martin 1992a, 1992b).

The business community has another critical influence on philanthropic giving and nonprofit organizations. Business leaders serve on the boards of or hold advisory positions in most nonprofit organizations, including foundations and review committees of local United Ways. Through these posts, business leaders advise foundations about funding priorities, influence the service choices of program administrators, and help select which community programs will receive United Way support. The importance of these linkages in directing funding support and program goals cannot be underestimated.

FEDERATIONS AND COLLECTION CAMPAIGNS

The United Way of America is the best known and largest of the giving organizations that operate federated fundraising campaigns. It functions as an umbrella organization with local affiliates around the country that provide funding support to member nonprofit agencies. Local United Way affiliates raise money primarily through fund drive collections and payroll deductions from government workers and local business employees. Many other federated campaigns operate in a similar manner. These include the Combined Federal Campaign, Catholic Charities, United Jewish Appeal, Combined Health

Appeal, United Black Fund of America, and the National/United Services Agencies. Although the resources generated from these campaigns benefit a wide variety of causes, some funding goes toward youth development services for young black males.

United Way affiliates and other fundraising campaigns have enormous leverage in pooling donations from individuals. Proceeds from the Combined Federal Campaign, which collects federal employee donations through payroll deductions, reached $204 million in 1991 (American Association of Fund-Raising Council Trust for Philanthropy 1992). State and local government campaigns raised another $200 million in 1991, while the remaining proceeds from campaigns amounted to over $2 billion raised in private sector and United Way campaigns nationwide.[4] United Way allocations for programs serving "at-risk" youth age 10 to 15 amounted to $196 million in 1985. This figure grew by 50 percent to $293 million in 1990, a figure that represented 12.7 percent of United Way's $2.3 billion total allocations to nonprofits that year (Stern 1992). In 1985, United Way agencies that reported to their Fund Distribution Survey by age and race directed $14.5 million to programs serving young black males. Agencies reporting detailed funding information in 1990 delivered $10.5 million to black males, a 28 percent decrease from the 1985 figure.[5]

One federated campaign, the United Black Fund, Inc. of Washington, D.C., was established in 1969 specifically to serve the needs of the black community. It was formed to provide access for black-oriented nonprofits that were being denied funds or equal distributions from the city's established federations. By its third year, the United Black Fund became the first black fundraising organization to receive payroll deductions from federal employees, a right acquired through legal action (United Black Fund, Inc. of Greater Washington 1992a). In FY 1991–1992, the United Black Fund raised $2.2 million for Washington, D.C., area programs, approximately 20 percent or $436,000 of which was allocated for youth development programs (United Black Fund, Inc. of Greater Washington 1992b). The United Black Fund, Inc. of Greater Washington, D.C., also created the United Black Fund of America, Inc., an umbrella organization with 37 chapters and affiliates.

CHURCHES, FRATERNITIES, SERVICE CLUBS, AND INDIVIDUALS

A discussion of private funding sources for nonprofit youth programs is incomplete without including churches, fraternities, service clubs, and individuals. Portions of the charitable donations from each of these groups are channeled through the above-mentioned vehicles. For instance, individuals are already partially accounted for through their contributions to foundations and United Way campaigns. Although individuals contribute the largest share of philanthropic capital in this country—a full 83 percent—it is impossible to estimate the amount of individual contributions made directly to programs for young black males.

Many African-American community institutions have tremendous resources to support youth development programs for boys. Churches, service clubs, fraternities, and sororities are fund providers, but even more valuable are these institutions' human capital and their stabilizing presence in almost every American community. Most of these African-American organizations have strong national networks that can provide powerful resources by linking their funds and human service capacity. One example is the Sigma Beta Club youth group for boys, developed by the Phi Beta Sigma Fraternity. This national-level club provides local activities to foster educational achievement, leadership development, self-pride, cultural awareness, community responsibilities, social and professional etiquette, and understanding of the free enterprise system and the workings of the global market place (Phi Beta Sigma Fraternity 1991).

Black churches operate programs internally, and donate funds and facilities to youth programs in the community. Churches provide services for youth through choirs and religious youth groups. Some sources estimate that up to 25 percent of giving to religious organizations is redistributed to non-religious activities such as human services and youth programs.[6] Many start-up community-based programs with no money rely heavily on the church for a meeting place and for recruiting volunteers as well as participants. Finally, service groups such as the Kiwanis Clubs and Links, Inc. have activities to raise money and donate portions or all of the proceeds to nonprofits. The dollar amounts tend to be small relative to foundation or government grants, but the impact can be larger when coupled with activities and voluntary service.

Summary

Given current funding patterns, it is unclear whether support for youth or minorities is reaching many of the development programs targeted at black males between age 10 and 15. While the federal government provides substantial resources to youth, government grants typically target programs aimed at treatment or problem behavior rather than general youth development. In contrast, private sector funding sources do tend to provide support for general youth development. However, the lion's share of private funding is directed to nationally affiliated youth organizations such as Big Brothers/Big Sisters of America and the National Urban League. While together these funding sources provide support to many laudable youth initiatives, the patterns of funding that exist pose severe obstacles for many youth development programs that serve adolescent black boys.

WHO IS REQUESTING FUNDING AND WHO IS PROVIDING IT?

Service providers of youth development for black males are all community-based, but can be divided into three categories: community-based programs affiliated with well-known national agencies such as the YMCA; black-focused national agencies such as the National Urban League whose funding patterns diverge from the bulk of national youth-serving agencies; and the independent initiatives exclusively serving young black males such as the programs described by Ferguson in chapter 4. Other programs with an African-American focus such as the Rites of Passage portrayed by Jeff in chapter 5 are nationally networked but not well known.

Well-known national agencies (such as the YMCA) provide important fundraising advantages to their affiliates, including name recognition, agency-owned systems for fundraising, and technical assistance. Name recognition may be the greatest advantage of national affiliation, because it helps local affiliates pass the tests of stability and program effectiveness often applied by funders. National agencies also provide well-developed systems of fundraising such as Girl Scout cookie sales, Boy Scout and YMCA membership dues, Red Cross fundraising projects, and Salvation Army consignment shops. Finally, the technical assistance provided to local affiliates, including help with proposal writing and with identifying funding sources, improves their capacity to raise funds.

As a result of these advantages, national affiliates receive the bulk of private funding for youth services. Perhaps because of the long-standing tradition and widespread appeal of national youth-serving agencies, these organizations have been the most successful at raising private funding. Many nationally affiliated youth development programs receive over 90 percent of their funding from private sector sources, particularly from foundations and United Ways. National affiliates that collect membership dues rely on those dues for between 8 percent and 30 percent of their funding (Stern 1992).

Agencies such as the National Urban League and the NAACP also enjoy name recognition, but are not strict youth-serving agencies. One-third of the total income of Urban League affiliates goes to children and youth programs, which include services to anyone between age 0 and 24 (Stern 1992). Some Urban League and most NAACP affiliates lack youth programs altogether. Another departure from the other national agencies is Urban League affiliates' heavy reliance on government resources. A breakdown of total Urban League funding for 1989 reveals that 56 percent came from the government, 23 percent from United Ways, and 14 percent from foundation and corporate support (Stern 1992).

It is useful to consider another national minority agency, ASPIRA (from the Spanish verb meaning "to aspire"), which serves the Latino community through programs for youth. Six local ASPIRA affiliates serve approximately 13,000 Latino youth and follow a funding pattern similar to that of the National Urban League. Almost 70 percent of ASPIRA's funding comes from government sources, 25 percent from foundations and corporations, and 5 percent from United Ways (Stern 1992).

Independent community-based programs vary greatly in size, program focus, and participants' racial, ethnic, and social profiles. Yet there is one unifying characteristic among these programs: their funding portfolios. Most independent programs rely heavily on government funders, while maintaining many other smaller funding sources (Weber 1992; National Network of Runaway and Youth Services 1991). Almost a quarter of independent programs surveyed in a study by Weber (1992) receive no government grants. Some programs such as Baltimore's Project RAISE and Philadelphia Futures have special partnerships with community foundations. The Baltimore-based Abell Foundation supports 60 percent of the funding needs for Project RAISE. However, two out of every five programs rely almost entirely on government funding. The distribution of funding sources for a typical independent community-based youth organization is as follows: 50 percent from government sources, 17 percent from various private sources, and 7.9 percent from United Ways. Remaining funding sources for these programs include fees for service, membership dues, and fundraising events (Weber 1992).

FUNDRAISING CHALLENGES FOR COMMUNITY-
BASED ORGANIZATIONS

The primary mission of every program discussed in this volume is to serve youth, yet fundraising concerns seem to rival that priority. Here I discuss some of the challenges to fundraising experienced by community-based nonprofit youth organizations, and highlight the additional obstacles faced by programs serving young black males. Interviews with a number of program directors and other practitioners serving youth consistently identified two major obstacles to funding: the time involved and funder restrictions. Youth development programs serving young black males face these obstacles but others as well, as discussed below.[7]

The Time-consuming Nature of Fundraising

"I could write a book about my funding problems," was the gist of the message from most program directors. Searching for funds is a constant responsibility of any community-based program. Few programs have budgets to support a full-time staff person to keep up with newly issued RFPs, research new and changing funding sources, or become expert in writing proposals. However, it is necessary to continually find new funding sources and renew old grants in a system that lacks continuing or long-term financial support. To win grants from competitive funding sources, fundraisers must become experts in writing proposals. Programs without full-time and/or accomplished fundraisers are at a disadvantage.

Typically, an agency must rely on numerous funding sources because grants to independent community-based organizations tend to be small.[8] Furthermore, funders do not generally guarantee repeated grants, compelling programs to seek many funding sources rather than rely on any one that may discontinue its support. Managing a full portfolio of donors requires time as well as accounting and data management skills. Grants are usually awarded on an annual basis, forcing programs to repeat their appeals annually to each source. National agency affiliates have the benefit of additional support to fulfill these tasks, and some even have a designated fundraiser. For programs that cannot rely on name recognition or a national headquarters, the job of "selling" the program to potential donors is even more difficult. In small organizations program directors tend to assume this responsibility. Having to devote substantial time to fundraising efforts forces directors to sacrifice attention otherwise focused on youth and program development.

Funder Restrictions

Among the challenges they face in fundraising, program directors cite the numerous obstacles posed by the grants themselves. Agencies are challenged by both creativity requirements and government grant restrictions. As one program director explained, funders often expect agencies to constantly come up with new and innovative programs. Although this director understands the importance of developing new services, her agency wanted to continue activities that were considered innovative in the past and were still found to be effective.

Agencies that provide general youth development services have difficulty fitting into government grant categories. Government grants are largely remedial. They focus on modifying a single behavior or targeting a deficit through the support of, for instance, drug and violence prevention programs. One project director explained that government grants are too restrictive and that without more flexibility government funding sources will remain inaccessible to many youth development agencies.

Another restrictive factor is the drop in support for general operating expenses. All foundations place limitations on the grants they award, and even though operating funds are essential, programs are often restricted from using resources for this purpose. The following sample phrases lifted from actual grant regulations reveal a common aversion to funding operating expenses: "no grants for equipment or materials;" "no grants for operating budgets;" "no grants for continued operating support, computers or vehicles;" "no support of general operating expenses, or salaries;" "no grants for operating budgets, seed money, or special projects," (The Foundation Center 1992). Subsidizing operations is not glamourous, but funders need to understand that organizations cannot run programs without at least a percentage of grants devoted to these expenses.

Challenges Unique to Programs for Young Black Males

In addition to the problems above, youth development programs serving young black males face obstacles of limited seed money, insufficient funder dedication, and fewer community resources.

Attention to the needs of young black males requires the development of new programs. But funders are hesitant to fund new efforts, preferring to endorse organizations with proven effectiveness and stability. For instance, historically United Ways have supported traditional programs such as those discussed in chapter 6, many of which are only beginning to serve minorities and youth in high-risk environments. United Ways have begun to reserve seed money for start-up organizations, but seed grants are often the first victim of dwindling resources and tight budgets. In the present tough economic climate, many such programs have been cut back.

One practitioner noted increasing difficulty in obtaining financial resources for programs serving adolescents or hard-to-serve youth. She attributed this to a recognition by funders of how hard it is to serve this population and an unwillingness to commit to the task. Unfortunately, perceptions regarding young black males, perpetuated by stereotypes and the media, complicate the process of obtaining funding.

Finally, the communities in which early adolescent black males reside have disproportionately fewer resources. The more closely targeted an organization is to high-risk environments, the more difficulty it may have in generating sufficient funding. The financial resources of the individuals and corporations on which nonprofits rely are scarce in these areas, as is physical capital such as buildings and safe places to hold program activities.

RECOMMENDATIONS FOR IMPROVING THE FUNDING SYSTEM

Despite the inadequacy of our knowledge of expenditures on youth development programs for young black males, we do know that present funding levels are low in relation to need. Counteracting the negative influences of high-risk environments confronting many young African-American boys surely deserves a greater national commitment. But additional resources are not the only answer. Substantial mismatches exist between the kinds of funding available and the needs of programs presently soliciting funds for the development of young black males.

Without adjustments to current funding practices, it is unlikely that existing funders will effectively reach black male youth development programs. Below I make several concrete suggestions for programs and funders to improve the funding of youth development programs that serve young black males.

Enhance Information Exchange and Knowledge Dissemination

A critical step toward improving the funding process is enhancing the flow of information between program directors and funders. Funders and fund seekers need to be brought together to learn from each other about how best to improve the system. Research institutions and national foundations could easily provide forums that would allow an exchange of ideas. These information sessions should include representatives of federal agencies, national and community foundations, corporate givers, the United Way, national youth-serving agencies, national minority organizations, and community-based program practitioners. The results of the forums could be disseminated in written form to a wide audience.

Better mechanisms also need to be developed to provide assistance to potential and struggling youth development programs that do or want to better serve black male adolescents. Many independent and even nationally affiliated agencies of this kind are sorely lacking in both the knowledge and resources necessary for fundraising. Information centers could be established or experts and successful practitioners mobilized to provide technical advice on fundraising activities. Networks for dissemination could also be developed to ensure that black communities have access to assistance and information. One innovative idea would be to provide loan relief to MBA students who agree to work in a community-based nonprofit organization for one to two years after graduation, as part of the Clinton administration's proposed legislation for national service. An MBA graduate with expertise in how to start and run a business is valuable to any nonprofit.

Another important way to improve the knowledge base regarding youth development for young black males is to require all programs to keep minimal records about program participants. Programs need not complete long and complicated forms; a basic tally of participants' age, sex, and race/ethnicity would be sufficient. Basic statistics about program participants would help funders and policymakers more accurately assess the need for funding, and would assist community-based organizations in leveraging funding.

Use Community Foundations as Intermediaries

To enhance support for youth development programs serving young black males, reformers should focus on what each funder does best.

The use of community foundations as intermediaries between large funders and community-based programs can facilitate this process.

National foundations prefer to address broad issues by supporting research and demonstration programs. National foundations have large assets that are not accessible to youth development programs delivering services to black boys. On the opposite side of the coin, community foundations focus their resources on local efforts, but most of these foundations have few assets to bestow upon their communities. Combining the assets of a national foundation or corporation with the local knowledge of a community foundation could allow for the proliferation of programs for young black males (Gibson 1992). An example of this method is under way. The Ford Foundation is implementing a community development initiative known as The Neighborhood and Family Initiative by sponsoring community foundations in four cities. The locally based community foundations act as mediators and work with neighborhood representatives using funds provided by Ford (Chaskin 1992).

Target Local Corporations

Local programs understand the need to meet funder requirements and preferences, but additional creative techniques could expand their funding options. The reality is that in order to successfully obtain corporate support, local programs have to match the interests of companies and consider their profit-motive structure. Corporations can be motivated to give when their funding achieves direct results such as increasing consumption of their products, or indirect results such as developing the corporation's positive image among employees and the community. To take advantage of corporate lending patterns, programs need to find innovative ways to tap into the multiple sources of money in each corporation. Marcienne Mattleman, director of Philadelphia Futures, solicited Meridian Bank's marketing department to sponsor the publication of *Guide to College and Financial Aid*. The guide is published yearly by the bank and distributed to every high school senior in the city. Philadelphia Futures hopes to counteract low matriculation into college by supplying information about tuition opportunities. The benefit for the bank is an opportunity to reach potential loan consumers.

The corporate sector offers tremendous potential for supporting black male youth development. Corporations with many young black male customers often provide philanthropic support targeted toward this consumer group. However, it is important to consider the limitations of corporate giving. The business sector is dependent on profits and the economy, which to some extent dictate the level of giving. But the business community wields influence that is dependable for the long term. The boards and allocation committees of foundations and United Ways are heavily populated by corporate representatives. Increasing the number of board members who understand the needs of the black community is a starting point for increasing commitment to young black males.

Develop More National Networks

Creating national networks can help currently independent agencies benefit from the lending preferences of many private sector funders. A current model, the National Network of Runaway and Youth Services, was formed by agencies providing innovative services to youth who were not benefiting from mainstream social service agencies (National Network of Runaway and Youth Services 1991). Not only can national networks provide advocacy and technical assistance, they can also help member agencies develop name recognition and they can guarantee funders that member agencies meet certain qualifications.

Provide Stable and Flexible Grants Mechanisms

A final and critical step that could help all youth development programs is to provide more stable and flexible grant mechanisms. The last decade was characterized by a decline in government resources for nonprofits (Salamon and Abramson 1992). The private sector measurably expanded its philanthropic support for nonprofits, but little of this was targeted at independent youth development agencies serving young black males. Community-based agencies face this uncertain financial environment every year while trying to maintain a funding base. One way to reduce this burden on agencies would be for public and private funders to provide long-term grants, and allow a portion of these funds to cover general operating costs.

Several concrete steps can be taken now to improve the funding process, steps that would level the playing field and allow equal access for independent community-based organizations with programs for young black males. In addition to modifying funding practices, we must also increase the level of resources available to ensure that we adequately nurture African-American boys and guide them through the difficult transitions that characterize adolescence.

Notes

1. Due to budget cuts in the 1980s, the real value of federal spending in 1992 was well below its 1980 level in areas crucial to programs serving young black males, such as education, training, employment, social services, and community development (Salamon and Abramson 1992). Some notable government initiatives begun in the second half of the 1980s provide significant support to nonprofit services for young black males. These initiatives include the Office of Minority Health and Office for Substance Abuse Prevention (within the Department of Health and Human Services) target grants that reach "high-risk" adolescents.

2. Figures are based on a database search of The Foundation Center's (1993) *Foundation Grants Index* 1990/1991, which yielded 150 records of youth development grants for young black males. The *Foundation Grants Index* includes only grants of $5,000 and over.

3. Based on phone conversation with Annette Perez, deputy director, United Black Fund, Inc., Feb. 18, 1993.

4. From materials furnished by the National/United Service Agencies, Inc. of Fairfax, Virginia, 1993.

5. Calculation based on data from United Way of America Research Services. This figure is only representative because the data are based on the United Way of America Fund Distribution Survey (1985 and 1990). Some United Ways fail to report to the survey, while others do not report the full detail of agency participants.

6. For a discussion of this estimate and alternative estimates see Salamon 1992, p. 30.

7. The program directors and practitioners interviewed for this section remain anonymous. Findings from several studies corroborate most of the findings here. These studies include Weber's (1992) survey of independent community-based youth organizations, the National Network of Runaway and Homeless Youth (1991) survey of member programs, and a survey of 20 national youth-serving agencies conducted for the Carnegie Council on Adolescent Development and reported in Stern (1992).

8. One agency affiliated with the National Network of Runaway and Homeless Youth reported having 64 different funding sources.

References

Abramson, Alan, and Lester M. Salamon. 1986. *The Nonprofit Sector and the New Federal Budget.* Washington, D.C.: Urban Institute Press.

American Association of Fund-Raising Council Trust for Philanthropy. 1992. *Giving USA.* New York: AAFRC Trust for Philanthropy.

————. 1991. *Giving USA.* New York: AAFRC Trust for Philanthropy.

Armbrister, Trevor. 1988. "When Companies Care." *Reader's Digest.* April.

Carnegie Corporation of New York. 1992. *A Matter of Time: Risk and Opportunity in the Non School Hours.* Report of the Task Force on Youth Development and Community Programs, Carnegie Council on Adolescent Development, December.

Chaskin, Robert J. 1992. *The Ford Foundation's Neighborhood and Family Initiative Toward a Model of Comprehensive, Neighborhood-Based Development.* The Chaplin Hall Center for Children, University of Chicago.

Council on Foundations. 1992. "Community Foundations in 1990: A Statistical Update." Council on Foundations Report, March.

The Foundation Center. 1993. *Foundations Grants Index, 1984–1993* edition, 12/92 Quarterly. Dialog Database File 27. New York: The Foundation Center.

————. 1992. *Foundation Directory, 1992.* Dialog Database File 26. New York: The Foundation Center.

Gibson, James. 1992. "Fostering Effective Community Strategies for Investment in African American Men and Their Families: Defining a Vision." Presented at conference on A Dialogue with Community Leaders on African-American Men and their Families, W. K. Kellogg Foundation, Nov. 30.

Hodgkinson, Virginia Ann, Murray S. Weitzman, Christopher M. Toppe, and Stephen M. Noga. 1992. *Nonprofit Almanac 1992–1993: Dimensions of the Independent Sector.* San Francisco: Jossey-Bass Publishers.

Klepper, Anne. 1992. *Corporate Contributions, 1991.* Report No. 1014. New York: The Conference Board, Inc.

Kovacs, Ruth, ed. 1992. *The Foundation Grants Index 1993.* 21st edition. New York: The Foundation Center.

Mauer, Mark. 1992. "Americans Behind Bars: One Year Later." Washington, D.C.: The Sentencing Project.

National Network of Runaway and Youth Services. 1991. *To Whom Do They Belong: Runaway, Homeless and Other Youth in High-Risk Situations in the 1990s.* Washington, D.C., February.

O'Connell, Brian. 1987. "Corporate Philanthropy: Getting Bigger, Broader and Tougher to Manage." *Corporate Philanthropy*, VII, 4.

Office of Management and Budget, Executive Office of the President. 1993. *Budget Baselines, Historical Data, and Alternatives for the Future,* Washington, D.C.: U.S. Government Printing Office, January.

————. 1991. *Budget of the United States Government: Fiscal Year 1992,* Washington, D.C.: U.S. Government Printing Office.

Office of National Drug Control Policy, Executive Office of the President. 1991. *Directory of Federal Anti-Drug Grants.* An Office of National Drug Control Policy White Paper, Washington, D.C., April.

Olson, Stan, Ruth Kovacs, and Suzanne Haile, eds. 1990. *National Guide To Funding For Children, Youth and Families.* New York: The Foundation Center.

Phi Beta Sigma Fraternity, Inc. 1991. "Programming for the Year 2000." Brochure. Washington, D.C.

Philadelphia Futures. 1991/1992. "Sponsor-A-Scholar." Brochure. Philadelphia, Pa.

Renz, Loren. 1991. *Foundation Giving: Yearbook of Facts and Figures on Private, Corporate, and Community Foundations*. 1991 edition. New York: The Foundation Center.

Salamon, Lester. 1992. *America's Nonprofit Sector: A Primer*. New York: The Foundation Center.

Salamon, Lester M., and Alan J. Abramson. 1992. "The Federal Budget and the Nonprofit Sector: FY 1993." A Report to Independent Sector, Spring.

Select Committee on Children, Youth and Families, U.S. House of Representatives. 1990. "Federal Programs Affecting Children and Their Families, 1990." Washington, D.C.: U.S. Government Printing Office.

Smith, Craig, and Nita Martin. 1992a. "Wooing Minorities." *Corporate Philanthropy Report* 7, 4 (December/January).

_____ . 1992b. "How Majority Nonprofits Get Minority Funding." *Corporate Philanthropy Report* 7, 4 (December/January).

Stern, Leonard. 1992. "Funding Patterns of Nonprofit Organizations that Provide Youth Development Services: An Exploratory Study." Carnegie Council on Adolescent Development, Task Force on Youth Development and Community Programs, February.

Taft Group. 1993. *Corporate Giving Directory 1993*. 14th edition. Rockville, Md.: The Taft Group.

United Black Fund, Inc. of Greater Washington, D.C. 1992a. *Directory of Members Agencies 1992–1993*. Revised edition, Sept. 30.

_____ . 1992b. *United Black Fund, Inc. Fact Sheet*. Revised edition, July.

United Way of America, Fund Distribution Survey 1990. Computer database.

_____ . Fund Distribution Survey 1985. Computer database.

U.S. Department of Justice, Office of Juvenile Justice and Delinquency Prevention. 1992. *Federal Agency Juvenile Delinquency Development Statements*. Washington, D.C., August.

Weber, Nathan. 1992. "Independent Youth Development Organizations and Exploratory Study." Prepared for the Carnegie Council on Adolescent Development Task Force on Youth Development and Community Programs, February.

EXAMPLES OF "NURTURING" PROGRAMS THAT SERVE YOUNG BLACK MALES

National Organizations

Advance Project
Personal Development Project
3245 Central Avenue
Memphis, TN 38111
(901) 320-1020

Alpha Phi Alpha Fraternity,
Inc. (National Headquarters)
2313 St. Paul Street
Baltimore, MD 21239
(410) 554-0040

Big Brothers/Big Sisters
of America (National
Headquarters)
230 N. 13th Street
Philadelphia, PA 19107
(215) 567-7000

100 Black Men
(National Headquarters)
127 Peach Tree Street, NE
Suite 704
Atlanta, GA 30303
(404) 525-7111

Boys' and Girls' Clubs of
America (National
Headquarters)
771 First Avenue
New York, NY 10017
(212) 351-5900

Boy Scouts of America
(National Headquarters)
1325 Walnut Hill Lane
P.O. Box 152079
Irving, TX 75015
(214) 580-2000

Child Welfare League of
America
440 First Street, NW, #310
Washington, DC 20001
(202) 638-2952

Concerned Black Men
(National Headquarters)
7200 N. 21st Street
Philadelphia, PA 19138
(215) 276-2260

Congress of National Black
Churches (National
Headquarters)
1225 Eye Street, NW
Suite 750
Washington, DC 20005
(202) 371-1091

Improved Benevolent Protective
Order of Elks of the World
(National Headquarters)
P.O. Box 159
Winton, NC 27986
(919) 358-7661

INROADS, Inc. (National
Headquarters)
1221 Locust, Suite 800
St. Louis, MO 63103
(314) 241-7488

Kappa Alpha Psi Fraternity,
Inc. (National Headquarters)
2322-24 N. Broad Street
Philadelphia, PA 19132
(215) 228-7184

National Association For the
Advancement of Colored
People (National
Headquarters)
4805 Mount Hope Drive
Baltimore, MD 21215
(410) 481-4100

National Black Child
Development Institute
1463 Rhode Island Avenue,
NW
Washington, DC 20005
(202) 387-1281

National Council of African
American Men, Inc.
c/o The University of Kansas
Center for Black Leadership,
Development and Research
1028 Dole Center
Lawrence, KS 66045
(913) 864-3990

National Network of Runaway
and Youth Services
1400 Eye Street, NW, #330
Washington, DC 20005
(202) 682-4114

National Trust for the
Development of African
American Men
908 Pennsylvania Avenue, SE
Washington, DC 20003
(202) 543-2407

African American Adolescent
Male Development Center
National Urban League, Inc.
(National Headquarters)
500 E. 62nd Street
New York, NY 10021
(212) 310-9084

Omega Psi Phi Fraternity, Inc.
(National Headquarters)
2714 Georgia Avenue, NW
Washington, DC 20001
(202) 667-7158

Operation Sisters United
National Council of Negro
Women
1667 K Street, NW
Washington, DC 20011
(202) 659-0006 ext. 20

Opportunities
Industrialization Centers of
America (National
Headquarters)
1415 N. Broad Street
Philadelphia, PA 19122
(215) 236-4500

Phi Beta Sigma Fraternity, Inc.
(National Headquarters)
145 Kennedy Street, NW
Washington, DC 20011
(202) 726-5434

SIMBA, Inc.
P.O. Box 27548
Oakland, CA 94602
(510) 839-4303

Community-Based Organizations

The Algebra Project
22 Wheatland Avenue
Dorchester, MA 02124
(617) 287-1508

Association for the Positive
  Development of African
  American Youth
6700 S. Oglesby
  Suite 1108
Chicago, IL 60649
(312) 493-0110

Atlanta Area Council, Boy
  Scouts of America
100 Edgewood Avenue, NE
  Fourth Floor
Atlanta, GA 30303
(404) 577-4810

Black Male Youth Health
  Enhancement Program
Shiloh Family Life Center
1510 Ninth Street, NW
Washington, D.C. 20001
(202) 332-0213

Blue City Cultural Center
205 N. Main Street
Memphis, TN 38103
(901) 525-3031

The Boys Choir of Harlem
127 W. 127th Street
New York, NY 10027
(212) 749-1717

By Our Own Hands
1206 Alcy Road
Memphis, TN 38106
(901) 942-5271

Challenge, Inc.
617 Seventh Avenue
Ft. Worth, TX 76104
(817) 877-1181

Concerned Men of Greater
  Indianapolis
Indianapolis Urban League
P.O. Box 88633
Indianapolis, IN 46208
(317) 639-9404

Crime Prevention Through
  Education
The Concerned Citizens for a
  Better South Memphis
1594 Latham Street
Memphis, TN 38106
(901) 785-6397

DC Youth Ensemble
3500 R Street, NW
Washington, DC 20001
(202) 393-3293

Detroit Urban League
15770 James Couzens Freeway
Detroit, MI 48238
(313) 863-0300

The Door
121 Sixth Avenue
New York, NY 10013
(212) 941-9090 ext. 274

Dunbar Center
3738 Herschel Road
College Park, GA 30337
(404) 659-4328

The Fifth Ward Enrichment
  Program
4014 Market Street
Houston, TX 77020
(713) 229-8353

Frontiers International
P.O. Box 3522
Springfield, IL 62708

The Godfathers Club
Progressive Baptist Church
1419 12th Avenue South
Nashville, TN 37212
(615) 292-3362

The HAWK Federation
High Achievement, Wisdom &
    Knowledge
Institute for the Advanced
    Study of Black Family Life
    and Culture
155 Filbert Street, Suite 202
Oakland, CA 94607
(510) 836-3245

IRAP (Intensive
    Resocialization and After
    Care Program)
1249 Washington Blvd.
    Suite 1200
Detroit, MI 48226
(313) 963-2022

Living Stage Theatre Company
Sixth and Maine Avenue, SW
Washington, DC 20024
(202) 554-9066

M.A.L.E. (Masculine-Aware-
    Loving-Educated)
Planned Parenthood of Idaho
4301 Franklin Road
Boise, ID 83705
(208) 345-0760

The Male Image Project
Youth Organizations, USA
19 Humphrey Street
Englewood, NJ 07631
(201) 894-1866

Male Responsibility Program
Detroit Urban League
208 Mack Avenue
Detroit, MI 48201
(313) 832-4600

The Male Responsibility
    Program and The African
    American Male Connection
    Program
Urban League of Portland
10 N. Russell Street
Portland, OR 97227
(503) 281-2612

The Mentoring Center
1221 Preservation Park Way
    Suite 100
Oakland, CA 94612
(510) 891-0427

Michigan Association of
    Leadership Development
77 Bagley Street
Pontiac, MI 48341
(313) 338-7880

Midtown Youth Academy
2206 14th Street, NW
Washington, DC 20009
(202) 483-3711

Network For African
    American Males
Oakland Unified School
    District
495 Jones Avenue
Oakland, CA 94603
(510) 562-0713

Oakland Men's Project
440 Grand Avenue
    Suite 320
Oakland, CA 94610
(510) 835-2433

Omega Boys' Club
953 De Haro Street
San Francisco, CA 94107
(415) 826-8664

Partnership/Mentorship
Greenville Urban League
15 Regency Hill Drive
Greenville, SC 29603
(803) 244-3862

Pennvisions
900 Massachusetts Avenue,
    NW
Washington, DC 20001
(202) 727-3984

Personality Enhancement
    Program
Warren Trumbell Urban
    League
290 W. Market Street
Warren, OH 44481
(216) 394-4316

Philadelphia Futures
230 South Broad Street
    7th floor
Philadelphia, PA 19102
(215) 790-1666

Planned Parenthood of
    Southern Arizona, Inc.
127 S. Fifth Avenue
Tucson, AZ 85701
(602) 628-3070

Project Chance
51 St. Edwards Street
Brooklyn, NY 11205
(718) 875-8018

Project Image
765 E. 69th Place
Chicago, IL 60637
(312) 324-8700

Project RAISE
Baltimore Mentoring Institute
605 N. Eutaw Street
Baltimore, MD 21201
(410) 685-8316

Real Men
Office of Community Outreach
    Services
LeMoyne-Owen College
807 Walker Avenue
Memphis, TN 38126
(901) 942-7327

Rites of Passage
Essex County Urban League
3 Williams Street
Newark, NJ 07102
(201) 624-6660

R.O.C.A. (Reaching Out to
    Chelsea Adolescents)
148 Washington Avenue
Chelsea, MA 02150
(617) 889-5210

S.O.S.A.D. (Save Our Sons
    And Daughters)
2441 W. Grand Blvd.
Detroit, MI 48208
(313) 361-5200

Simba Program
Planned Parenthood of
    Connecticut
129 Whitney Avenue
New Haven, CT 06510
(203) 865-5158

Teen Fathers Program
National Institute for
    Responsible Fatherhood
8555 Hough Avenue
Cleveland, OH 44106
(216) 791-1468

The Untouchables
P.O. Box 26292
Alexandria, VA 22314
(703) 838-5075
(703) 550-4007

Washington DC Metropolitan
  Area Rites of Passage
  Collective
P.O. Box 55273
Washington, DC 20040-5273
(301) 856-8568

W.E.B. Du Bois Academy/
African American Institute for
  the Positive Living
323 Salem Avenue
Dayton, OH 45406
(513) 223-8255

**School-Based or
School-Linked Programs**

The "A-MEN"
Arlington High School
4825 N. Arlington
Indianapolis, IN 46226
(616) 771-6577

Black Male College Explorers
  Program
A&M College of Education
300 AGEC
Tallahassee, FL 32307
(904) 599-3483

Black Manhood Training
  Program
Urban League of Greater
  Richmond
101 Clay Street
Richmond, VA 23219
(804) 649-8407

The Children of the Sun
A Program of the National
  Trust for the Development
  of African American Men
Greater Tampa Urban League
2313 E. 28th Avenue
Tampa, FL 33605
(813) 229-8117

Fulton Academic and
  Athletics Magnet
San Diego City Schools
7055 Skyline Drive
San Diego, CA 92114
(619) 262-0777

Inroads/Wisconsin Youth
  Leadership Academy
Milwaukee Public Schools
231 W. Wisconsin Avenue
  Suite 903
Milwaukee, WI 53203
(414) 272-1680

My Brothers Keeper
Detroit's Woodward
  Elementary School/
Michigan State University
Department of English
221 Morrill Hall
East Lansing, MI 48824-1936
(517) 353-9252

Morehouse College's
  Community Service Projects
  at Oglethorpe and Dean
  Rusk Elementary Schools
830 Westview Drive, SW
Atlanta, GA 30314
(404) 681-2800 ext. 2856

Project 2000
Center for Educating African-
  American Males
Morgan State University
Jenkins Building—308 B
Baltimore, MD 21239
(410) 319-3275

Project First Class Male
Urban League of Broward
  County
11 NW 36th Avenue
Fort Lauderdale, FL 33311
(305) 584-0777

School/Community Helping
  Hands Project
Wake County Public Schools
3600 Wakeforest Road
Raleigh, NC 27609
(919) 850-1660

Toussaint Institute Fund
98 Fort Green Place
Brooklyn, NY 11217
(718) 875-5469

Ujamma Institute
Medgar Evers College
131 Livingston Street, #204B
Brooklyn, NY 11210
(718) 935-3904

This list includes programs that have been brought to the attention of researchers at the Urban Institute; it is *not* meant to be an exhaustive list.

The following people assisted in the research and compilation of this list: Michael W. Andrews, field manager, Northeast Area Office, Big Brothers/Big Sisters of America; Michael R. Adams, Urban Youth Initiatives Consultant, and co-founder, Memphis Prevention Network Team; and Gregory Hodge, Urban Strategies Council, Oakland, California. In addition, program information was gathered from the "National Directory of African American Male Focused Organizations" by Keith B. Fulton and Richard J. Brown.

ABOUT THE EDITOR

Ronald B. Mincy is a senior research associate at the Urban Institute, directing the Underclass Research Project since 1990. He is also serving as a member of the Clinton administration's Welfare Reform Task Force, advising the U.S. Department of Health and Human Services on absent parent policy. Dr. Mincy has been on the economics faculties of Purdue University, Bentley College, the University of Delaware, and Swarthmore College. He has worked for the U.S. Department of Labor and has served on the Minimum Wage Study Commission. He specializes in the study of public policies for the working poor, public and private interventions that support families with adolescents in high-risk environments, the effects of urban opportunity structures on low-skilled workers and minorities, and in issues concerning measurement of the underclass. His most recent publications include "Ghetto Poverty: Black Problem or Harbinger of Things To Come?" and "The Underclass: Concept, Controversy, and Evidence."

Ronald F. Ferguson is an associate professor of public policy at the John F. Kennedy School of Government at Harvard University. He has been a visiting associate professor of urban studies and planning at the Massachusetts Institute of Technology (M.I.T.) and, before moving to Harvard, taught both economics and African and Afro-American Studies at Brandeis University. He earned his Ph.D. in Economics from M.I.T. Professor Ferguson's publications address economic and social issues including the fiscal health of cities, youth employment, the quality of public education and education finance, drug problems, and state and local economic development policy. His ongoing research examines the effects of teachers' skills on school achievement among children, the impacts of racial differences in reading and math proficiency on earnings disparities, and initiatives to improve the quality of life for teenagers and young adults in low-income black neighborhoods.

Andrew B. Hahn is associate dean of the Heller Graduate School and Human Services Research Professor at Brandeis University. Most of his research and policy work has concerned the self-sufficiency challenges facing disadvantaged groups including youth employment, dropout prevention, and welfare reform. He is coauthor of *What Works in Youth Employment* and *Dropouts in America: Enough Is Known for Action,* and is associated with a number of projects in Brandeis's Center for Human Resources and teaches graduate-level courses in the Heller School.

Morris F. X. Jeff, Jr. is an Afrocentric social worker and director of the City Welfare Department, New Orleans, La. He is the founder and creator of the Louis Armstrong Manhood Development Program, and past president of the National Association of Black Social Workers.

Courtland C. Lee is an associate professor and director of the Counselor Education Program at the University of Virginia. He has edited several books on multicultural counseling and is the author of a book on African-American male development. He has published numerous articles on adolescent development and counseling across cultures, is former editor of the *Journal of Multicultural Counseling and Development*,and serves on the advisory board of the *International Journal for the Advancement of Counseling*.

Karen J. Pittman is director of the Center for Youth Development and Policy Research and senior vice-president of the Academy for Educational Development in Washington, D.C. She has extensive experience in research and advocacy through her past work at the Children's Defense Fund. She has written extensively about youth development and has been active in mobilizing community stakeholders and policymakers around youth issues.

Jane Quinn, program director at the DeWitt Wallace-Reader's Digest Fund, was previously with the Carnegie Council on Adolescent Development, Washington, D.C., where she directed a study of youth development programs and services in the United States, and was principal author of *A Matter of Time: Risk and Opportunity in the Nonschool Hours*. Quinn served from 1981 to 1990 as director of program services for Girls' Clubs of America in New York. She has held positions at the Center for Population Options and the District of Columbia Department of Human Resources. In addition, she was a caseworker for the Juvenile Protective Association of Chicago and for the Family Counseling Center, Catholic Charities of Buffalo, N.Y.

Susan J. Wiener has been a research associate with the Urban Institute's Underclass Research Project since 1989. She specializes in the study of poverty, in estimates of the size, growth, and characteristics of the underclass, and in youth development programs. She has recently published "Guiding Boys through the Transition to Adulthood: The Role and Potential of Mentoring," and "The Under Class in the 1980s: Changing Concept, Constant Reality" (with Ronald Mincy).

Shepherd Zeldin is director of research at the Center for Youth Development and Policy Research at the Academy for Educational Development. He has authored numerous reports on youth programs based on his past work as a senior legislative assistant and as an evaluator and trainer in the field of adolescent development. He specializes in experiential learning and informal education in community settings.